PHILIP PAYTON

Philip Payton

THE FATHER OF BLACK HARLEM

Kevin McGruder

Columbia University Press
New York

Columbia University Press
Publishers Since 1893
New York   Chichester, West Sussex
cup.columbia.edu
Copyright © 2021 Columbia University Press
All rights reserved

Library of Congress Cataloging-in-Publication Data
Names: McGruder, Kevin, 1957- author.
Title: Philip Payton : the father of black Harlem / Kevin McGruder.
Description: New York : Columbia University Press, [2021] |
Includes bibliographical references and index.
Identifiers: LCCN 2021002789 (print) | LCCN 2021002790 (ebook) | ISBN 9780231198929 (hardback) | ISBN 9780231198936 (trade paperback) | ISBN 9780231552875 (ebook)
Subjects: LCSH: Payton, Philip, 1876–1917. | Real estate developers—New York (State)—New York—Biography. | African American businesspeople—New York (State)—New York—Biography. | Real estate development—New York (State)—New York—History—20th century. | African Americans—Housing—New York (State)—New York—History—20th century. | Discrimination in housing—New York (State)—New York—History—20th century. | Harlem (New York, N.Y.)--History. | Harlem (New York, N.Y.)—Biography.
Classification: LCC HD268.N5 M34 2021 (print) | LCC HD268.N5 (ebook) | DDC 333.33092 [B]—dc23
LC record available at https://lccn.loc.gov/2021002789
LC ebook record available at https://lccn.loc.gov/2021002790

Cover design: Julia Kushnirsky
Cover photographs: Photographs and Prints Division, Schomburg Center for Research in Black Culture, New York Public Library

*To the memory of
Dr. Judith Stein, advisor, mentor, friend
and
Dr. Martia Graham Goodson, friend and mentor*

CONTENTS

ACKNOWLEDGMENTS ix

Introduction 1

Chapter One
The Paytons Before and in Westfield 11

Chapter Two
The Provincial in New York City 30

Chapter Three
Entering the Field of Battle 54

Chapter Four
Battles in the Streets and the Courtroom 73

Chapter Five
To Liberia and Back 102

Chapter Six
Fifty Years of Freedom National 124

Chapter Seven
The Last Big Deal   145

Epilogue   166

NOTES   179

CHRONOLOGY   199

BIBLIOGRAPHY   201

INDEX   211

ACKNOWLEDGMENTS

I am very appreciative of the assistance I received from many in completing this project. Kristopher Burrell and David Golland read drafts of the manuscript and provided me with feedback as part of a reading group, through which we shared and commented on one another's work, returning to familiar territory that we shared as students in the doctoral program in history at the Graduate Center of the City University of New York. Robert E. Penn, Len Richardson, Sur Rodney Sur, and Michael Sherrell also read drafts of the manuscript and gave me critical feedback regarding its reception by general readers as part of Other Countries, the New York City–based (but now virtual) black gay men's writing workshop.

 A special note of gratitude goes to Dr. Robert Brown, who retired as director of the Westfield Athenaeum, located in Philip Payton's hometown of Westfield, Massachusetts. On a winter morning a few years ago, shortly after he had made a presentation on the Payton family, Brown sat with me at the Athenaeum for two hours and shared his extensive knowledge of Payton's life in Westfield. This information allowed me to connect many elusive archival dots, which was particularly helpful in explaining how, as a young man in his early twenties, Payton was able to gain acceptance into the inner circle of Booker T. Washington, then considered the leader of black people.

ACKNOWLEDGMENTS

I appreciate the insights on Maggie Payton and her family, particularly after Payton's death, provided by Cecil R. Forster. Forster is the grandson of Bessie Hobby, the niece whom Philip and Maggie Payton raised. The filmmaker Jeruvia, who is working on a project about the early years of Black Harlem that will initially focus on Philip Payton, posed questions regarding who Payton was, what motivated him, and how to accurately bring him to life on the screen. These queries helped me to similarly consider, in a different light, my equally challenging project of bringing Payton to life on the page.

Two of my mentors did not live to see this completed manuscript, but their guidance over the years contributed greatly to it. Judith Stein, retired professor of history at CUNY Graduate Center, convinced me that a biography of Philip Payton, who did not leave personal or business papers, might be a little ambitious for a dissertation topic. She provided valuable feedback on my actual dissertation, which in revised and expanded form became *Race and Real Estate: Conflict and Cooperation in Harlem, 1890–1920*. That project created the foundation and a wealth of unused archival material that I drew on for this book. Martia Goodson, retired associate professor in the Black and Latino Studies Department at Baruch College, opened the door to academia for me in the early 1990s by alerting me to an opportunity to teach as an adjunct at Baruch. That experience eventually led me to consider pursuing doctoral studies. Over the years, Martia and I worked on many projects as members of the Archives and History Ministry at the Abyssinian Baptist Church. At the same time, we traded notes on our personal research projects, grounded in our mutual desire to bring this information to the widest audience possible.

Last but not least, I thank my editor Stephen Wesley for shepherding this book through the process to become a publication of Columbia University Press.

PHILIP PAYTON

INTRODUCTION

In the first two decades of the 1900s, the upper Manhattan community of Harlem was transformed from a middle class, predominantly white enclave to a new residential frontier for New York City's growing black community. White residents, some of whom had arrived to the newly developed urban neighborhood only ten or twenty years before, watched in horror as Little Africa—133rd, 134th, and 135th Streets east of Lenox Avenue, to which black people had been confined since the late 1800s—soon outstripped its bounds and began to expand westward, spurred by the arrival of black people seeking what most had never had in New York City: quality housing. Real estate operator Philip Anthony Payton Jr. played a pivotal role in this expansion. A black man born in 1876, Payton grew up in predominantly white Westfield, Massachusetts. He had an unremarkable scholastic career in the public schools, although he did make a name for himself on the football field. After dropping out of high school, Payton worked in his father's barbershop for a few years. In 1899, possibly prompted by the success of his younger brother James, who would soon graduate from Yale, he set out for New York City seeking his fortune. There, like most black men, he worked in a series of menial positions, until a job working as a porter in a real estate office pointed him in the direction of what would become his life's work.[1]

In 1903 Payton formed the Afro-American Realty Company (AARC), whose name illustrated the fact that serving black people was central to its mission. A year later he reorganized the company from a partnership to a corporation and framed the business as a liberator vanquishing New York's residential segregation practices:

> The idea that Negroes must be confined to certain localities can be done away with. The idea that it is not practical to put colored and white tenants together in the same house can be done away with. . . . Race prejudice is a luxury and like all other luxuries, can be made very expensive in New York City, if the Negroes will but answer this call of the Afro-American Realty Company. . . . Prejudice, so far as it relates to the Negro tenancy in New York City, will in time become so very expensive that it will become impractical, and like all impracticable things, will die a natural death. A respectable law-abiding Negro will find conditions can be so changed that he will be able to rent wherever his means will permit him to live.[2]

In this appeal, Payton was asking black people to buy ten-dollar shares in the company in order to achieve his goal of eradicating racial discrimination in the New York City housing market. In the following years he used a range of tactics to "open" white neighborhoods to black residents, primarily in Harlem. But he also confronted the economic challenges of operating a race enterprise, a business owned and operated by black people with a stated mission of bettering their housing conditions by eradicating residential segregation, while also attempting to maximize the profits of his business in an economic environment in which access to capital was limited for black people.

This book is the first full biography of Philip Payton Jr. It demonstrates how he used his family contacts, media, and his natural assertiveness to become a leader of black businessmen in New York City before he was thirty years old. As a child Payton watched his parents, a hairdresser and a barber, work together to build thriving businesses with a base of white customers. Living above their shops, in a building they owned on one of Westfield's main streets, Payton also saw the way that his parents' business success translated into the respect accorded to them by the town's white residents.

When Payton decided to embark on his own entrepreneurial career in New York City, he was able to draw on contacts made as a young man, and on his talent for making friends, to quickly become part of the inner circle of black leader Booker T. Washington. Payton soon developed his own network of black entrepreneurs and leaders, which he cultivated and nurtured through frequent dinner parties hosted with his wife, Maggie, at their Harlem townhouse. He had a keen understanding of the value of publicity in shaping his image, and with *New York Age* editor Fred R. Moore as a friend and business partner, these affairs were regularly chronicled in the *Age*, almost always with a guest list, and often with a record of the menu for the evening. But behind this vision of black prosperity, Payton eventually struggled to respond to the white backlash to the increasing black presence in Harlem. He quickly strayed from his ambitious mission of eradicating racial discrimination to one that maximized his profits, provided better opportunities for his businesses, but actually set the stage for increasing racial segregation in Harlem, by specializing in renting all-black buildings.

The goal of providing access to quality housing was achieved for many of the black people who moved to Harlem in the first two decades of the 1900s. The segregated buildings that Payton "opened" to black people represented progress in access to better housing, but they also represented scarcity since they illustrated that housing choices for black people were still limited to such "open" buildings. As white property owners in Harlem had done before and after, Payton and other black real estate operators exploited this strong black demand for the scarce housing available to them by charging black people more than the previous white residents of the buildings had paid. Residential segregation, first on a building level and then by block and neighborhood, became an essential component of the business model for Payton's business and for the other Harlem property owners and managers, black and white, who followed him. Payton did not explicitly plan to set the stage for segregated neighborhoods, but his business model centered on racially segregated buildings. In many cases, as he gained control of buildings in an area, he evicted white tenants and replaced them with black ones, rather than moving black tenants into buildings with existing white residents, as he had proposed in the AARC prospectus. In the succeeding years, other real estate dealers, white and black, followed his practice, and the residential buildings on a block and eventually in a neighborhood became all-black buildings.[3]

Payton's access to additional buildings depended on white residents' and owners' fear of black residents, driven by a growing narrative in Harlem and other northern areas that linked black residents with lower property values, noisy neighborhoods with bars and prostitution, increased crime, and even disease. All these characteristics existed in the Tenderloin and in San Juan Hill, black neighborhoods in New York from which many black Harlem residents had moved. But in those neighborhoods and others in northern cities, those characteristics were not the result of the race of the residents, but the decisions of real estate owners, in most cases white investors, to provide no more services than absolutely necessary. Building owners were often guided by implicit city policies to locate bars, hotels, and restaurants attracting those in the "sporting life" in black neighborhoods, and they often made under-the-table payments to corrupt police to incentivize them to ignore illegal activity in these districts. By the 1910s Philip Payton's initial vision of black and white people living in the same Harlem buildings was a forgotten memory.

Payton's business and personal life illustrate the compromises that many race-based business owners made and continue to make when faced with a choice between maximizing profits and promoting racial equity. They operate in the capitalist system but are constrained because their businesses face the limits of the system that sociologist Gargi Bhatcharyya calls "racial capitalism," the characteristic of capitalism that uses the different treatment of people to privilege white actors and create obstacles for nonwhite ones. Bhatcharyya argues that differentiating people by race is an example of this characteristic, and that this practice has become so intrinsic to the capitalist system that it now seems immutable. Racial capitalism is an important vehicle for maintaining the racial hierarchy in which black people are least favored and white people are most favored. Race enterprises, such as the Afro-American Realty Company, operate in an economic system in which differentiation based on race is embedded. Race enterprises serving black people consciously target this portion of the market and differentiate it from other customers. But capital markets of potential lenders and investors differentiate race enterprises from other businesses. This differentiation separates those who, because of their race, are favored by capitalism with access to capital and opportunities to accumulate wealth and protect it, sometimes over generations, from those who are not privileged and can be exploited because they have little, or very limited, access to such opportunities.[4]

Philip Payton came from a background of relative privilege compared to his black peers in New York in 1899, the year he moved to the city. His entrepreneurial parents had the financial resources to provide him with a good education even though, unlike his brothers, who both graduated from Yale, he chose to end his formal education before he graduated from high school. But the Paytons' modest wealth, which included ownership of a building on one of the main streets in Westfield, was not sufficient to finance their son's business. Beyond perhaps modest assistance, he was on his own to navigate the terrain of racial capitalism. His decision to develop a race enterprise—one that in the late twentieth century would have been called "for us, by us"—reflected race pride but also the racial reality of the era. His decision to capitalize his business by seeking to sell shares in his company to black people reflected his understanding that even though these people's own access to wealth was limited, he had an affinity to them and they to him because of their shared racial identity that could allow him, as a new business entrant, to obtain their investment dollars.

Born at the end of the Reconstruction period, Payton was part of a generation of black men, including Booker T. Washington (born in 1856), who firmly believed that in the post-Emancipation era, the American creed of success through hard work was as equally available to black people as it was to white people. In a profile about his success, Payton recounted in Washington's anthology *The Negro in Business* (1907): "I have not found my color an obstacle to my success. On the contrary white people have in many cases been disposed to encourage me and as soon as they learned I was able to do the work they wanted done as well as or better than others, there was no longer any question of color between us, as far as business was concerned."[5] While Payton and his contemporaries were aware of racial hostility, particularly as lynching and other acts of violence against black people increased during the first two decades of the 1900s, without the benefit of hindsight they could not see that these acts were part of broader efforts to construct and maintain practices of white supremacy meant to ensure that black people would remain at the bottom socially and economically, regardless of how hard they worked, and that white people would continue to profit from this state of affairs.

This book combines scholarship on urban history, business history, and biography. James Weldon Johnson's *Black Manhattan* (1930) chronicled the movement of black people in Manhattan in the nineteenth and early twentieth centuries through the lens of the arts. The chapters focusing on the twentieth century describe the movement of black people to Harlem, for which Johnson, brother-in-law of real estate dealer and former AARC employee John E. Nail, had a unique perspective. Gilbert Osofsky's landmark of urban history, *Harlem, the Making of a Ghetto: Negro New York, 1890–1930* (1966), was the first comprehensive treatment of this period when large numbers of black people moved to Harlem. It includes a chapter, "Race Enterprise: The Afro-American Realty Company," summarizing the activity of Payton's business, which until now has been the most detailed history of Philip Payton's business activities. *Philip Payton: Father of Black Harlem* provides more detail about who Payton was, why he took the actions that he took in building the Afro-American Realty Company and later enterprises, and how these actions affected him and Harlem, the community where he lived and worked.[6]

In the past decade several books on Harlem history have provided additional knowledge about Harlem as a black community. My previous book, *Race and Real Estate: Conflict and Cooperation in Harlem, 1890–1920* (2015), provides a detailed analysis of the real estate transactions that undergirded the change in the racial composition of Harlem in the first decades of the 1900s and the tensions and instances of cooperation between black and white principals, including Philip Payton. Shannon King's *Whose Harlem Is This, Anyway? Community Politics and Grassroots Activism During the New Negro Era* (2015) focuses on the activist responses by black Harlem residents to the deterioration of their living conditions in the 1920s and 1930s as Harlem became overcrowded and the Depression severely affected an already poor population. *The Roots of Urban Renaissance: Gentrification and the Struggle Over Harlem* (2017), by Brian Goldstein, answers the question posed both by the title *Whose Harlem is This Anyway?* and in Johnson's *Black Manhattan*: "How long will black people be able to hold it?" Goldstein's narrative chronicles the choices made by black Harlem leaders as they promoted various redevelopment plans from the 1960s to the 2000s and effectively opened the floodgates of capital that had been held at bay for so long because of racial capitalism.[7]

This book takes its place alongside recent studies of black business history that have provided insight on the strategies used and challenges faced by black entrepreneurs in the twentieth century. In *Banking on Freedom: Black Women in U.S. Finance Before the New Deal* (2019), Shennette Garret-Scott describes the tenacious work of Maggie Lena Walker, a Payton contemporary, who built the St. Luke Bank in Richmond, Virginia, into a powerhouse among black banks. Scott describes the system of racial capitalism in which Walker and Payton operated: "Capitalism itself was a double-edged sword, built on the exploitation of others' labor and shaped by the racial exclusionary logics of Jim Crow. . . . Black entrepreneurs capitalized on the separate black economy but were simultaneously limited in their access to and ability to compete in wider markets."[8] Brandon K. Winford's recent *John Hervey Wheeler, Black Banking, and the Economic Struggle for Civil Rights* is a business history that demonstrates how Wheeler, born more than a generation after Philip Payton, was able to build on his business successes to become a civic leader in Durham, North Carolina, but was challenged by the difficult choice he made in supporting an urban renewal initiative that many in the city viewed as a betrayal of the black community, a large portion of which it demolished under the plan.[9]

The later evolution of the racial segregation process in real estate in which Payton was a participant is chronicled in one of several recent books that have examined the role of race in the real estate industry. *Colored Property: State Policy and White Racial Politics in Suburban America* (2007) by David Freund explores the resistance of white suburban residents to racial integration in suburban post–World War II communities. Focusing on a period four decades after Payton's death, Freund illustrates the ways in which writing race into housing practices and policies, in its infancy during Payton's time, was codified into federal policies and suburban home marketing practices. Keeanga-Yamahtta Taylor's *Race for Profit: How Banks and the Real Estate Industry Undermined Black Homeownership* (2019) looks at the forces described by Freund with a particular focus on the roles of the banking and real estate industries in perpetuating and creating barriers to black homeownership in the 1960s and 1970s. These studies mark the later evolution of processes that were just beginning to be developed during Philip Payton's life.[10]

Most histories of black Harlem make a passing reference to Philip Payton, often describing him as the person who opened Harlem to black residents. This book describes how and why Payton felt compelled to undertake this effort. Chapter 1 illustrates how the roots of Payton's later success can be traced to a web of relationships that were established decades before his birth and were tied to his father's roots in North Carolina and to his hometown of Westfield, Massachusetts. This chapter establishes the basis of some of the privileges, later downplayed by Payton, that contributed to his entrepreneurial nature and facilitated his access to leading figures in black life, which he maintained during his career.

The second chapter describes how, in four years, Payton went from being a porter doing menial work in a real estate dealer's office to speaking at the annual meeting of the National Negro Business League about his new business, the Afro-American Realty Company, which he led in partnership with several black men who were decades older than him. The chapter demonstrates Payton's early embrace of free market capitalism and his initial belief that his economic success would make his race inconsequential in business transactions.

Chapter 3 illustrates the collision of Philip Payton's real estate ambitions in Harlem with the attitudes of white New Yorkers who already lived there. Payton successfully adopted a publicly assertive stance regarding the right of black people to live in Harlem, but that stance set the stage for the new black residents to be confined to segregated housing in Harlem. This chapter demonstrates the growth of a vocal antiblack element in Harlem that required a strategic response if African Americans were to retain and build a presence in the community.

The period spanning 1905–1908 is covered in chapter 4. During this time Payton experienced the sometimes contradictory challenges of leading a race enterprise while also attempting to maximize profits. The chapter illustrates the pressures he faced to maximize profits for his investors by ignoring his promise to develop racially integrated buildings. The tension culminated with a lawsuit from a group of disgruntled AARC investors that tarnished Payton's image and hampered his business efforts.

The fifth chapter describes Payton seeking to recover from the negative press associated with the lawsuit by cultivating new relationships and business opportunities, using the black press to recover his image as a race champion. Payton demonstrates his continued commitment to race enterprise as a field for business success by traveling to "the little black republic" of Liberia for several months. Upon his return, he took over leadership of a new company, the Philip A. Payton Jr. Company.

Chapter 6 depicts Payton faced with headwinds from new black competitors and increasingly hostile white residents, struggling to develop a counterstrategy and to maintain a public image of prosperity and success. The chapter demonstrates the limitations of race enterprise he was experiencing after early years of reaping the benefits. Chapter 7 demonstrates that although it may have appeared that Payton's career was beyond recovery, he would prove doubters wrong with the announcement of the largest deal of his career, the leasing of six large Harlem apartment buildings as exclusive housing for black people. Payton's last big deal was structured as a race enterprise, down to naming the six apartments after six black historical icons. The deal announced Payton's return to preeminence among black real estate dealers in Harlem.

The title of this book, *Philip Payton: Father of Black Harlem*, is a derivative of the posthumous title given to its subject in eulogies and other tributes soon after his death in 1917: "Father of Colored Harlem." The New Negro era of the 1920s would introduce Harlem to the nation and the world, and the neighborhood would become known as the Black Capital of America, so it is through this lens that it seems more accurate to describe the neighborhood in which Payton had such a significant role in creating as Black Harlem rather than Colored Harlem. Both terms imply that another Harlem existed before Philip Payton's real estate activities. A small number of black people had been in Harlem since its formation as a Dutch farming community in the 1600s. The Village of Harlem in Upper Manhattan was annexed by New York City in the 1870s. When Payton arrived in New York in 1899, there was already a small black community there, identified as "Little Africa." White residents also lived on these streets, and a few lived in the same buildings as black residents. These streets represented what was probably decades of a practice of confining black residents to the area. As in other areas of New York, they were charged rents higher than white residents and paid the rents in order to be within walking distance of employment. The broader image of Harlem of this era was that of a white middle- and upper-middle-class residential community of stately brownstones, moderate-sized apartment buildings on the east-west streets, and mixed-use buildings with stores on their first floors and apartments above on the wider north-south avenues.[11]

The pressure of the growing black population in New York in the first decades of the twentieth century meant that black people were going to overflow their mid-Manhattan Tenderloin and San Juan Hill boundaries, but it was not inevitable that they would go to Harlem rather than Brooklyn, or move to the areas of Manhattan contiguous to San Juan Hill, expanding north into streets numbered in the 60s and 70s rather than leapfrogging to streets in Harlem. Without Payton's branding of Harlem as favorable to black people from 1904 to 1917, they may still have arrived there, but at a later date. Instead, though there was still a substantial white population in the neighborhood, by the 1910s black people had claimed central Harlem (then 125th to 135th Streets, and Fifth to Eighth Avenues) as their own, and by the 1920s they would brand it as the wellspring of black cultural life in America.

Black Harlem soon became important to the nation and to the world because it was the center of the Negro Renaissance of the 1920s that also was underway in Chicago, Washington, D.C., and other cities. Because artists in New York, even then the media center of the nation, were able to produce a wide range of plays, novels, and artwork, and New York–based Renaissance "midwives" such as W. E. B. Du Bois, Jessie Fauset, Charles S. Johnson, and Carl van Vechten promoted these activities, the Negro Renaissance was closely identified with Harlem. Payton's efforts two decades before enabled black people to be firmly established in the area and create a cultural movement that would introduce Harlem to the world.[12]

This is the dual legacy of Philip Payton. Through an appeal to race pride, he facilitated the creation of the Black Capital of America while also reifying and perpetuating racial residential segregation in Harlem as a concession to racial capitalism. The black residents of his buildings paid more than they would have paid in a free market in which one could live "wherever his means will permit him to live."[13] But the housing available to many in the first generation of Payton-inspired segregated buildings in the first two decades of the 1900s was better than that available to them in the past. Their residential concentration enabled black residents to build institutions they could control, place black people in elective office to represent their interests, and establish strong social networks that enabled them to cultivate the relationships that would act as springboards for creative work, mentoring, business enterprises, and the intangible feeling of belonging that makes life worth living.

Chapter One

THE PAYTONS BEFORE AND IN WESTFIELD

The tree-lined streets of Westfield, Massachusetts, seem an unlikely training ground for one of the boldest African American entrepreneurs of the early twentieth century. For almost two decades Philip Anthony Payton Jr. had a meteoric career in New York City's real estate industry. As a young man, in five years he went from a job working in his father's Westfield barbershop to leading the Afro-American Realty Company, which he formed in New York to facilitate the movement of large numbers of black people to Harlem. When Payton later described his success, he often framed it as that of a self-made man.[1] But as with most self-made people, his success was due in part to luck, but even more to a web of relationships that can be traced to places hundreds of miles from New York, where Payton made a name for himself, to the states of North Carolina and Virginia. These relationships had their roots in his father's generation. During and after the Civil War, important ties between Westfield, where Payton was born and raised, and both whites and blacks were established. These ties provided two generations of Paytons and other black people with opportunities that would extend far beyond the South to New England and New York.

Washington, North Carolina, at the junction of the Tar and Pimlico Rivers in the eastern part of the state, was a city of industry: in the late 1700s northern industrialists had begun to use it as an entry port to ship their goods inland to North Carolina cities, and Washington in turn sent lumber, agricultural products, and naval supplies, such as tar, to the North. By the 1840s the economies in the Upper South states were no longer dependent only on plantation slavery, having developed light industries that resulted in somewhat diversified local economies. Philip Anthony Payton Sr. was born in 1845, a middle child of eight children born to Uriah and Winnie Payton in Washington. While North Carolina was a slave state, in 1840 it had a free black population of 22,732, an enslaved population of 753,419, and a white population of 484,277. Whether the Paytons were enslaved or free at the time of the birth of Philip Sr. is not known.[2]

In the 1850s, when Payton Sr. was a child, the decades-long tension involving the slaveholding southern states, which were seeking to preserve and expand slavery, was growing in intensity. Northern states had become increasingly resentful of the political power of the South, which had elected the overwhelming majority of U.S. presidents. From the perspective of those in the North, the South had reached into their territory with the passage of the Compromise of 1850. The law, meant to thwart obstacles to slavery while placating free states, had admitted California to the Union as a free state but had strengthened the Fugitive Slave Law by making it a crime to thwart the work of slave catchers in the North, or to refuse to assist them in capturing an enslaved person if their aid was requested. Many northerners viewed the new Fugitive Slave Law as a brazen effort to ensure that slavery was a national institution preserved even in states where it had been abolished.

In the election of 1860, as Philip Payton Sr. entered adolescence, the divisions of the nation were in full view. The Democratic Party split into northern and southern wings, each offering a candidate: Stephen Douglas and John Breckenridge, respectively. A third party, the Constitutional Union Party, nominated John Bell. Abraham Lincoln, the nominee of the antislavery Republican Party, making its second appearance in a presidential election, was on the ballot only in northern states. Lincoln's victory in November 1860 led some southerners to conclude that, with his inauguration in March 1861, they would have an enemy in the White House. In South Carolina, at a December 20 secession convention, 169 delegates voted unanimously to leave the Union.[3]

North Carolina had substantial secessionist and Unionist populations. By 1860 the state had an enslaved population of 331,059, with 34,658 slaveholders out of a white population of 629,942. The state had 30,463 free blacks. While North Carolina slaveholders interpreted the election of Abraham Lincoln as a threat to their wealth and to their way of life, they were far outnumbered by nonslaveholders in mountain districts of the West and swamp regions of the East, where Philip Payton Sr. and his family lived. Nonslaveholders saw no benefit to making rash decisions that could irreparably impair the region. With soil that prevented it from becoming a major cotton state, North Carolina had fewer large slaveholders to dominate state political life, and the state did not initially join states such as South Carolina in seceding from the Union because of Lincoln's election. Instead, North Carolinians adopted a more moderate "watch and wait" stance.[4] In February 1861 the North Carolina electorate voted down a proposal to hold a secession convention by a margin of 650 votes out of over 93,000 cast. The close margin undoubtedly inspired secessionists to continue their work in various regions, arguing for the need to fight perceived northern dominance even while denying support of the slaveocracy.[5]

After Confederate troops fired on Fort Sumter off the coast of Charleston, South Carolina, on April 12, 1861, as a Union ship attempted to resupply the fort, the momentum toward secession accelerated. North Carolina governor John Ellis refused Lincoln's call to the states for seventy-five thousand troops. At a state secession convention on May 20, North Carolina delegates voted unanimously to secede from the Union, joining the nine states that had previously made the decision.[6] The outbreak of the Civil War in 1861 disrupted the young life of Philip Payton Sr., but it also became the vehicle that placed him on pathways toward true freedom and unusual opportunities.

For the Confederate Army, Virginia was the first line of defense against northern aggression, as well as a launching site for incursions on the nation's capital and northern states. North Carolina was next in line, with valuable territory and industries. The Union Army viewed both Upper South states, in close proximity to the District of Columbia, as logical starting places to force the Confederate states back into the Union. In North Carolina in the months after secession, the state appropriated funds for ammunition and equipment, and state militias began recruiting soldiers to contribute to the Confederate Army. Local factories produced uniforms, and women sewed unit flags.[7]

Northern states responded to President Lincoln's request for troops after the assault on Fort Sumter with a rapidity that reflected both the states' military readiness and governors' views of the prospect of military confrontation against the South. Massachusetts, asked to provide fifteen hundred troops, immediately provided two regiments. By the fall of 1861, as it became clear that an extended war was possible, the 27th Regiment from the western counties near Springfield, including the nearby town of Westfield, was assembled. The regiment left Massachusetts on November 2 and traveled by sea to Annapolis, Maryland, reaching the city on November 5. After several weeks of drilling, the regiment left the city on January 6, 1862, for Fortress Monroe on the North Carolina coast. On January 12 it moved on to join General Ambrose Burnside's Roanoke Island campaign. The 27th Regiment's first large confrontation with Confederate forces took place on the island, the site of a failed 1585 English settlement. On February 8, 1862, General Burnside led ten thousand troops on a motley assembly of eighty boats from the North Carolina coast to the twelve-by-three-mile island, where the Confederate Army had established a fort and other defensive elements. Arriving under the cover of night, the Union troops far outnumbered the 1,800 Confederate troops and soon seized control of the island. Five men from the 27th Regiment were killed in the island campaign, and fifteen were wounded.[8]

After a month living on ships off the coast of Roanoke, on March 11 the regiment traveled to the North Carolina coast in a flotilla that included army transport ships and thirteen gunships, with the first troops landing on the March 12 and the 27th Regiment arriving the next day. The troops marched toward New Bern, North Carolina. Civil War historian David Eicher notes that "this small town of 5,432 citizens represented a gateway for the Yankees from which to strike eastward into the heart of North Carolina, demolishing the railroads, and to move southward on Beaufort."[9]

On the morning of March 13 the 27th Regiment, along with other regiments making up the Department of North Carolina force of eleven thousand assembled by Burnside, confronted Confederate troops, ousting them from the area after a short time and giving the Union Army control of the second-most important city in North Carolina (after Wilmington, 1860 population of 9,552). The troops remained in the area through the spring and summer.

To the enslaved in New Bern and vicinity, the arrival of the Union troops and their occupation of the eastern region represented the arrival of freedom, even though the federal government's policy had not determined that

THE PAYTONS BEFORE AND IN WESTFIELD

result. As slaveholders on surrounding plantations fled, some took the enslaved with them, but many enslaved people used the coming of the troops as an opportunity to seize their freedom. Soon they were descending on New Bern in the hundreds from nearby plantations and towns. It is quite possible that Philip Payton Sr. and his family were in this number if they were enslaved. For enslaved and free blacks, in addition to freedom, the Union troops represented opportunities to earn money doing manual work or to attend the schools that Union soldiers and northern volunteers soon established.[10]

The "jubilee" moment in New Bern was short-lived. In May 1862, when Edward Stanley was appointed military governor of North Carolina, he quickly instituted policies that he thought would appeal to area Unionists by following the letter of military regulations. These included ruling formerly enslaved as contraband of war who were to be emancipated only if it could be proven that their owners had been supporters of the Confederacy. Stanley also closed the contraband schools, noting that his purpose was to reestablish the social hierarchy that had existed before the war. Some of the formerly enslaved panicked at the thought that their short taste of freedom might be revoked, but many were adamant that they would not return to enslavement. Stanley's tactics divided Union troops as well. Through interactions with the formerly enslaved in New Bern, many Union soldiers learned of the harsh realities of slavery for the first time. For some, appalled by the conditions described to them, the experience pushed them from disinterested neutrality on the issue into the ranks of the abolitionists. For others, their assumptions of black inferiority were confirmed as they witnessed uneducated, unskilled black people struggle to adapt to a new world. In September 1862 two companies of the 27th Regiment were ordered to Washington, North Carolina, Philip Payton Sr.'s hometown forty miles from New Bern. The regiment remained in the New Bern region until June 1863, occasionally traveling to Washington and other surrounding towns.[11] After the New Bern campaign, the regiment saw action in Virginia, where in May 1864 some were captured and imprisoned. With a three-year enlistment, the 27th remained in North Carolina until September 1864, when the remaining 179 troops returned home to Massachusetts, where they were mustered out of the army on September 27.[12]

While the details of Payton Sr.'s life during the war are not known, if he was not already literate before Union troops arrived in the New Bern area, the campaign may have provided him with the opportunity to learn to read and write. After the war, as a twenty-year-old, he traveled to Washington, D.C., where he enrolled in Wayland Seminary, established in 1865 by the American Baptist Home Mission Society. The school was first housed in Nineteenth Street Baptist Church, a black congregation established in 1802 and relocated in 1866 to a building on I Street. The ministry was a common pursuit for literate black men in the nineteenth century, and in the aftermath of the Civil War most Christian denominations instituted aggressive missionary campaigns to expand their reach in the South by establishing more churches. Wayland was one of several seminaries established to educate the future leaders of these churches.[13]

Documents are not available to determine the outcome of Payton's time at Wayland, but he does not seem to have entered the ministry. By 1870 he was living in a New York City apartment in lower Manhattan, with Richard Bowen and Annie Maria Hammonds Ryans. Payton and Bowen were working as porters in a store; Ryans worked as a dressmaker. All three reported to the 1870 census taker that they could read, but it was reported that Annie could not write. A native of Baltimore, she was born in 1847 to Jacob Hammond and Caroline Ryans. Payton and Ryans moved to Westfield, Massachusetts, in 1872, and Payton found work as a barber. The couple was married in Westfield on February 24 by Rev. J. S. Barnes. The marriage was the first for Philip, age thirty, and the second for Annie.[14] In all likelihood, Payton's familiarity with Westfield came from his interaction with 27th Regiment troops who had occupied New Bern and Washington, North Carolina, in the early years of the Civil War, when he was a teenager.

Founded in 1646, Westfield had a proud colonial heritage. It was located in the Connecticut River valley in Hampden County in the western part of the state. People of African descent had been present in the county since at least the 1650s following the settlement of the area by English colonists. Both enslaved and free people of African descent had worked in the area as farmers. During the War for Independence, free blacks enlisted to fight the British, and some enslaved blacks were offered freedom in exchange for service to the American cause. Following the war, free African Americans continued to reside in the area as landholding farmers as well as day laborers for white farmers. Ten miles from the larger city of Springfield, by the nineteenth century Westfield had become known as a center for the manufacturing of horse whips, with over thirty-five businesses devoted to this product based there by the 1870s. These businesses were complemented by manufacturers of steam heaters and radiators, textile manufacturers, and paper companies. The industries spurred the growth of the town's population, which by 1870 numbered over 6,500 people. The black population, however, although present for almost two centuries, was minuscule at 36 people.[15] By the time Philip and Annie Payton were married, Westfield had all the attributes of a New England town: a town square bordered by the Methodist church, the court house, and a private library, all shaded by stately trees, and a main street on which the merchant class displayed the proceeds of their industry through two- and three-story wood-frame homes with wide porches that provided residents with ideal venues to while away temperate summer evenings.[16]

Tuesday, July 4, 1876, in Westfield dawned as a clear, humid day. Anticipation filled the air as residents looked forward to celebrations marking the centennial of the signing of the Declaration of Independence. By seven a.m. crowds had gathered along the downtown streets, looking forward to the first glimpse of the "Ancient and Horribles Parade," a New England tradition but a first for Westfield, in which residents dressed up in silly costumes and poked fun at those in power. The parade stepped off at eight a.m., with the three hundred parade participants led by the Westfield Brass Band. The procession was the kickoff of a day of music offered on the village green at the intersection of Main, Broad, Court, and Elm Streets.[17]

During the era of slavery, many African Americans commemorated the signing of the Declaration of Independence on July 5 rather than on July 4 as a way of quietly protesting the fact that the nation had not lived up to its creed that "all men are created equal." Eleven years after the end of slavery, the centennial celebrations of the signing of the Declaration of Independence ironically highlighted black citizens' continued subordinate status. In 1874 Congress had appropriated three million dollars for a Centennial Exhibition in Philadelphia, but black people were for the most part excluded from local planning committees as well as the narratives chronicling how the previous one hundred years of independence had been made possible. In 1876 the nation was in the throes of an economic downturn, and some questioned whether the funds would have been better spent on those suffering from the bank failures and business closures that had begun in the early 1870s. In the South, the Reconstruction era that blacks thought had permanently secured for them the vote and had led to the election of two black senators, several members of the House of Representatives, and many local elected officials, was drawing to a close, the victim of election fraud and terroristic violence targeting black people and their allies. While there were still six black representatives and one black senator serving, their influence was minimal as whites in the North and South expressed fatigue with Reconstruction, and as blacks were dissuaded from voting by intimidation and violence.[18]

Considering the ambivalence with which blacks faced Independence celebrations, the Paytons would have had good reasons to refrain from participating in Westfield's festivities in 1876. But as local business owners with a predominantly white clientele, their position as full citizens of the city would be further established by such celebrations. It is very likely that they were among those gathered to watch the festivities and hear the addresses.[19]

In Westfield, Philip Payton Sr. had quickly established his trade as a barber, occupying a series of shops on Elm Street, one of the city's main streets. Some of the women of Westfield were customers of his wife. Annie operated a millinery store in the same building as Philip's barbershop, where she sold hats, hat trimmings such as bows and ribbons, women's wigs and wiglets, and men's toupees. Philip's barbering skills and Annie's hair and millinery businesses were complementary, and they ran annual advertisements in the *Westfield Directory* promoting their products and services.[20]

In addition to maintaining an image for their business activities, they would have been further incentivized to attend the Independence Day festivities by the fact that they were parents of black children of the Emancipation era. On that day they most likely would have been accompanied by their one-year-old daughter Susan and their infant son Philip Jr., who had been born in February. If the family had returned for the evening festivities, they would have witnessed the fireworks display that concluded the Independence Day celebrations. Afterward they could have exited on the Elm Street side of the village green to make the short three-block walk to their home, the apartment above their shops at 342 Elm Street.[21]

The following year, 1877, as the Reconstruction period ended in the South and state-sanctioned black oppression was given full sway, the Paytons welcomed a third child, James. Three years later, Westfield had grown to a population of over 7,500, among them 59 "colored" (designating black) people and 4 people who were Chinese or Japanese. That summer the Paytons and three other black families were enumerated in the manuscript census.

THE PAYTONS BEFORE AND IN WESTFIELD

Residing at 342 Elm Street, Philip Sr. was listed as a barber, and his wife, Anna M. as "keeping house." Their children, Susan, Philip, and James, were listed as ages five, four, and two. A fourteen-year-old black servant, Allis McArther, lived with the family. Providing a window on Westfield racial mores, Joseph White, a twenty-five-year-old white barber, also lived with the family and undoubtedly worked with Payton in his shop.[22] The Elkays, another of the city's black families, lived across the street, at 357 Elm Street. Head of household Lewis Elkay, born in Canada, was a laborer, while his wife, Susan, born in Connecticut, was described as "keeping house," like Annie. Their daughter, Georgina, born in 1864, worked as a servant. Their son Albert, age twelve, born in 1868, was listed as attending school but also as having "consumption" or tuberculosis, a common affliction of black people in urban areas in the nineteenth century. Their twin sons, Evan and Frank, were three months old. The widow Margaret Pell, also black, was forty-four and lived at 206 Linn Street with her daughters: Ann, twenty-four, who worked as a servant; Jane, eleven; Lucy, eight; and son Frederick, four. An additional eight black people lived as servants in households throughout the city.[23]

In 1880 Westfield had four Chinese residents, who lived at 389 Elm Street as boarders in the household of merchant William H. Fork, aged forty-two. Also in the household were Fork's wife, Josephine, forty, who was "keeping house," the Fork's eight-year-old daughter, Grace, and twenty-year-old servant William McElligent. The Chinese men were born in China and listed as "in school." Che Yew Tong was eighteen, and Leang Luy Wong, Chaung Yang, and Cheun Lin Paun were all sixteen. They were said to have been sons of Chinese officials and were reportedly sent to the United States by Child of the Sun Society in China. Two years later the federal Chinese Exclusion Act would make it almost impossible for such immigration to occur.[24]

The Paytons welcomed a fourth child, Edward, in 1882. As parents they were undoubtedly concerned with providing their children with a stable home in which to grow, as well as resources to thrive. Philip's barbershop continued to prosper, and in 1883 he purchased a two-story building at 83 Elm Street for $5,250. The Paytons' businesses occupied the first floor, and the family lived in a second-floor apartment. Through thrift and hard work, they built thriving businesses that served Westfield's black and white residents. The purchase of the building indicates that the Paytons were at the top of the economic ladder in relation to other black residents, and well along the economic ladder for Westfield's overall population. By the late nineteenth century the Payton name was well regarded by white and black residents of Westfield. Because of Westfield's small black population, and New England's relatively new tradition of integrated schools, the Payton siblings attended schools with white classmates at the Green District School, at Washington and School Streets, two blocks away from their home. With all the trappings of Victorian architecture, the imposing three-story brick building with mansard roof had tall windows that brought generous amounts of light into the high-ceilinged classrooms. While many U.S. towns had no secondary education options, New England's long tradition of literacy had resulted in the establishment in 1802 of the Westfield Academy, a private school on Broad Street, a two-story brick building with a four-story tower at one end that was constructed in the mid-1800s as an expansion of the Westfield Academy. The buildings were purchased by the city of Westfield in 1867 and became Westfield High School.[25]

In the fall of 1893 Philip Payton Sr. became concerned about his oldest son's future during Philip Jr.'s third year of high school. Concluding that

FIGURE 1.1 Susan Payton's Green District School class, 1888 (Susan in *back row, center*). *Source*: Westfield Athenaeum Archives.

THE PAYTONS BEFORE AND IN WESTFIELD

his son was associating with the wrong group of friends, Payton Sr. decided to send him to complete his junior and senior years of high school at the secondary school arm of Livingstone College in Salisbury, North Carolina. In the late 1800s, as black colleges were established in the South, their administrators understood that most of their potential students from the region had limited opportunities for education beyond grammar school. North Carolina's public school system was established following the enactment in 1839 of a law establishing common schools for white children. After the Civil War, when a new school system was established during the Reconstruction period, black and white students were educated in separate schools.[26] Public education of black children was not a priority for the white leaders of the South. Where grammar schools for black children existed, they adjusted their schedules to accommodate the agricultural calendar so that the children could help their families, often sharecroppers, in the fields. Most southern towns and cities did not provide high schools for black students, who were barred from segregated white high schools. Responding to this reality, many of the new black colleges complemented their collegiate curricula with secondary curricula available to students from around the region who attended as boarders. This also created a feeder system of natural recruits for the collegiate arms of the schools. Philip Payton hoped that the close supervision of the Livingstone College faculty, and the influence of conservative fellow students from small towns in the South, would help his son to find some direction in his last years of secondary school.[27]

Payton Sr. wanted all his children to attend college. At the end of the nineteenth century, college education was rare for any American. Only 2 percent of young adults were then enrolled in college. His decision to take such a drastic step, sending his son more than 750 miles away to school, was an effort to keep alive this goal for his eldest son. In considering the decision to send Philip Jr. to North Carolina, Payton Sr. understood the lasting impact that youthful indiscretions could have on the future of a young black man in a small town.[28]

Salisbury, North Carolina, must have been something of a shock to Philip Payton Jr. in the fall of 1893. Although North Carolina did not adopt a Jim Crow law affecting trains until 1898, many of the laws being enacted throughout the South codified practices that had been in place for years; therefore it is quite likely that he encountered these practices on his train ride from Westfield to Salisbury. If so, as the train entered the South, most likely in Virginia, he and other travelers of color would have been directed from their standard coach car to the Jim Crow car directly behind the locomotive. In this car the smoke and cinders from train entering the open windows in late August would have made the air uncomfortable. The reduced status of the car was reinforced by the fact that it was also the smoking car. The white passengers in that car who weren't smoking may have been chewing tobacco and periodically spewing its juice into the spittoons that were placed in the car.[29]

By southern standards, Salisbury's climate was fairly temperate, not drastically different from what Payton was used to in Westfield. Dunn Mountain to the west of Salisbury may have reminded him of the Berkshires that framed Westfield.[30] While the Jim Crow accommodations on the train may have been a temporary shock to him, other shocks would have been more pleasant. With his arrival at Livingstone College, for the first time in his life Philip Jr. was living in a predominantly black community and was away from home. In Westfield it had been rare that he went anywhere in its vicinity without someone knowing him or his family.

Livingstone College had roots in the African Methodist Episcopal Zion (A.M.E.Z.) Church, a denomination dating to the establishment of Zion Methodist Church in New York City in 1796. Established in 1879 as Zion Wesley Institute and moved to Salisbury in 1882, the school changed its name later in the decade to honor the Christian Scottish missionary David Livingstone. The college's founding president, Joseph C. Price, was a friend of Payton Sr., possibly from childhood. Born in Elizabeth City, North Carolina, in 1863, he traveled with his mother, who was born free (his father was enslaved), 120 miles to New Bern at the time the Union troops occupied the area. Price later attended Lowell Normal School in New Bern and Shaw University in Raleigh, before entering the ministry. His success in fundraising in England on behalf of the Zion Wesley Institute in 1881 enabled the organization to purchase the grounds and buildings in North Carolina that became Livingstone College. Price was part of a national network of black leaders who met and corresponded regularly to develop strategies to advance the causes of black people. With New York–based publisher T. Thomas Fortune and others, in 1887 he cofounded and served as the first president of the Afro-American League, a short-lived effort to create a civil rights organization with chapters across the country. Its goal was to obtain full citizenship and equality for African Americans.[31]

At a time when black and white leaders debated whether a vocational or classical education was most appropriate for black youth, Livingstone reflected Price's vision for providing a broad education. W. E. B. Du Bois later explained that Price was building the "Harvard of the Colored South at Livingstone."[32] Although northerners might have looked down on the education provided by these new colleges, Philip Payton Sr. undoubtedly understood the educational opportunity that Livingstone would provide for his son and was interested in providing him with greater exposure to education grounded in African American culture. The commencement program from 1888, five years before Philip arrived, reflected these goals. Miss Bettie E. Riddick of Coffeeville, Mississippi, offered an essay on "How We Should Like to Be Remembered," followed by an oration on "Some Aspects of Life and Its Chief Aim" by F. McNeill, of Bunn's Level, North Carolina. Other speeches were given by young men and women, including a Latin salutatory address by W. L. Henderson of Salisbury, followed by a mathematical oration by Miss E. Dade of Philadelphia. Musical performances were interspersed throughout the program, including a solo by Miss D. Hamilton of Spartanburg, South Carolina. A musical quartet selection preceded the valedictory oration by C. D. Howard of Tarboro, Tennessee.[33] A Livingstone commencement program from 1902 suggests that rather than restrict educational choices to vocational or classical areas, Livingstone's curriculum offered both, with Departments of Mechanical and Agricultural; a Grammar School Course of four years; a Normal Course (for teachers and college prep) of three years; a Classical Course of four years; and a Theological Course.[34]

By the summer of 1893, when Philip arrived at Livingstone, white supremacists were triumphant across the South. They had successfully reestablished the racial hierarchy of white supremacy that the decade of Reconstruction had disrupted, and North Carolina was no exception. Hostile whites in most southern states prohibited black voting through various mechanisms such as poll taxes and literacy tests added to state constitutions, as well as by violent intimidation. Segregated public education was firmly entrenched, and for African Americans, their schools often followed schedules designed to ensure that students would be available for farm work.[35]

Life at Livingstone was regimented, as Payton Sr. undoubtedly knew. Young Philip lived in the men's dormitory with the college-aged students. Befitting a school with religious roots, the day began with mandatory devotion services. Considering that his father had attended seminary, religion had been emphasized in the Payton household, but the incorporation of religious themes in the classroom was new to Payton. At Livingstone, most of the teachers were either ministers or otherwise affiliated with the AMEZ church, so their presentation of educational material was infused with references to religion and its importance to African Americans.

As Philip settled into his studies in October, the optimism of the start of the school year at Livingstone was clouded with the news that its president, J. C. Price, was ailing and confined to his home. Considering the nature of medical care at the time, particularly in black communities, the presence of illness was not unusual. But the campus was stunned on October 25 when news arrived that the thirty-nine-year-old Price had died. His funeral took place at the chapel on campus three days later, and Price was interred in a mausoleum constructed on campus. Livingstone College and black people across the nation mourned the loss of a leader who had seemed on a trajectory for great achievements.[36]

In spite of his New England origins, Payton's gregarious personality most likely helped him get acclimated to his fellow students. Many of them were children of farmers, young men pursuing the Mechanical/Agricultural curriculum, or young women interested in pursuing teaching with plans to return home after finishing their schooling to use their education to build lives better than their parents had known. Those taking the Normal Course planned to seek teaching positions, a field in which men were still well represented. Students pursuing the Classical curriculum faced a more uncertain future with few professional jobs available to black people. A few of the women might find jobs as librarians or as clerical workers in black businesses, such as insurance companies, that were being established in response to harsher segregation practices. The young men might follow similar paths, and some might open their own businesses. In questioning the pursuit of a liberal arts education, Booker T. Washington, the leader of Tuskegee Institute in Alabama, would soon warn that classically trained students might end up in positions such as train porters, relatively well-paid but frustrated that the color line was preventing them from using their intellects. Payton, pursuing the high school course, felt less pressured than the college students to chart a course for his life. He was uncertain regarding his future plans. He could go into barbering, but he knew his mother wanted him to be more ambitious. He was enjoying his boyhood freedom and was not sure what he wanted to do in the future.[37]

While Payton Sr. may have wanted Livingstone to be a break from Westfield, his son was able to continue to indulge his interest in football at Livingstone. The previous year, on December 27, 1892, Livingstone had faced Biddle University in the first college football game among black colleges. Although Livingstone was on the losing side in a 5–0 game, excitement over the new game continued the following year when Philip arrived. As a high school student he may not have had an opportunity to play on the Livingstone team, but he undoubtedly watched practices and attended games.[38]

After the 1893–1894 year in North Carolina, Philip satisfactorily demonstrated to his father that he was becoming more serious-minded, and he was allowed to return to Westfield to complete his senior year of high school with friends, white and black, whom he had known since early childhood. But rather than the triumphant return that he probably dreamed of during his days at Livingstone, during his senior year he was faced with new challenges, as he later described: "On returning home, I again entered High School the following fall. During that term I met with an accident, while playing football, which laid me up for the best of a year, and I was compelled to leave school. Thus ended my education, much to the disgust of my father who had always intended that each of his children should have a college education."[39] Payton was a high-profile member of the Westfield football team (figure 1.2), as noted by the *Springfield Republican*: "Philip A. Payton, one of the best players on the high school football team, will not be able to play any more this season on account of an injury at Northampton Friday. The bones of his right wrist were dislocated, and a small bone was broken."[40] In addition to providing an indication of Philip's prowess on the gridiron, the article shows a one-year gap in the narrative of his high school career. Entering Livingstone in his junior year in the fall of 1893, if he had returned to school at Westfield at the beginning of the next academic year, the fall of 1894, he should have graduated in the spring of 1895. The article indicates that Payton was still in school in the fall of 1896 and possibly would have graduated in the spring of 1897.

Perhaps he returned to Westfield after a year at Livingstone but did not immediately enroll in school. The gap also may explain why he did not

FIGURE 1.2 Westfield High School football team, 1895 (*left to right, front row*: James W. Payton, K. M. Bradley, G. W. Hannum, L. D. Taylor, Philip A. Payton; *middle row*: H. H. Pettibone, G. T. Chapman, F. B. Sizer, W. G. Parenteau; *back row*: J. B. Ely, W. T. Eldridge, B. W. Gladwin, J. B. Bates, H. J. Bush). *Source*: Westfield Atheneum Archives.

return to school after his wrist healed. He may have begun to feel that he was getting too far behind, since his brother James, one year younger, had graduated in the spring of 1896. Nevertheless, high school graduation was important enough to Philip that although he was not included in the official high school portraits for the Class of 1896, he had his own individual Class of 1896 graduation photograph made (figure 1.3), perhaps an early hint of his talents at managing his image.[41]

While Philip Jr. faced obstacles to his schooling, his older sister Susan was making good progress with her academic career. She graduated from Westfield High School in 1894 and enrolled at Westfield State Normal School. Established in 1838 through the efforts of Horace Mann, then the state secretary of education, the school trained teachers, drawing students primarily from the surrounding towns. It admitted black students, and by the 1890s there were usually one to three black students in each matriculating class. Susan's local origins were unusual for black students at the

FIGURE 1.3 Philip Payton Jr. "graduation" photo. *Source:* Westfield Atheneum.

Normal School. More typically, black students at the school were from the South, having been recruited through relationships, like those of Payton Sr.'s, that extended to before the Civil War. In the 1880s Booker T. Washington had established ties with the school that would become significant for Philip Payton Jr. Westfield's links to Washington most likely were the result of his mentor, General Samuel Chapman Armstrong, who founded Hampton Institute in Virginia in 1868. Armstrong's mother, Clarissa, was born in Blandford, Massachusetts, eleven miles from Westfield, and was a graduate of Westfield Normal School. The ties between Washington and Westfield State Normal School were further solidified when one of Washington's protégés, Samuel Courtney, enrolled there in the 1880s. Born in 1861 in Malden, West Virginia, Courtney, like Washington, was the son of a white planter and a biracial enslaved woman, Cornelia Courtney. In 1865 Washington, who was five years older than Samuel Courtney, moved with his mother to Malden. He enrolled at Hampton Institute in 1872 and became one of Armstrong's star pupils. After graduation, following a brief detour at Wayland Seminary, the same Washington, D.C., seminary that Payton Sr. attended, Washington returned to Malden. He worked as a schoolteacher there between 1876 and 1878 and prepared several young men, including Samuel Courtney, to enter Hampton. Courtney graduated in 1879 and moved to Weston, Massachusetts, to work in the household of Ellen B. Sears and Horace Sears.[42]

In 1881 Samuel Chapman Armstrong recommended Booker T. Washington to Alabama legislators seeking someone to establish a vocational school for black youth in Tuskegee, Alabama. Hampton Institute, with its emphasis on vocational training or work with the hands, served as the model for Tuskegee Institute. Westfield Normal School, possibly at Armstrong's suggestion, would serve as a place of instruction for Tuskegee's most promising students. Perhaps the benefits of the school were affirmed when Washington's protégé Samuel Courtney entered Westfield in 1882 and completed his studies in 1885. Because the school had dormitories only for women students, male students boarded with Westfield families. It is possible that Courtney may have boarded with the Paytons, considering that there were only a handful of black families in the city. Even if he did not, he would most likely have been acquainted with them during the time when Philip Payton Jr. was in elementary school.[43]

For two years following his graduation, Courtney served as a chief organizer for Tuskegee, traveling throughout the North to raise funds. He left his employment at the institute in 1887 and entered Harvard Medical School, graduating in 1894. By the time Susan Payton entered Westfield Normal School in that same year, Courtney was serving as the house physician for Boston Lying-In Hospital. The next year, in 1895, Booker T. Washington would step onto the national stage at the Atlanta Cotton States and International Exposition and be seen as a leader of black Americans after making his "Atlanta Compromise" speech, recommending that, socially, the races "remain as separate as the fingers, but one as the hand on those things essential to mutual progress."[44]

Philip Payton's prospects did not measure favorably against the academic opportunities that were being seized by his sister and other ambitious black youth of the time. After recovering from his football injury, he began working in his father's barbershop. His brother James enrolled at Yale in the Class of 1900, where he majored in the classics. Philip languished for a few years in the barbershop, but with his brother's college graduation a year away, sibling rivalry may have prompted him to consider his options. He noted that in "April, 1899 when realizing that I was not making much of myself, and that I was not growing any younger [he was twenty-three], and if I intended to do anything in this life, it was time I started, I decided to try a new field." It is likely that as Philip worked in his father's barbershop, his parents drew comparisons to his current situation as a barber, an accomplishment for his father's generation, with those of his siblings, who were seizing the new opportunities as part of the generation born in emancipation who had better access to education and employment options. It would have been particularly galling for Philip that his younger brother, who had competed on the high school football team with him, seemed poised to carry the family name forward in the field of education, where he had faltered. Philip's decision to seek a change of scenery that might offer the possibility of success is understandable. He later explained that "on Sunday morning April 10, 1899, I left Westfield, pack and baggage for New York City, much against the wishes of both of my parents."[45] While his parents clearly had ambitions for him, they probably had hoped that he would seek them close home. At twenty-three, Philip was still somewhat undisciplined, but he carried with him an ambitious personality, inspired by the successes he had seen his parents create for themselves in Westfield. Although he was leaving the place of his birth, New York at the turn of the century had the potential to present many more challenges than Westfield, as well as infinite potential for success for a young man seeking his fortune.

Chapter Two

THE PROVINCIAL IN NEW YORK CITY

The opening lines of chapter 7 of Paul Laurence Dunbar's novel *The Sport of the Gods* (1902) capture what Philip Payton Jr. most likely experienced when he arrived in New York City in April 1899: "To the provincial coming to New York for the first time, ignorant and unknown, the city presents a notable mingling of the qualities of cheeriness and gloom. If he have any eye at all for the beautiful, he cannot help experiencing a thrill as he crosses the ferry over the river filled with plying craft and catches the first sight of the spires and buildings of New York."[1]

In 1899 passengers traveling to New York on trains from the east disembarked at the Long Island Railroad's terminal at Hunter's Point, Long Island City, on the East River, retrieved their luggage, and then took the Hunter's Point ferry across the river to the 34th Street pier.[2] If their train travels continued, they could take a streetcar or carriage to Grand Central Terminal at Lexington Avenue and East 42nd Street. For those with New York destinations, they could begin navigating the streets of New York. Upon arrival in New York, Philip Payton in all likelihood made his way, possibly on the 34th Street Crosstown Railway streetcar line, from the 34th Street terminal on the East Side of Midtown Manhattan to the West Side, toward the city's large black neighborhoods. Disembarking there, he most likely stopped at a neighborhood restaurant or a bar for a meal as well as to get suggestions for lodging in one of the area's hotels or rooming houses. Dunbar's *Sport of the Gods* suggests how someone like Payton might have experienced his first evening in New York:

> Later, the lights in the busy street will bewilder and entice him. He will feel shy and helpless amid the hurrying crowds. A new emotion will take his heart—as the people hasten by him,—a feeling of loneliness, almost of grief, that with all of these souls about him he knows not one and no one cares for him. After a while he will find a place and give a sigh of relief as he settles away from the city's sights behind his cozy blinds. It is better here, and the city is cold and unfeeling. This he will feel for the first half-hour, and then he will be out in it all again.[3]

The Sport of the Gods, a chronicle of the turmoil that awaited the young adult members of the Hamilton family, African Americans who moved with their mother to New York from the rural South, expressed the age-old fears of the city held by those living in America's rural areas and small towns. Many black people shared these beliefs, having in the decades after emancipation watched their children, other relatives, and friends leave familiar communities for opportunities in cities unknown to them. Dunbar's text most likely conveyed the concerns behind the disapproval of Annie and Philip Payton Sr. regarding their son's decision to seek his fortune in New York, but for them, the concerns may have been based on their familiarity with that particular city. The couple had lived in New York in the early 1870s, before their marriage, and undoubtedly knew firsthand of the opportunities available there, compared to smaller towns and cities in the North or South, but they were also very aware of the multiple risks, laid out in tragic detail in Dunbar's novel, from crime and gambling to health challenges, facing young black people in the city. Compared to their homes in Baltimore, Maryland, and in Washington, North Carolina, New York may have been attractive to the Paytons in the Reconstruction era of the 1870s, but the fact that they left before the middle of the decade indicates that, for them, there were limitations to New York's charms. From the lens of their prosperous life as parents in tranquil Westfield in 1899, they probably could not comprehend why their son, raised with advantages that most young black men did not have, would be attracted to such a place.

April 10, 1899, the date of Payton's departure from Westfield, was a Monday. Perhaps he selected that date both to get a last round of income from weekend barber work and to make his fresh start in the city at the beginning of a new workweek. One can imagine that, during that last weekend before his departure from Westfield, he visited friends to say final goodbyes. The weekend may have been capped by a going-away meal, perhaps joined by younger brother James from Yale, sister Susan from Westfield Normal School, and brother Edward, who by then was getting settled into his studies at Westfield High School. The trip from Westfield to New York City, approximately 150 miles, would have taken only a few hours by train.

After his first night in New York, on Tuesday morning, April 11, if Payton had wanted to get a view of world events by paying three cents for a *New York Tribune*, he would have read on the front page about the White House ceremony taking place later that day to mark the ratification of the peace treaty ending the Spanish American War. Ironically, to the left of that story he would have read about the U.S. attack on the city of Santa Cruz in the Philippines. The treaty may have ended the conflict with Spain, but the early phases of what would be the four-year Philippine War were just beginning. An adjunct to the Spanish American War, it would be marked by U.S. atrocities and the eventual military deaths of 20,000 Filipinos, and 4,196 Americans. Scanning to the right on the front page, Payton would have read that Governor Theodore Roosevelt of New York had sent a staff report on an investigation of fraud in canal contracts to the New York State legislature and expected prosecutions to follow. Further to the right on the front page, he would have learned about a riot in a Pana, Illinois, mining camp sparked by attempts by camp guards to prevent several black families from departing the camp for Iowa. One hundred deputy sheriffs were called out, and four black men, a black woman, and two white men were killed in the ensuing confrontation. The final story on the *Tribune* front page was a local story of the fraud investigation of the New York City Building Department focusing on the Croker family and their ownership of shares in the Roebling Construction Company, which "has a practical monopoly in fireproof concrete materials."[4]

Shifting from world and local events to his own purpose in moving to New York, Philip Payton's description of his first weeks in New York suggests that his parents' concerns about his move to the city were well founded: "On reaching New York I spent what little money I had, sight-seeing while looking for employment. After drifting around a few weeks, I struck a job in one of the large department stores as an attendant for the "penny-in-a-slot" weighing and picture machines at six dollars per week."[5] Later that year a visit to Westfield during the week of Labor Day precipitated a challenge for Payton. When he returned to New York, his job was gone. Reluctant to go back to Westfield and the embarrassment of facing his friends as a failure, he found a job at a Manhattan barbershop. He also became friends with William Ten Eyck, age twenty-nine, who worked as a porter in a liquor store, and soon he began sharing an apartment at 348 West 17th Street with Ten Eyck, his wife Bessie, a dressmaker, and their four-year-old daughter, Gretchen.[6]

At the beginning of 1900 Payton found a position as a porter in the office of Charles E. Schuyler, who in an 1898 history of the New York City real estate industry was described as "the most prominent real estate dealer in the upper west end of the city." How Payton made the journey from the New York barbershop to a job as a porter for one of the top real estate dealers in the city is not known, but it is possible that Westfield connections may have played a part. Schuyler was a member of the Yale Class of 1882, although he left college before graduating. Westfield had a tradition of sending its top students, including Payton's brother James, to Yale, less than seventy miles away in New Haven, Connecticut, so it is quite possible that a Yale alum from Westfield connected Payton to Yale alum Schuyler. Traveling to Schuyler's office at Broadway and 107th Street, where he earned $8 per week, Payton had an opportunity to see the Upper West Side of Manhattan under development. Between his menial tasks, Payton glimpsed Schuyler and his colleagues contribute "greatly to the development in high class residential property along Riverside Drive, West End Avenue, the Boulevard [Broadway] and Morningside." The work gave Payton a new perspective on the possibilities for him in New York.[7] "It was while there that I conceived the idea of going into the real estate business. I married in June of that year and on the first day of October, I started out in the real estate business on my own hook, with a partner. We opened an office in West 32nd Street near 8th Avenue."[8]

Although Payton's mention of his marriage is delivered almost as an aside, sandwiched between details of his business plans, perhaps that is because it was not a spur-of-the-moment decision but the result of a plan following a relationship of some years. Payton's bride, Maggie Lee, a native of North Carolina, lived in Westfield before her marriage, where she worked as a servant for Abiah Root Strong, a pastor's widow whose large brick Greek Revival home at 63 Broad Street was on one of the prominent streets in Westfield.[9] In her teens, Mrs. Strong briefly attended Amherst Academy, where she had been a close friend of the poet Emily Dickinson, maintaining a correspondence for several years after she left the academy. Why Maggie had relocated from North Carolina to Westfield is unknown, but it is possible that her relationship with Payton had begun during his year of high school at Livingstone College in Salisbury, North Carolina, approximately 130 miles from Maggie's home in Raleigh. A thin woman, her fair skin contrasted with Payton's brown complexion. Even though at the time of their marriage Payton had an unknown future, for Maggie the marriage into the prosperous Payton family offered the potential to embark on a new, more secure life. In the Westfield marriage register, she noted that her parents were Henry and Mary Currill, names that do not appear in the U.S. Census for North Carolina in the latter decades of the 1800s. It is unknown why Maggie, born in 1874, concealed the fact that she was the daughter of Henry Lee, a furnace tender, and Mary Knight. She had an older sister, Julia, born in 1872, and younger twin brothers, John and Joseph, born in 1875.[10]

As newlyweds, Philip and Maggie Payton would have had several options of areas to live in New York, in addition to the 17th Street area where Philip had been living. Like other northern cities, New York did not have segregation laws, but customs had developed regarding where black people could live. In the late 1700s and the early 1800s, when New York's black population was less than 2 percent, several Lower Manhattan streets, such as Anthony and Church, had concentrations of black residents and the earliest independent black churches. By the 1830s a larger black community developed centered around Grove Street in what is now Greenwich Village. The area became known as Little Africa, and when a black theater company was developed there, it was called the African Grove Theater. In the mid-1800s the city's black population grew, but because the white population grew even more dramatically due to European immigration, the black population remained less than 2 or 3 percent of the total population. The growing black population outstripped the Greenwich Village community, and an African American neighborhood in Midtown Manhattan developed from approximately 25th Street up to streets numbered in the 60s. The lower part of this area became known as the Tenderloin, because some claimed that corrupt police knew they would prosper from assignments in the district and gain access to choice opportunities for graft payments. The northern area was known as San Juan Hill, supposedly because the many fights between black and white residents in the area reminded people of the San Juan Hill battlefield in Cuba during the recently ended Spanish American War. The somewhat fluid customs related to race and residential areas in New York were hardening as the city's black population increased at the turn of the century. Philip and Maggie found lodging in San Juan Hill.[11] "When we first married we lived in three rear rooms in a tenement on West 67th Street where we paid $12 per month rent. During the first two weeks of our married life, we slept on the floor. We had a bed which my father gave us as a wedding present, but it was missent in shipping it from Westfield, hence the predicament."[12]

Before they had time to get settled, in August 1900, two months after the Paytons' marriage, the Tenderloin neighborhood to the south of their apartment erupted in violence. As with many community disturbances, the spark was an innocuous incident: a black woman standing on a street corner. She was May Enoch, the common-law wife of Arthur Harris, a black laborer who was a native of Washington, D.C. Harris and Enoch had been taking an evening stroll when he decided to enter a corner store to buy a cigar. He asked Enoch to wait for him on the street, but when he exited the store, he was angered to see a white man accosting her. Harris challenged the man, and they began to fight. In the course of the struggle, Harris pulled out his knife, a common implement for Tenderloin residents, and stabbed the man, who fell to the ground wounded. Harris and Enoch fled. The wounded man was Robert J. Thorpe, a policeman who, in plainclothes, had been on patrol. Seeing Enoch on the corner in an area in which prostitution was common, he had assumed she was a prostitute. Thorpe, like a substantial portion of the police force, was of Irish descent, and was engaged to marry the daughter of the captain of the precinct, covering the Tenderloin. As word of the stabbing spread through the neighborhood and police responded to alarms, Thorpe was taken to Roosevelt Hospital. A tense vigil of police officers, friends, and family members began in the evening and spanned into the next day, broken by the news that Thorpe had died from his injuries.[13]

With news of Thorpe's death, black people on midtown streets became targets for violence by white men who chased them down streets and pulled them off streetcars as the police, grieving for their fallen brother, looked the other way or in some cases aided the rioters. News of the riots was carried in newspapers across the country. Philip Payton's parents must have been in despair, knowing that their son and daughter-in-law lived not far from the area under attack. After two days the violence subsided, but not before scores of people were injured. Black residents soon formed a grievance committee, led by black ministers, to seek compensation for their losses. The police commissioner and Police Board president Bernard York brushed aside their complaints, noting that in order to "preserve the peace, and in unusual extreme conditions, they [police officers] are required to act vigorously and in so doing much must be left to the good judgment of the officer in immediate command at the place of disturbance."[14]

As Tenderloin residents nursed their wounds and grew frustrated over their ignored complaints, in October Philip Payton moved forward with his plan to enter the real estate business. He formed a partnership, the firm of Brown and Payton. His partner was Albert N. Brown, a native of Springfield, Massachusetts, near Westfield. Brown was three years older than Payton and most likely a childhood friend.[15] With offices at 248 West 32nd Street, they opened in the heart of the Tenderloin neighborhood as it recovered from the August riot. The neighborhood consisted of four- to six-story tenements on the side streets. On Eighth Avenue, bars, pool halls, and other businesses occupied first-floor spaces, with residential spaces on most upper floors. The black institutional and commercial center of the area was twenty blocks north on 53rd Street, where, between Sixth and Seventh Avenues, the Marshall and Maceo Hotels attracted black musicians, the sporting crowd such as heavyweight champion Jack Johnson, and academics such as W. E. B. Du Bois.[16]

Payton described the struggles of the firm of Brown and Payton: "We stayed there the entire winter [of 1901], and altogether I think we took in less than $125. Our rent was $20 per month, then there was our telephone and other expenses."[17] Brown and Payton enters the historical record in only one notice. On May 8, 1901, in its "In the Real Estate Field" column of recent transactions, the *New York Times* noted: "Brown and Payton in conjunction with George R. Thompson, have sold for Louis Aaron, the three five-story brownstone-front flats 215, 219, and 221 West Fortieth Street."

The advertisement does not note the sales price of the buildings, but estimating that three story flats may have sold for $10,000 each, the sale might have generated $30,000. At the time, broker's fees for sales in New York might have generated 1 percent. If they had to split this with broker George Thompson, the result would have been $150, approximately the amount that Payton noted.[18]

In spite of the large number of potential customers in the area, Brown and Payton struggled to obtain buildings to manage or sell in their first year of business. On his porter's wage of eight dollars per week, it is unlikely that Payton could have saved enough to cover initial costs associated with securing the office space or advertising and other startup expenses, so it is likely that Brown brought capital and possibly prior experience to the partnership. In a community dominated by residential renters, it is also likely that Brown and Payton initially sought agreements with landlords to find tenants for their buildings for 2 percent of the first year's rent, the standard fee at the time. If they were given responsibility to collect rents and otherwise handle the management for a building, their fee would have been 5 percent of the annual rent collected in the building. With Tenderloin monthly rents in 1900 typically ranging from $12 to $20 per month for apartments, renting an apartment for a landlord would have resulted in monthly per apartment income for Brown and Payton of approximately $0.24 to $0.40. Collecting rents in a ten-unit building of apartments with rents averaging $15 per month would have resulted in annual income of $90 to Brown and Payton. To be successful, the new firm needed to generate a substantial volume of business.[19] Although real estate sales were documented by the New York City Register and in the local press, leases, even for entire buildings, were rarely documented publicly; therefore, compiling a record of Brown and Payton's business activity related to leasing, in the absence of corporate records, is not possible. After that first year, and the one sale, Albert Brown abandoned the business and Philip Payton had to persevere alone.

Perhaps because of the instability of the Tenderloin after the August 1900 riot, with Brown gone from the partnership, Payton soon moved to a small office in the Temple Court Building at Nassau and Beekman Streets in Lower Manhattan. Completed in 1882, the ten-story red-brick building with cream-colored limestone trim was one of the nation's first skyscrapers. It took its name from the distinctive glass canopy hidden behind the exterior walls that created its famous interior court, a popular feature of late nineteenth-century buildings. The office building was noted for attracting architects, attorneys, and physicians.[20] But behind the public façade of prosperity, Philip Payton struggled. On some days he walked the ten miles to his office from his new home on West 134th Street in Harlem because he did not have the five cents for streetcar fare.

It is not surprising that, in the aftermath of the 1900 riot, Philip and Maggie moved to Harlem. Although the midtown Tenderloin and San Juan Hill districts were the largest black communities in New York at the turn of the twentieth century, a small black community had developed in the late nineteenth century along West 135th Street in Harlem. White residents continued to rent apartments in the two- and three-story walkup tenement buildings in the area, but by the time the Paytons moved to the area, 133rd, 134th, and 135th Streets were substantially black. While increasing racial animus accounted for the increasingly restrictive racial segregation practices in New York City, white property owners took advantage of the growing black population to create a racial market that enabled them to benefit, as segregated neighborhoods like that in the 135th Street area grew. Black residents were steered to these neighborhoods by the property owners who specifically advertised for "respectable colored families" and then charged up to 25 percent more for rent, which the owners understood would most likely be paid because of the limited choices available to the prospective black tenants in the racially segregated housing market that was solidifying. Many times the black tenants took in roomers or rented as extended families to cover the high rents on their meager wages from menial jobs. In Harlem, Philip Payton, who was a new entrant to the real estate business when he moved to the community, had an opportunity to observe firsthand the workings of the racial real estate market in New York City.[21]

The real estate market in Manhattan was less than a century old. David Scoby described the process in *Empire City: The Making and Meaning of the New York City Landscape*:

> First of all, space was transformed into a standardized, alienable commodity. That transformation had begun in 1811, when New York's [then only Manhattan island] famous street plan, with its uniform block and lot lines inscribed the principle of calculable exchange on the uneven terrain of Manhattan. Yet the laying of the grid merely inaugurated a longer process by which farms, estates, and municipal landholdings were disaggregated into city lots and brought to market, a process that climaxed during the midcentury boom . . . real estate became an efficient medium of capital

accumulation, and the New York City landscape served as a "savings bank" for national capitalist growth.[22]

The development of Manhattan real estate as a commodity required a coordination of the flow of information and capital, and in 1862 the Exchange Salesroom was established at 111 Broadway as a centralized market for owners, developers, builders, auctioneers, and brokers to exchange information regarding real estate transactions. In 1868 an industry publication, the *Real Estate Record and Builders' Guide* (*RRBG*), was established, providing weekly reports on real estate transactions in the city. The number of transactions continued to grow, and in 1885 a new Real Estate Exchange and Auction Room was established at 5½ Pine Street, replacing the old Exchange Salesroom. A photograph of the opening of the new building shows a group of brokers assembled on the street in front of the building in top hats and black suits.[23]

Philip Payton may not have been aware of this history, and he probably understood that black brokers may not have been welcome at the Exchange Salesroom. But as the son of entrepreneurs, he would have thought it natural for him to become his own boss by going into business. Sibling rivalry may have also contributed to his quick dissatisfaction with his menial jobs. By 1901 his younger brother James had graduated from Yale and was a professor of classics at Wiley College, a black college in Marshall, Texas. Working in a real estate office as well as living in Manhattan for several months would have given Philip some familiarity with the unique characteristics of Manhattan real estate. With the growing tide of black migrants from the South and immigrants from the Caribbean entering the city, and the challenges they and longtime residents faced finding housing, a year after arriving in New York, Payton's decision to enter the real estate business seemed like a timely proposition.

The Paytons continued to struggle in Harlem. As Philip remembered: "We remained in this house until April passed. We were dispossessed for not being able to pay our rent and our entire scanty belongings were set out on the sidewalk. I managed to secure charge of another house after a while on the same street, and we moved in there. Seemingly this was the turning point in my business career. Things began to pick up. I began to get charge of more houses." The business momentum continued to move in Payton's favor.

One fine day I made a deal that netted me nearly $1,150. I could hardly believe it true. My wife refused to credit it until I showed her the checks. From that time things grew better. I opened an office in 134th Street, still keeping my office in Temple Court. I bought the flat house in which I was living. I bought two more flats and kept them five months when I sold them at a profit of $5,000. I bought another, kept it a month and made $2,750, another and made $1,500, another and made $2,600, and so on.[24]

In August 1902, riding this wave of prosperity, Payton traveled to Richmond, Virginia, to attend the third annual meeting of the National Negro Business League (NNBL), an organization formed and led by Booker T. Washington, head of Tuskegee Institute in Alabama. The college, founded by Washington in 1881, emphasized industrial and vocational training for African Americans and, as a result of Washington's skilled leadership and cultivation of white patronage, became a model for black education that attracted white support in the South and North. Tuskegee Institute helped to launch Washington to national leadership when in 1895 he was asked to speak at the Cotton States Exposition in Atlanta, a gathering meant to market the post–Civil War "New South" to potential investors. Washington's speech, soon called "The Atlanta Compromise," counseled black southerners to remain in the South, work the land, save their money, and defer participation in politics. His suggestion that for white and black people, "in all things purely social we can be as separate as the fingers, but one as the hand on those things essential to mutual progress," comforted white segregationists concerned that black progress in emancipation would lead to racial intermingling and demands for black equality. Following the speech, white philanthropists sought Washington out, provided funds to Tuskegee, and began asking him for advice when they considered making donations to other black institutions. Republican politicians also consulted Washington as they made decisions and dispensed lower-level appointments to black people. But behind the public face of conciliation, Washington funded several challenges to southern segregation.[25]

Although based in Alabama, Washington traveled frequently along the East Coast raising funds for Tuskegee or meeting with members of his Board of Trustees, which in the early 1900s represented the white captains of industry. A master at using the media, similar to Frederick Douglass, in his autobiography *Up from Slavery* (1901) Washington chronicled his journey from his birth in Virginia in 1856 to education at Hampton Institute, to his creation of the Tuskegee Institute. The book fit closely to the rags-to-riches narrative made popular by the Horatio Alger stories, but in this case with a black protagonist recounting his life story. The public would develop an appetite for books by Washington, which he cultivated by using ghostwriters to regularly provide them with new publications. The publications were advertised in the black press, and these advertising dollars gave Washington access to and eventually power over black editors across the country.[26]

Five years after Washington's Atlanta Compromise speech brought him to national attention, he had issued a call for a national meeting in August 1900, noting:

> The need of an organization that will bring the colored people who are engaged in business together for consultation and to secure information and inspiration from each other has long been felt. Out of this national organization it is expected will grow local business leagues that will tend to improve the Negro as a business factor. Boston has been selected as the place of meeting because of its historic importance, its cool summer climate and general favorable conditions. It is felt that the rest, recreation and new ideas which business men and women will secure from a trip to Boston will more than repay them for time and money spent.[27]

Another likely reason for the selection of Boston as the site of the first meeting of the NNBL was that it was the home of Washington's childhood friend and protégé Samuel Courtney. After graduating from Westfield Normal School, Courtney had worked for Tuskegee for a time and then in 1888 had entered Harvard Medical School, from which he graduated in 1894. By 1900 he had a thriving medical practice and was well established in Boston's black community. Courtney chaired the local committee for the first NNBL annual meeting, and when the meeting opened he was the initial speaker, reading the call that had brought over three hundred delegates to Boston from across the country.[28]

The second annual meeting of the NNBL had been held in 1901 in Chicago. At the third meeting, in August 1902 in Richmond, Payton joined two hundred other delegates from across the country. Over the course of three days, they heard speeches that included Fred R. Moore of Brooklyn describing the "new Negro," who knew better than to follow ignorant preachers,

Fannie Barrier Williams of Chicago urging young women to "make character their goal, rather than rich garments and jewels," and Judge Robert Terrell of Washington, D.C., explaining "The Lawyer's Relation to Business Development." For a new entrepreneur, the meeting provided Philip Payton with a unique opportunity to learn from those with much more business experience, and to meet the men and women who were forming a national black business network.[29]

But upon his return to New York, tragedy interrupted Philip Payton's march of success. In October 1902 his brother James became ill with typhoid fever while in Westfield on a visit home from Wiley College in Texas. The disease was common and feared at the time. Associated with symptoms of high fever, rash, headache, and severe abdominal discomfort, its source, the bacillus *Salmonella* typhi, often spread through water or milk contamination, but a treatment had yet to be identified. Typhoid fever patients could struggle with the disease for three to four weeks, and 10 percent of the afflicted died.[30] This unfortunately was the fate of James Payton. He died on October 15 at the age of twenty-five. His death was felt far beyond the Payton family and the Wiley community. In 1900, while a senior at Yale, James had succinctly described his four years at Yale in an article titled "Some Experiences and Customs at Yale," written for the *Colored American Magazine*. The magazine began publication from Boston in 1900 through a partnership among black Bostonians Walter Wallace, H. A. Fortune, Jessie Watkins, and Peter B. Gibson, through the Colored Co-operative Publishing Company. It is considered the first general purpose African American magazine published in the United States.[31] James Payton's article described freshman-year excitement at attending a speech on campus by William Jennings Bryan, at which the upperclassmen heckled Bryan's advocacy of the silver standard, and developing habits of study and leisure as an upperclassman who "now smokes his pipe with much ado, even if he has not yet learned to enjoy it." James provided a glimpse at college life for readers, some of whom may not have graduated from high school. Aware of his audience, he closed the article with a note of encouragement, although most likely not totally aware of the relatively privileged life he had led before entering Yale:

> The chances at Yale, for a poor boy, are as good and perhaps better than at any other college. There are numerous ways in which a fellow can "get by"

and make his "ends meet." Board can be easily obtained by waiting on table at different student "joints." ... Room can be obtained at very reasonable prices on campus or at private houses. ... As regards tuition, the college offers numerous scholarships and prizes of which a fairly bright fellow can always get a share. ... Any young man who refrains from entering college because he has not enough money to carry himself through, or even part way through, is very foolish.[32]

With his photograph in a cap and gown on the cover of the magazine, which was then published in Washington, D.C., the article brought national attention to James through his advocacy of college life for young black men.

In this context, it is understandable that the *Colored American Magazine* would seek to honor James in death, just two years after his article had appeared in its pages. The "Here and There" column of December 1902 featured a tribute to James in which the writer recognized the potential that had been interrupted by death:

> Mr. Payton had planned to eventually take up law, and it was toward this end that he studied. ... His education compared favorably with the learning of educational leaders, and he conversed fluently in English, Greek, French and German, besides being an authority in Latin. ... Prof. J. W. Payton was a young man who seemed to have understood life's deeper meanings and set himself to work in the uplift of fallen humanity after thoroughly preparing himself by graduating with high honors from Yale University.[33]

A resolution from Wiley College and James's Yale graduation photograph (figure 2.1) accompanied the profile.[34]

James Warren Payton was buried in Elm Hill Cemetery in Westfield. Philip Payton returned to New York, but grief did not deter him on his path toward success. In November 1902 his wife Maggie purchased apartment buildings at 106 and 108 West 134th Street, assuming mortgages of $36,000 and $5,000 on the buildings. The transaction could suggest that Maggie was playing an active role in the real estate business, or it could represent an early recognition by the young couple of the need for them to diversify their assets, with her having wealth distinct from Philip's.[35] A March 2, 1903,

FIGURE 2.1 James Payton Yale graduation photo. *Source: Colored American Magazine,* December 1902.

advertisement in the *New York Times* noted, "Colored Tenements Wanted. Colored man makes a specialty of managing colored tenements: references; bond. Philip A. Payton, Broker 67 W. 134th Street; telephone 1919 Harlem Branch, 119 Nassau Street; telephone, 380 Cortlandt St." In addition to purchases and sales, Payton developed a thriving business as a specialist in "colored tenements." In April 1903 the *Real Estate Record and Builders Guide* noted under "Real Estate Notes":

Philip A. Payton Jr., the young colored broker and agent of 67 West 134th St, with branch office at 119 Nassau St., has by intelligent and indefatigable work built up an extensive and profitable business. His specialty is the management of colored tenements. Recent sales completed by Mr. Payton included the 3-sty dwelling, Nos. 250 West 130th st, 60 West 134th st and 102 West 126th st [should be 136th St.], and the 5-sty flats, 106 and 108 West 134th st. [that had been purchased by Maggie Payton in 1902] sold to J. Chainowitz, and resold to C.F. Bogen; also Nos. 109, 185 and 194 West 134th st and four lots on the east side of Park av., between 117th and 118th sts for Moritz Bauer to Robt. Altman. Mr. Payton bought 13 West 121st [should be 131st St] a 3-sty dwelling for his own occupancy.

Payton's business fortunes improved so much that in March 1903 he purchased 13 West 131st Street (figure 2.3), a brick townhouse on a quiet brownstone block between Lenox and Fifth Avenues, three blocks from his office on West 134th Street. In 1900, West 131st Street between Lenox and Fifth Avenues, like many other areas of residential Manhattan, was lined on both sides of the street with the brownstone-faced row houses that Edith Wharton had complained created a city that was "hide-bound in its deadly uniformity of mean ugliness."[36] A few moderate-sized apartment buildings provided occasional breaks in the landscape. The residents of the block were a diverse mix of people of European descent, some native-born in the United States, others immigrants from Germany, Ireland, Sweden, and other parts of the world. The Payton home contrasted the block's brownstone aesthetic with a gold brick facade. It had a standard floor plan with a kitchen a few steps down from the street level. One entered the home first through the parlor floor several steps up from the street. Carved wood double doors led into an alcove opening to another set of wood doors with large beveled glass

PHILIP A. PAYTON, Jr., Tel., 4391 Cortlandt
Real Estate Broker and Agent.
Management of Colored Tenements a Specialty.
119 NASSAU ST.   Branch, 31 West 134th St.

FIGURE 2.2 Payton Real Estate advertisement. *Source: Real Estate Record and Builders Guide,* June 28, 1902.

FIGURE 2.3 The Paytons and their home, 13 West 131st Street, New York City. *Source: The Negro in Business*, 1907.

panes. In the main entry hall, the entrance to the front parlor was at the left, with a stairway to the two upper floors, containing bedrooms, at the right.[37]

Philip Payton purchased David Klein's house, taking over payments on a $9,000 mortgage and providing Klein with "one dollar" and other "lawful money." Unless other black residents moved onto the block after the 1900 census, Philip and Maggie were the only black people living on the block. As a symbol of their prosperity, they had moved from an apartment on 134th Street dominated by tenements occupied by poor and working-class people, some of whom doubled up to cover the cost of the rent, to a block of single-family homes occupied by professionals, craftspeople, and entrepreneurs. Their new home was three blocks away from Payton's Harlem office on West 134th Street and the apartment that they had occupied in the same building. In a condensed dimension of time and space, the move represented the standard trajectory of a successful striver, but in this case it occurred over the span of three years rather than a more likely three decades. The residential move into a different social class and racial cohort required a relocation of a mere three blocks.[38]

As his ambition to make his mark in the real estate field grew and he cultivated relationships with New York's black business class, in June 1903 Payton established a new company, noting the importance of the National Negro Business League to his business plans: "It was while in attendance at the meeting of the National Negro Business League in Richmond, Virginia, in 1902, that I received the inspiration for the organization of the Afro-American Realty Company."[39] The company was a partnership, with stated plans of "renting and re-renting, leasing and subleasing, tenement houses, flats, or other buildings, for residences and other purposes, in the City of New York."[40]

While there is no surviving explanation for the name choice of the company, the name "Afro-American" alone was distinct and embraced an image of black culture rooted in the African continent in an affirmative manner that "Colored Realty" or "Negro Realty" would not have done, even in 1903. Identification with Africa by black Americans ebbed and flowed in the centuries that followed the arrival of Africans in the Americas. Initially most came the African continent, either directly or by way of the Caribbean, where many of the newly arrived enslaved were "seasoned," learning the language of the enslavers along with the labor practices that would dominate their lives. During this period there was no need to specify that the enslaved had come from Africa. Instead, their ethnic origin, such as Igbo, Ashanti or Yoruba, was often used to describe them.[41]

As the direct connection with Africa receded over the generations of enslavement and after 1808 was separated by law when the transatlantic slave trade was outlawed, there did arise a need to describe the people, both enslaved and free, most of whom had never seen the African continent but whose skin tone, hair texture, and facial features continued to connect them to people on the continent. Could they accurately be described as Africans if they had no physical association with the continent and were unlikely to ever have one? Sometimes they were described as black, although this was not accurate for most, who were really various shades of brown. The term "black" served to distinguish them from the European enslavers who had begun to identify themselves as "white," a term that didn't accurately reflect their true complexions either.

By the nineteenth century other terms used by both black and white people to describe black people included "Ethiopian," "Abyssinian," and "People of Color." In the 1860s a paper serving New York City's black community was called the *Anglo-African*, acknowledging the influence of English culture on people with blood links to Africa. By the mid-nineteenth century the term "Afro-American" was used occasionally as an alternative to "colored." Many argued that if European immigrants such as Italian-Americans could retain references to their lands of origin, black Americans should be able to do the same. By the late 1800s T. Thomas Fortune, editor of the *New York Age*, the newspaper of record for the city's black community, was advocating use of Afro-American, which he put into action as a leader, along with Livingstone College president J. C. Price, of the group that formed the Afro-American League in the 1890s. It is quite possible that Payton's school year at Livingstone, during which remembrances of the achievements of Price would have been ubiquitous following his October 1893 death, gave Payton a greater familiarity with the term Afro-American.[42]

In 1903, when Payton chose to name his partnership Afro-American, blackness had been under attack for decades in the post–Civil War era in the North and the South. The emancipation of the enslaved came in stages. Some sought their freedom with the opening of the Civil War in April 1861; others were inspired to leave slavery behind by the Emancipation Proclamation of January 1863. The end of the Civil War in April 1865 and the ratification of the Thirteenth Amendment outlawing slavery in the nation in December led to the emancipation of four million people. Managing these people, and in many cases limiting their movements, became a top priority for many white Americans accustomed to the tight controls of slavery. In the South, Black Codes were developed requiring black people to enter into labor contracts or be jailed, limiting their movement and inhibiting their freedom in other ways. The rationale for the laws centered on a notion that black people were unprepared for freedom because they were peculiarly inclined to indolence, lust, and riotous living. The irony of this charge was clear by the sobering facts that even in "emancipation," white men regularly targeted black women for sexual assault, and that in the latter decades of the nineteenth century southerners constructed the convict lease system to entrap black men convicted of spurious charges to work as uncompensated laborers in tasks that most white men would have refused to do even for pay. The charge that black people were a pathologized race was used to justify lynching of black men and women, as well as the imprisonment of thousands of black men under the South's prison system that leased these convicts to owners of mines, plantations, and other businesses.[43]

At the turn of the twentieth century, with the movement of thousands of black people from the South to the North, an area that previously had only a small number of black residents, a hardening of somewhat fluid racial customs created a more hostile environment for black people seeking employment, education, or housing. The Afro-American Realty Company (AARC) was formed to meet the growing housing needs of black people in New York City, so it is appropriate that, in naming his company, Payton both embraced the link with the African continent that the people he sought to serve had and emphasized through the use of the term "American" that these people were citizens of the United States. The latter fact was something that was implicitly denied by the discriminatory practices being implemented with increasing regularity against black people in New York and other U.S. cities by 1903.

From 1885 through 1888, W. E. B. Du Bois attended Fisk University in Nashville, Tennessee. He had vivid impressions of his time there and traveled throughout the South. His impressions, viewed through the lens of his childhood and youth in predominantly white Great Barrington, Massachusetts, would lead him to publish *The Souls of Black Folk* in 1903, at the beginning of a long career, as a celebration of African American culture and possibility. Philip Payton, eleven years younger than Du Bois, had been enveloped in the black community at Livingstone College in Salisbury, North Carolina, during the 1893–1894 academic year, his junior year of high school. It is quite possible that Payton's school year living in a black community made a similarly strong impression on him and inspired a strong appreciation of African American culture and the opportunity to prosper in the course of meeting the growing housing needs of black New Yorkers. While Payton did not publish a book upon his return to the North, his company's name and later marketing campaigns would place it firmly in the context of black culture as a "race enterprise" with a mission that he claimed would benefit all African Americans.[44]

The Afro-American Realty Company was a partnership, an agreement between individuals to work together toward a common business goal, sharing the losses, profits, and liabilities that might result from the business activity. Payton, who served as business manager for the company, assembled seven members of New York's small but growing African American business class to join him as partners in the company. It is fascinating to consider this group of men that the twenty-seven-year-old high school dropout, who four years earlier had been a barber working in his father's shop, was able to assemble.

James C. Thomas, president of the AARC, had come to New York from Texas in the 1880s, and while working menial jobs he had taken courses in embalming and acquired his undertaker's license. His arrival coincided with the incremental growth in New York's black population as black people moved to the city in greater numbers from the South and the Caribbean. Thomas established an undertaking business in 1897 on Seventh Avenue in the Midtown Manhattan Tenderloin district, understanding that for many poor black people, a decent funeral following a hard life was something that they longed for, either imploring their relatives to provide for them or making provisions through burial insurance paid to fraternal organizations or mutual aid societies, the forerunners of black insurance companies. As the city's black community grew, with an unfortunately disproportionately high death rate due to diseases associated with poverty, poor living conditions, and violence, Thomas's business thrived. By the time he joined the AARC partnership, he was believed to be one of the wealthiest black people in New York City.[45]

James Garner served as secretary/treasurer of the company. Born in Maryland, he came to New York in 1876 and worked as a porter in a drugstore and then as a waiter in a well-known restaurant. He started a housecleaning business in 1880 and by 1903 had built it into the Manhattan House Cleaning and Renovating Bureau, located at 220 West 28th Street. His clients included the Waldorf-Astoria Hotel, Tiffany & Company, and the *New York Times*. He employed six office workers as well as a work crew averaging twenty-five but growing to seventy-five during busy seasons. Walter E. Handy, the manager of the housecleaning arm of Garner's business, was also an AARC director. Born in 1872 in New York City, Handy, was an age-group peer of Philip Payton and a graduate of City College of New York. Similarly, another director, John Stevenson, born in Pennsylvania in 1873, was an age-peer of Payton. Joseph H. Bruce, a thirty-nine-year-old native of Washington, D.C., was a butler. Payton's former apartment mate, William Ten Eyck, thirty-five and still working as a porter, was also a director.[46]

The directors of the Afro-American Realty Company ranged from older, experienced businessmen to young men who, like Payton were still looking to make their mark in New York. One younger director, Wilford Smith, thirty-seven, had arrived in the city in 1902 from Galveston, Texas. A native of Mississippi, he graduated from Boston University Law School in 1883. Returning to Texas, he developed a thriving practice in criminal and civil law, most notably with several civil right cases. In 1901 he became the personal attorney to Booker T. Washington, by then principal of Tuskegee Institute. It was probably just a matter of time before a lawyer of such unique talent would become acquainted with Philip Payton among New York's small group of black professionals.

It is also possible that Samuel Courtney, friend of Booker T. Washington and organizer of the National Negro Business League, who had attended Westfield, Normal School during Payton's youth, had facilitated the connection between Payton and Smith that led to their association in the AARC. Payton's formal affiliation with Smith, likely prior relationship with Courtney, and membership in the NNBL placed his real estate business activities in the view of Booker T. Washington and gave them the potential for national influence.[47]

Later in 1903 Payton attended the NNBL's fourth annual meeting, held in Nashville on August 19 and 20. An indication of the growth in the status of the NNBL in the few years since its first annual meeting in 1900 is the fact that the proceedings took place in the chamber of the Tennessee House of Representatives and attracted over six hundred delegates. Opening-day speakers included representatives of various professions and lines of business in Nashville, with many of them encouraging listeners to respond to racial discrimination with industry. But Richard Hill, a Nashville businessman, strayed from the conciliatory message that Booker T. Washington had perfected. In the heart of the segregated South, where most blacks had been intimidated from going to the polls, he stated "that the right to vote is the highest privilege [available] to an American citizen and should be exercised by every brave and true man." He concluded by reminding his listeners of the horrors of slavery:

> In the name of those who believed 300 years of unrequited toil have given the negro the right to deny that this is "a white man's country," and in the names of the mothers whose blood had been lashed from their backs in streams by the cruel whips of the slave driver, and whose hearts are still dripping because of the unbridled licentious conduct of that slave driver's sons;

in the name of our mothers and daughters for whose virtue we are willing to do or die, I welcome you to Nashville.[48]

During the evening session of the first day of the convention, attended by more than two thousand who were crowded into the lobby and the gallery, Washington brought the audience back to the message that he had honed since his Atlanta Compromise speech in 1895:

> We shall succeed in winning our way into the confidence and esteem of the American people just in proportion as we show ourselves valuable to the community in which we live, in all the common industries, in commerce, in the welfare of the state, and in the manifestation of the highest character. The community does not fear as a rule the vote of the man, no matter what his color, who is a large taxpayer. It is not the negro who owns a successful business, or works at a trade who is charged with a crime.[49]

Also in 1895, journalist Ida B. Wells had presented evidence that contradicted Washington's suggestion that black prosperity was a protection from being viewed as a threat to white people. In *The Red Record: Tabulated Statistics and Alleged Causes of Lynching in the United States*, she presented statistics and cases demonstrating that no black person was safe from false accusations. But in the setting of the Tennessee State Capitol, Washington's optimistic message was undoubtedly appealing to many in the audience.[50]

On the second day of the convention, less than four years after leaving his father's Westfield barbershop and only a few months after forming the Afro-American Realty Company, Philip Payton stepped onto the national stage as a speaker. In his address, entitled "Possibilities for the Negro in the Real Estate Field," speaking with an authority that belied his brief two years of business successes, Payton suggested that the available opportunities he had observed in learning the Manhattan real estate market could be extrapolated to other parts of the country. He encouraged the use of mortgage financing to acquire property and claimed that real estate would yield annual returns of 8 to 10 percent (at a time when a 6 percent return was standard). Taking a page from the Washington playbook, he encouraged real estate owners to banish fear of the day when tax or interest payments were due. Most mortgage loans of the time were interest-only loans, with principal being paid by the sale of the property or the refinancing or renewal of the loan. Payton advised his listeners who owned real estate to consistently set aside money for these payments. In somewhat of a deviation from a core part of Washington's philosophy, which emphasized the strong work ethic of black laborers, Payton observed that black people would need to use their heads, not their brawn, to become wealthy. But in his closing statements he affirmed a philosophy very much in alignment with Washington's belief that economic interests could overcome racial prejudice:

> I have this to say of my business, that at no time in my experience have I ever found myself handicapped because of my color, and in many instances, I have been benefitted, as usually the better class of white people are always willing to help the Negro who will first help himself, and the other who are not so broad and generous will forget that you are a Negro if you can offer them a good business proposition.[51]

In the coming years, Philip Payton would experience examples supporting his statement but also learn that no amount of money would gain the cooperation of some white people. In 1904 he would reorganize his business and experience significant successes that would generate a backlash, challenging his goal of providing housing to black people in Harlem.

Chapter Three

ENTERING THE FIELD OF BATTLE

The *Evening World* described New York City's New Year's Eve celebrations in 1904:

> The din resembled several election nights and a Fourth of July celebration rolled into one. . . . It was a good natured crowd. Some had come down [to an area in front of Trinity Church in lower Manhattan] to hear the chimes because they had done so for years and had a sentimental interest in this form of observance of the new year. Some were there for the first time. . . . the programme of Trinity was made up of "Old Dog Tray," "Blue Bells of Scotland," "Little Maggie May," "Since I First Met You," "Put Me in my Little Bed," "Auld Lang Syne," and "Home Sweet Home" as a recessional.[1]

As 1904 began, Philip Payton leased two buildings at 156 and 158 West 98th Street, on behalf of another client, in the middle of another of Manhattan's small black enclaves. At the beginning of February, he sold to Mercy Seat Baptist Church a fifty-by-one-hundred-foot plot of land on the north side of West 134th Street between Madison and Fifth Avenues, on behalf of August Ruff. It was reported that Mercy Seat would construct a church on the plot. The continued growth of Payton's business was the manifestation of a much broader development trend in Manhattan.[2]

ENTERING THE FIELD OF BATTLE

In New York in 1904, the last frontier of vacant land in northern Manhattan was disappearing, the result of a building boom. Only a few years before, there had been substantial areas of vacant land in Upper Manhattan. In 1897, 110th and 111th Streets between Seventh and Eighth Avenues were almost totally vacant. Continuing northward, partial rows of brownstones began to fill blocks such as 112th and 113th Street. Most of Seventh Avenue between 110th and 116th was vacant. Many of the streets east of the avenue were vacant or sparsely developed with apartment houses. Above 116th Street up to 135th Street, the blocks and avenues were more densely developed, but areas of vacant land remained in the middle of some blocks or along some avenues.[3]

With the end of armed conflicts with Indigenous people and continued settlement in western territories in the 1890s by European immigrants and Euro-Americans, pronouncements had been made that the nation's western frontier had disappeared. Laments soon followed that without a frontier, American ingenuity would be hampered.[4] The waning of the Manhattan frontier was celebrated in 1904 by the *Harlem Reporter and Bronx Chronicle*:

> The marvelous growth of Harlem, both as a residential and business center has not been equaled by any one particular section on Manhattan Island. It was but a few years ago that our principal thoroughfare, 125th Street, was a street devoted to a few private residences with large gardens on all sides. Look at it today: the progressive spirit of this part of Harlem has been exemplified by the establishment of branch offices of well-known corporations having headquarters downtown.[5]

The development boom in Harlem was sparked by the construction of New York's first subway line, which investors claimed was essential to continuing the dramatic growth in the city's population due to European immigration. Real estate investors recognized an opportunity to finally extract a substantial return from never-developed Manhattan land. The African American population of New York was also growing dramatically, as black southerners moved north to escape lynching and the drudgery of farming that did not pay and others traveled from the Caribbean seeking refuge from that region's racial and economic limitations.

Manhattan had streets and some neighborhoods with high concentrations of African Americans, but they were present as residents in all the borough's wards. Before 1900 the city's white residents had not perceived their small numbers as threatening. While the racial segregation laws that had become common in the South over the previous twenty years were not enacted in northern cities like New York, the increased presence of African Americans in these cities led to a hardening of racial segregation customs that had previously been relatively invisible. As black New Yorkers' numerical presence increased, resistance to their movement to some neighborhoods increased as well.

By 1904 people of African descent had lived in Harlem for almost three hundred years. Small, scattered numbers of African Americans, enslaved and free, were in the area beginning in the early 1600s, from its time as a community of farms during Dutch settlement through governance by the English begun in the 1660s. While larger numbers of African Americans eventually lived in Lower Manhattan, the established city of New York, by the mid-1800s small numbers continued to live in the northern Manhattan village of Harlem.[6]

With the end of slavery in 1865, decade by decade, the African American exodus from the South increased the black population in New York. Most of these new arrivals settled in the existing African American enclaves in mid-Manhattan, but some found homes in the growing enclaves of Harlem. In the latter part of the 1800s, as walk-up apartment buildings were built in Harlem in the area East of Fifth Avenue, African Americans lived side by side with Jews who had moved from the Lower East Side and from Eastern Europe, as well as Italians who had moved from Lower Manhattan and from Italy. During this period the African American population remained below 2 percent of the city's population. In the 1890s the walk-up apartment buildings on West 135th, 134th, and 133rd Streets between Lenox and Fifth Avenues became an area of concentration for African Americans in Harlem. Residents rented their apartments from white owners, just as other African Americans did in the mid-Manhattan areas.

In the 1880s and 1890s, in Harlem west of Fifth Avenue, brownstones were built on many blocks complemented by larger apartment buildings on the avenues. The brownstones were occupied by middle- and upper-middle-class people of European descent, second and third generation Germans, Irish, and others, some of whom had businesses in the area, and others with skilled or professional jobs. The white real estate investors who had constructed these buildings had spent decades lobbying for a subway line, arguing that the elevated train lines on Eighth and Third Avenues were slow and detracted from property values. In 1904, in anticipation of the realization of their dream when the subway line was scheduled to open, owners of properties in the African American enclave at 135th Street and Lenox, where a subway stop would be located, concluded that their African American tenants were blocking their way to higher rents or newer, larger buildings on the now more valuable land.[7]

In 1904, West 135th Street between Lenox and Fifth Avenue was a study in contrasts. The north side of the street was almost totally vacant, except for a row of apartment houses on the eastern end facing Fifth Avenue. Many of the other blocks to the immediate north were empty parcels of land. The southern side of 135th Street was almost fully developed, with rows of walk-up tenement apartment houses and a few row houses. The blocks to the south were similarly developed.[8]

In the nineteenth century Manhattan's residential property owners adopted the practice of renewing all residential leases on May 1, which quickly became known as Moving Day as poor and working-class people carried or drove their belongings through the streets seeking new lodgings, often to take advantage of a free month's rent offered by landlords during dips in the real estate market. On Moving Day 1904, scores of African American families were evicted from their homes near West 135th Street between Lenox and Fifth Avenues. As described in the May 2 edition of the *New York Herald*: "There is nothing but trouble in a section of Harlem where a community of negroes that has grown rapidly in a few years, is being made to disintegrate and 'move on' through the concerted action of landlords. One hundred families will be on the move-today, and six hundred other families are perilously near eviction."[9] The opening of the first subway line, expected in the fall, had disrupted the settled lives of these residents. Owners of the properties they rented on these streets made handsome profits since black tenants were customarily charged more than white tenants because of the limited housing choices for black people. Even though the premium rents stretched black tenants economically, often resulting in them accepting boarders to cover the rent, such enclaves provided them with a refuge. The eviction effort would bring this to a close.

The impetus for the eviction effort was the Hudson Realty Company, a firm formed in 1893 by investors who saw, as Philip Payton did in 1900, the opportunity that Manhattan real estate provided. The company's president was Maximilian Morgenthau, brother of banker and future diplomat Henry Morgenthau. Born in Baden, Germany, in 1847, he immigrated with his parents and siblings to the United States in 1865. After pursuing a business career, he attended New York University, graduating and passing the New York City bar in 1877. In 1883, along with his brother Gustav and Joseph Bausland, he formed Morgenthau, Bausland & Co., operating a dry goods store in Chicago that became known as the Bee Hive. In forming Hudson Realty in New York in 1893, Morgenthau joined with Joseph Bloomingdale, a scion of the family behind Bloomingdale's department store. Hudson Realty bought, sold, and developed properties throughout Manhattan. By the turn of the century its attention was increasingly focused on the Upper Manhattan neighborhoods of Harlem and Washington Heights. In the course of the decade, the company, which by 1904 had bought and sold land and buildings in Lower and Midtown Manhattan, was beginning to shift its attention to Harlem. Its proprietors would have fit Payton's definition of the "better class" of white people, but their actions in Harlem would create the first major obstacle to Payton's plans for his business in Harlem.[10]

Real estate investing was a common pursuit for wealth creation in New York and elsewhere in the late 1800s and early 1900s, and Manhattan's remaining vacant land represented a unique opportunity to those with capital. Reflecting this opportunity, in 1902 the Hudson Realty Company revised its Articles of Incorporation to increase the stock the company could raise in $100 shares from $100,000 to $1,000,000. In addition, it voted to expand the company's purpose from leasing of property to include the sale of stocks, bonds, and securities, the making of mortgages, and the issuing of bonds. Soon afterward, the company embarked on its acquisition campaign focused on Harlem. In early April 1904 it purchased seventeen vacant lots on the north side of 135th Street and six lots on the south side of 136th Street. On April 23, a week before Moving Day, the company purchased more buildings at 40, 42, and 44 West 135th Street, on the south side of that street. Since they were most likely occupied, they would have been central to the eviction effort, but since Hudson did not own other occupied properties in the area, other property owners must have joined in to result in the potential movement of hundreds described by the *Herald*.

ENTERING THE FIELD OF BATTLE

In the days before Moving Day 1904, scores of African American families on 135th, 134th, and 133rd Streets received eviction notices.[11]

In response to the 135th Street eviction effort, some tenants moved quietly, but others refused to go. When pressed for an explanation for the mass evictions, owners responded that the African Americans in the area were unruly and that the area was crime-ridden. This was a common characterization for the Midtown African American enclaves, but until this time Harlem's enclave had been viewed as the home of prosperous, well-behaved Negroes. Adding the insult of alleged criminality to the injury of eviction was the last straw for African American residents. A meeting of area residents was held on May 1 at Mercy Seat Baptist Church at 46 West 135th Street. Mercy Seat's pastor, Norman Epps, and seven members had formed the church in 1897, with initial meetings held at a building at 427 West 127th Street near Amsterdam Avenue. The church moved to the 135th Street location in 1899. By 1904 Rev. Epps was well-acquainted with the practice of filing a public grievance. On a September evening in 1901, while he and his brother Philip were chatting on 41st Street near Eighth Avenue in Midtown, they were told to move on by policeman Frank T. Lane. They moved fifty feet down the block, which was not far enough for Lane, who pursued them and struck Epps on the back of the head with his club, knocking him to the ground. When Epps recovered, he ran down the street to avoid the officer, who eventually caught and arrested him. After being bailed out later that evening, Epps filed a grievance against the officer, and the next month Lane appeared before Deputy Police Chief William S. Devery, where he explained that "his Captain, Cooney had ordered that colored men be not allowed to congregate on that particular corner, which was a storm centre in last year's race riot." No punishment was reported for Lane. As in the Harlem eviction effort, the allusion to black criminality, in this case for a riot that had occurred a year earlier in which black people were overwhelmingly the victims of white criminals, was used to justify an effort at black removal.[12]

At the May 1 meeting in 1904, Rev. Epps had his hands full maintaining order among the people of all ages. Their vacate date of April 30 had already passed, but their anger seemed as strong regarding their characterization as criminals as at the potential loss of their housing. Epps affirmed residents' complaints that their evictions were premised on the false accusations that they were noisy and disorderly, noting that "the prospective opening of the subway has enhanced the desirability of the locality, and so . . . the very landlords who had once invited the [N]egro tenants are now trying to drive them out!" The occupants of the 135th Street properties may have moved, but they did not go quietly.[13]

The Mercy Seat meeting ended with no clear resolution or stated plan, but behind the scenes Philip Payton, the undertaker James Thomas, and Julia Liggan, another African American real estate broker, were beginning to work. For Payton, countering the eviction effort was personal and professional. Earlier that year he had purchased 67 West 134th Street, an apartment building in which he housed the uptown office of the Afro-American Realty Company. In the following weeks Thomas, Payton, and Liggan purchased several properties in the area.[14]

Not all the white owners of property in the 135th Street area were in accord with Hudson Realty and the other property owners leading the eviction effort. Over the course of the next six weeks, owners of three of these properties entered into agreements to transfer properties they owned in the 135th Street/Lenox Avenue area to African Americans. On May 2, the day after the indignation meeting, Mercy Seat signed a five-year lease for 46 West 135th Street, next door to the row of buildings purchased by Hudson Realty. The monthly rent was $100, and the lease gave the church the option to purchase the building at a price of $16,000 "at any time during the term of this lease, with the appurtenances." The lessor was Louis Partzchefeld. Three days later, on May 5, Charles and Katie Kroehle sold 30–32 West 135th Street to James Thomas, president of the Afro-American Realty Company. On May 12th Mercy Seat purchased lots at 45 and 47 West 134th Street for $16,000 from August and Mena Ruff. The sales agreement for the Ruffs' lot included a covenant indicating the first building constructed on the property would be a church for Mercy Seat. On May 12 Charles Satchell Morris, pastor of Abyssinian Baptist Church, a black congregation then on West 40th Street, transferred to Abyssinian a building located at 61 West 134th Street that he had purchased eight months earlier, in September 1903. Two days later James C. Thomas purchased 30 and 32 West 135th Street from Charles Kroehle. On June 29 Thomas transferred a half interest in the properties to Philip A. Payton Jr. A month later Thomas sold the other half interest to Payton as well. As if playing a game of chess, these purchases by black investors blocked Hudson Realty's acquisition campaign.[15]

The group that transferred control of their properties to African Americans were German American, like Maximilian Morgenthau and James

Bloomingdale of the Hudson Realty Company, but they were of a different social class. Born in Germany in 1851, Louis Partzchefeld owned a metalworking company specializing in roof installation. He lived at 4 West 136th Street, one block north of the Little Africa enclave, with his German-born wife, Luisa, and their American-born sons—Louis, who at twenty-two did structural work, and Ernst, eight years old, who attended Felix Adler's Ethical Culture School (Maximilian Morgenthau was a good friend of Adler's). Charles Kroehle was forty-six years old and his wife was forty-two. Both were born in New York, but their parents were born in Germany. They lived with their daughters, Matilda (thirteen) and Marianne (ten), at 992 Second Avenue, near East 53rd Street, the heart of an East Side German American enclave. August and Mena Ruff were born in Germany. August had arrived in the United States in 1867, and in New York he was fully ensconced in the thriving German American community. He was an officer in a German American singing society, Schwaebisher Saengerbund, and was active in Democratic politics. He was a builder who lived at 52 West 120th Street.[16]

Phillip Payton was proud of his success in turning back the tide of eviction. Booker T. Washington, in New York at the time of the May anti-eviction meeting, wrote him a congratulatory note: "I have read in yesterday's *World* how you turned the tables on those who desired to injure the race, and wish to congratulate you on this instance of business enterprise and race loyalty combined."[17]

The 135th Street eviction tragedy turned to triumph in June 1904 with the announcement of the incorporation of the Afro-American Realty Company, whose name made clear who it planned to serve. A year earlier, in June 1903, the AARC had been quietly formed as a partnership "for the purpose of engaging in the business of renting and re-renting, leasing and subleasing, tenement houses, flats, or other buildings, for residences and other purposes, in the City of New York."[18] The eviction efforts of the spring of 1904 required more of the AARC than mere leasing, or the apartments that African Americans had settled into in the 135th Street area would become a faint memory and residents would be returned to the usual hand-me-down housing of the Tenderloin and San Juan Hill districts of Midtown Manhattan. The company was incorporated in 1904 to "buy sell, rent, lease, and sub-lease all kinds of buildings, houses, houses and lots, and other improved real estate in the City of New York . . . and to tear down and re-build houses and construct new houses on unimproved lots."[19] Buying property was a significant addition to the company's portfolio since it provided a much greater ability to control the future of properties compared to leasing properties owned by others. Incorporation provided the means to raise up to $500,000 in capital through the sale of stock at ten dollars per share.

The company's Certificate of Incorporation with its staid language remained in the office of the New York County Clerk, but for the public Philip Payton produced an eight-page, pocket-sized prospectus that revealed his understanding of how to market to African Americans and announced the revolutionary mission of the AARC. In explaining the company's purpose, the pamphlet homed in on the recent eviction effort: "When the movement was started to put the colored people out of West 135th street, this co-partnership being unable to lease any houses on this street, voted to buy and did buy two 5-story flats valued at $50,000 and thereby stemmed the tide, which had it been successful in West 135th street, would surely have extended to West 134th street, which is almost entirely given over to our people." By using business tactics, Payton and the AARC's investors resolved to fight fire with fire in head-to-head confrontations with the white-owned businesses and real estate investors who sought to oust African Americans from Harlem. The pamphlet stated that "race prejudice is a luxury and like all other luxuries, can be made very expensive in New York City, if the Negroes will but answer the call of the Afro-American Realty Company."[20]

The company prospectus differed from the plain pamphlets developed by most other businesses. The *Colored American Magazine* described it as "bound in chocolate colored covers and adorned with the imprint of an African's head."[21] Its cover (figure 3.1) was dominated by a design in black and white that included an ornate pendant accented by curlicues. The lower portion of the pendant included a drawing of the face of a black man. The man's image was not a caricature but a realistic drawing of a half-smiling, pleasant-looking person who, beneath full eyebrows and medium length curly hair, looked over his broad nose directly at the reader. In the wider, upper portion of the pendant, the name of the company was spelled out in white capital letters: "AFRO-AMERICAN REALTY COMPANY." Below the name, in slightly smaller capital letters: "CAPITAL STOCK $500,000."

Inside the pamphlet, the title page noted that the company was "Incorporated Under the Laws of the State of New York" and that $100,000 had

FIGURE 3.1 Afro-American Realty Company prospectus cover, 1904. *Source*: Manuscripts and Rare Books Division, Schomburg Center for Research in Black Culture, New York Public Library.

already been invested in it. The following pages explained the 135th Street eviction showdown that was the impetus for the company's formation. The text then explained "Negro Colonization to be Done Away With." In the midst of hardening residential segregation practices in New York City, the pamphlet suggested that "the idea that Negroes must be confined to certain localities can be done away with. The idea that it is not practical to put colored and white tenants together in the same house can be done away with." The prospectus explained the cause of racial segregation and the comparative advantage of the AARC: "The reason for the present condition of the colored tenancy in New York City to-day is because of the race prejudice of the white owner and his white agent. When the owner becomes colored and his agent colored, then there is compelled to come an improvement of the condition." The text then linked the mission of the company to the profit motive: "Prejudice, so far as it relates to the Negro tenancy in New York City, will in time become so very expensive that it will become impracticable, and like all impracticable things, will die a natural death.... A respectable law-abiding Negro will find conditions can be so changed that he will be able to rent, wherever his means will permit him to live."[22] Promising returns on investment of 7 to 10 percent, in one of the closing sections the text made clear that the AARC was a race enterprise—a business owned by black people designed to serve black customers:

> An earnest appeal is hereby made to the colored people of this country to unite for our mutual benefit and protection. The Negro is being gradually crowded out of all lines and is pursued by a relentless race prejudice. It remains for him alone to stop this. Judging from the rapidity with which the balance of the unsold stock of the company is being taken by our people, we can but say our appeal is being answered, and the colored people are awake to the needs of the situation.[23]

The *Colored American Magazine* noted that "not a white person is connected with the company in any capacity: even the typewriter keys are being manipulated by colored ladies who are very businesslike and obliging. The company is devoted to the cause of African ownership and tenancy."[24] The directors of the company were most of the men who had been part of the Afro-American Realty partnership of the previous year, but three new directors were added: Winston Dabney, a thirty-eight-year-old house cleaner; Frank A. Steuart, a twenty-eight-year-old hotel bellman; and Rev. Richard R. Wilson, the fifty-year-old pastor of Timothy Baptist Church, on 30th Street, and a porter in a jewelry store.[25] Payton was twenty-eight years old. Almost all his fellow investors were his elders.

While the 1904 purchases of Payton and his colleagues were strategic—properties in the middle of the area that was the focus of eviction—and daring, they required surprisingly small amounts of capital. Most of the purchases were sealed with the payment of $100 (the equivalent of $2,880 in 2020 dollars).[26] Typical financing terms called for the company to assume the payments on existing loans on the properties. These were usually interest-only payments at a rate of 6 percent for a period of approximately five years, after which the outstanding principal of the loan would be due. The financing terms are particularly revealing. The AARC did not have to expend much of its newly raised capital for the purchases because the sellers provided financing. That they were willing to do so for African Americans at a time when other white property owners were attempting to evict the same group suggests the possibility that the German American sellers saw beyond the racial lines of 1904 and viewed Payton, Thomas, and Liggan as small, striving business people like themselves to whom they were willing to extend financing to make their purchases possible. The sellers chose to deal with Payton and his African American colleagues rather than associate themselves with the Hudson Realty Company and other white owners undertaking the eviction efforts.

While Hudson Realty was not the only entity pushing for eviction, its holdings were the largest in the area, and it stood to gain the most through the eviction of African Americans. The German American sellers of properties purchased by Payton, Thomas, and Liggan—a stable owner, a contractor, and a blacksmith—were of a lower social class than the Hudson Realty principals and may have viewed Hudson's actions as hostile not only to African Americans but to the smaller white business owners who did not have the capital to redevelop their properties as Hudson most likely planned to do once the African Americans were evicted. The sellers may have been more inclined to deal with the black New Yorkers striving to move up rather than white New Yorkers seeking to dominate those below them in the social hierarchy.

In contrast to Booker T. Washington's congratulatory message when the Afro-American Realty Company's incorporation was announced in June 1904, the *New York Times* lodged a complaint on its editorial page.

Under the headline "To Make the Color Line Costly," the editorial suggested that the AARC was formed "to depress real estate values in order to bring desirable apartment houses into the market as homes for negroes promises to be a business mistake." The editorial predicted that white residents would leave and "that the number of unobjectionable negro tenants standing ready to take their places is not great enough to prevent neighborhood deterioration." The *Times* editorial writer drew on existing housing market theory that the presence of African Americans in an otherwise white neighborhood resulted in a reduction in property values, implicitly suggesting the undesirability of African Americans as neighbors.[27]

At the National Negro Business League Convention in Indianapolis, which met from August 31 through September 2, 1904, Philip Payton, then on the NNBL's Executive Committee as first vice president, offered a speech on "Meeting the Realty Needs of the New York Negro," repeating the message from the AARC prospectus that "race prejudice is a luxury, and like all luxuries can be made very expensive in New York City if Negroes will but answer this call of the Afro-American Realty Company. . . . Prejudice so far as it relates to the Negro as a tenant in New York City will in time become impracticable, and like all impracticable things will die a natural death."[28] The strategic purchases by the African Americans in Harlem in the spring of 1904 seemed to support Payton's assertion.

In the fall of 1904 the Hudson Realty Company sold all the properties it had purchased earlier that year in the 135th Street area, conceding defeat in this particular battle. But the anti-eviction effort was the first salvo in an ongoing war. The hostile response to the formation of the AARC did not surprise Payton. He knew that there would be a backlash to his efforts, but he also believed that the hostile reaction had to be confronted, and that eventually such beliefs could be changed. Payton was beginning an upward journey that would bring his efforts in Harlem to the attention of African Americans across the nation. His efforts would brand Harlem, one of the most desirable areas of the city, as a community where African Americans could and would live. In establishing the Afro-American Realty Company as a corporation, Payton, still not yet thirty years old, exuded a confidence and faith in his abilities to bring about change.[29]

In 1905 Payton's business activities would continue to be chronicled in local and national newspapers. The *Sun* described the New Year's Eve celebrations in 1904 of over two hundred thousand people gathered for the event, then centered in front of Trinity Church in Lower Manhattan:

> This will go down as the New Year of the cowbells. That particular variety of nerve destroyer first made its appearance in last year's celebration. This year they were sold in the thousands. People who were flush bought whole strings of them. The genuine noise fiends operated a horn with one hand and a cowbell with the other . . . at 12 the noise doubled. Every horn and rattle and cowbell and hazoo and drum and bugle was shot off in a volley and 1904 was hurried off into space.[30]

Between February and April Philip Payton made five real estate transactions, and the AARC made one. Most properties were concentrated in Harlem, although one was on 63rd Street in San Juan Hill, and another on 99th Street in the other developing black enclave on the West Side of Manhattan. Most of these transactions were brokerage activities, purchases or sales on behalf of clients.[31] The AARC generated publicity through its network of contacts in the black press. It was the focus of a cover story in the May 1905 issue of the *Colored American Magazine*. In 1904 Fred R. Moore had purchased a controlling interest in the magazine and moved the publication to New York. Moore was a director in the AARC and served as national organizer for the National Negro Business League. Consistent with these ties, the magazine's article on the AARC gave the company lavish attention. The cover featured a drawing of its president, undertaker James C. Thomas. The author, Roscoe Conklin Simmons, a nephew of Booker T. Washington, was a noted orator and publicist of the NNBL.[32] These skills were on full display in the article, "The Afro-American Realty Company: Has it Justified the Support Given It?," which began with a series of questions:

> It is now almost one year ago since the Realty company was incorporated and offered its stock for sale; and it is a good time to inquire, Has the Company justified itself? Has it rendered sufficient service to warrant further indulgence and support? Were its supporters dreamers? What proof is there that its future is secure, and the capital invested therein safe? Is there need in New York for such a corporation?[33]

In the following twelve pages, Simmons presented evidence that would have led most readers to answer his questions in the affirmative. Photographs of buildings AARC owned or leased, individual photographs of several company directors, including Moore and Payton, as well as individual photographs of key AARC staff provided an indication of the scale of the company's activities (figure 3.2). "The Company now controls thirteen pieces of valuable New York property, a part of which it owns, and upon the remainder it holds leases of long duration" (figure 3.3). Simmons presented the activities of the AARC as a team effort, with Payton, as general manager, playing an important but not pivotal role in the company.[34]

In mid-July 1905 Philip Payton's old neighborhood of San Juan Hill was the site of another race riot. Mary White Ovington, who worked at a settlement house in the area and would go on to become one of the white founders of the National Association for the Advancement of Colored People (NAACP), noted:

> The riot of 1905 commenced on San Juan Hill one Friday evening in July with a fracas between a colored boy and a white peddler; both races took a hand in the matter until the side streets showed a rough scrambling fight.... the police however instead of keeping the peace, angered the Negroes, urged on their enemies and by Monday night found that they had helped create a riot, this time bitter and dangerous. Overzealous to proceed against the "niggers," officers rushed into places frequented by peaceable colored men whom they placed under arrest. Dragging their victims to the station-house they beat them so unmercifully that before long many needed to be handed over to another city department—the hospital.[35]

FIGURE 3.2 Afro-American Realty Company directors (*left to right*: James C. Thomas, president; Philip A. Payton Jr. vice president and general manager; James E. Garner, secretary-treasurer; Wilford H. Smith, attorney). Source: *Colored American Magazine*, May 1905.

FIGURE 3.3 Afro-American Realty Company buildings (*top row*: 30-32 W. 135th Street; 65-67 W. 134th Street; 57-59 W. 98th Street; *bottom row*: 156-158 West 97th Street; 330, 332, 334, 336 West 59th Street). *Source*: *Colored American Magazine*, May 1905.

As with the riot in 1900 in the Tenderloin district to the south of San Juan Hill, after the 1905 violence ended, San Juan Hill residents organized a grievance committee to present their complaints to city officials. Payton, who had just recently moved his residence and office from the area, was elected president of the organization, the Colored Citizens' Protective League, and as people offered initial contributions to the organization, he donated one hundred dollars.[36] Some of the funds were dedicated to an action against 68th Street police precinct leaders Captain John Cooney and Officer Robinson for assaults against black people brought to the station during the rioting. Affidavits were collected by attorneys Wilford Smith and Gilchrest Stewart, leading to the temporary transfer of Captain Cooney, pending a more complete investigation. In November Police Commissioner William McAdoo and Police Inspector William McLaughlin heard testimony at a hearing at the 68th precinct station.[37] Writing about the hearing, the *New York Age* suggested that some black witnesses had been pressured to "whitewash" their testimony by claiming they had memory lapses or did not see any violence. The newspaper noted that

> as a result of the investigation Captain Cooney's transfer was made permanent and a tacit understanding was reached that as long as the present management of the police department continued he will never be placed in charge of any precinct having many Afro-Americans in it. An official reprimand was given him for being absent from the station on the night of the riot. . . . If some of the witnesses had had better memories more would have been accomplished.[38]

Payton's prominence leading the Protective League brought him to the attention of another media-savvy promoter who was also using race to market his offerings, but from the other side of the color line. A month after Cooney was transferred, on a Saturday evening in mid-December, a U.S. Mail special delivery messenger delivered a package to Payton's home on West 131st Street. Similar packages were also delivered that evening to the homes of Rev. Charles S. Morris, pastor of Abyssinian Baptist Church, Rev. C. Leroy Butler, pastor of St. James Presbyterian Church, and Rev. M. W. Gilbert, pastor of Mount Olivet Baptist Church. The packages contained promotional material for *The Clansman*, a play by Thomas Dixon scheduled to arrive at New York's Liberty Theater in January 1906. Dixon, a former minister, based the play on the book he had published earlier in 1905, *The Clansman: An Historical Romance of the Ku Klux Klan*. The book dealt with the Civil War and the Reconstruction period from the perspective of a southern plantation family and a northern family, linked by the romance between their children. It depicted black Union soldiers and a biracial politician as threats to white womanhood, black Reconstruction era politicians as buffoons, and the Ku Klux Klan as heroes. Historian Ralph Luker describes Dixon's actions in 1905 targeting black leaders as a "campaign of self-promotion by racial vituperation."[39] An early phase had included an attack on Booker T. Washington for his "inappropriate" familiarity with the families of northern white philanthropists, and on his leadership of Tuskegee Institute, which Dixon claimed was educating black students to compete with white workers. Skilled at the use of the media and too savvy to take the bait of an obvious media manipulator, Washington ignored the criticisms. The special delivery packages that arrived in New York that December evening were the next phase of Dixon's campaign to gain publicity by raising the ire of black Americans. Philip Payton, also skilled at the use of media, may have been inclined to follow Washington's strategy of ignoring Dixon, but the timing of the delivery of the packages, Saturday evening, took the matter out of his hands. The following Sunday morning several of the pastors who received them entered the pulpits of their churches and preached sermons against *The Clansman*.[40] They encouraged other black pastors to do the same on the following Sunday, and the opposition effort that Dixon was clearly hoping for to gain publicity for his play was set in motion.

At a meeting of the Colored Citizens' Protective League held at the downtown offices of the AARC on Maiden Lane, with Payton presiding, a resolution was passed condemning *The Clansman* as "detrimental to public morals, historically incorrect, slanderous to the memory of the Union soldier and patriot, and vilifying the [N]egro." The next week the league appointed a committee to meet with Mayor George B. McClellan, Jr., the son of a Civil War general, and to protest the play on the "grounds of its immorality and its tendency to embitter racial feeling and antagonism, if not directly leading to more riots."[41] The concern that the play would inspire more rioting explains why Payton, leader of the Protective League, unlike Washington, was unable to ignore Dixon's campaign.[42]

On December 17, 1905, the *New York Times* brought its readers' attention to Payton's practice of evicting white tenants in the buildings he opened to black residents. Under the headline "Real Estate Race War Started in Harlem," it noted that "White folks, hat in hand, filed into the real estate offices of a [N]egro named Philip A. Payton, Jr., in West One Hundred and Thirty-fourth Street, yesterday, and pleaded that they might be left in undisturbed possession of their little flats over the holidays. They were scrutinized by the colored clerks and usually told that their cases would receive attention." The article recounted the irony of the fact that the white "working men of small incomes" in three buildings on West 135th Street were experiencing what black tenants evicted by the Hudson Realty Company in 1904 had experienced, and that the Afro-American Realty Company had responded to that situation by purchasing homes in the area from which the white tenants were being evicted. It noted that Hudson Realty had sold its properties on West 135th, and that on one site apartments were nearing completion that would reportedly be rented exclusively to white tenants. It explained that on the other side of the street, Philip Payton, after evicting white tenants, would soon begin renting apartments to black tenants in buildings owned by an unknown client, but which the *Times* suggested was the AARC. Given the articles' inflammatory headline, it ended on a note that, while complimentary, reflected the low expectations many white New Yorkers had for these black people moving into buildings controlled by black people: "The Payton realty office is now the centre of one of the largest [N]egro neighborhoods in the city, but they are all decent, hardworking [N]egroes. Even the private houses there are occupied by colored families or colored business establishments."

The article foreshadowed growing tensions. In 1906 Philip Payton's publicity of Harlem for prospective black residents, and his boldness in opening Harlem buildings to black residents by evicting white residents, would generate a backlash from some white New Yorkers. He would also face a battle on a second front as some Afro-American Realty Company investors would challenge his efforts to assert control over the company.

Chapter Four

BATTLES IN THE STREETS AND THE COURTROOM

In New York, the celebration of the coming of the year 1906 marked a new beginning, in location as well as in time, as noted in the January 1 edition of the *New York Times*:

> A goodly portion of the crowd that used to gather in thousands around old Trinity Church to welcome in the New Year by all the tricks and noises that can be invented by a celebrating throng of merry-makers, came uptown this year to Times Square. In the old days the chimes of Trinity did their level best to lift a little note above the clamor of the crowds below, but rarely were they ever successful. Last night Times Square came to the aid of the chimes by deflecting a large part of the celebrants.[1]

Adolph S. Ochs, publisher of *Times*, had facilitated the shift in the New Year's celebration to commemorate the paper's new skyscraper headquarters at Broadway/Seventh Avenue, between 42nd and 43rd Streets, which had opened in 1905. Soon after the opening, Mayor George B. McClellan signed a resolution that renamed the area, previously known as Long Acre Square, Times Square.[2] The *Times* article described the New Year's revelry:

> On the stroke of twelve last night the figures "1906" were flashed from the tower of the Times Building. Far out across the skies, visible for miles away,

the electric symbol of the New Year shot its way. The entire Times Building was illuminated. Electric streamers were displayed from the four corners of the tower.... When the New Year was announced from the tower, the hysterical crowd below became, if possible more hysterical. Their utmost strength of lungs was given to a welcoming blast to 1906.... Conventions were forgotten, and good folk who had never yet been within a thousand miles of an introduction screamed wildly at one another: "Happy New Year!"

The development of Times Square as an office and transportation center that in 1906 had become a logical location for the New Year's celebration foretold the development pressures that black residents in the tenements on blocks in close proximity to Times Square had begun to face by 1906. These residents were a ready market for the Afro-American Realty Company. In the January 4, 1906, issue of the *New York Age*, the company ran a two-column advertisement with the headline "The Pride of the Negro Race Is the Half-Million Dollar Afro-American Realty Co.," with text noting that "the company has as its principal object the better housing of the Negro Tenant Class," followed by text noting that "buildings with values totaling $690,000 had come under the company's control in the last year.... What this Company is doing in New York City it intends ultimately to do in every large city in the United States where its people are found in any considerable number. Invest now and help this great movement onward." Philip Payton and the AARC entered the New Year with a flurry of activity in New York consistent with the ambitious vision outlined in the advertisement. The activity provided Payton with an opportunity to fulfill his vision outlined in the AARC's 1904 prospectus. The company's increased visibility generated additional business but also enemies who questioned whether Payton was really a race champion or manipulating the real estate market to make a quick dollar.

In late January 1906 Payton handled the sale of two five-story, four-family apartment buildings on West 37th Street in the southern section of the Midtown African American Tenderloin district, and the sale of 2232 Fifth Avenue, near 135th Street, a five-story apartment building with stores, for Weil & Mayer. In early February he sold land at the northeast corner of Lenox Avenue and 135th Street for a client, McKinley Realty and Construction Company.[3]

In February the *Colored American Magazine* turned its attention once again to the AARC in an article entitled "Growth of the Afro-American Realty Company." The second page of the article featured a full-page photograph of Philip Payton, now listed as "President and General Manager." With no author credited, the writer of the article framed its purpose as a status report in the months since Roscoe Conkling Simmons's May 1905 article had suggested that the company would be of interest to African Americans in the know: "The annual report before us should be gratifying to the supporters of the Company, and the colored people as a whole, for it discloses an unusual able administration of funds entrusted to it, and points out minutely its present status and future possibility." The writer noted that of the $500,000 in available capital stock, $67,786.90 had been purchased, and indicated the following financial activity for the year:

Gross income from rentals	$45,000
Direct expenses (lease rents, taxes, interest, repairs)	35,400
Gross profit	9,600
Annual expenses	5,500
Earnings	$4,100[4]

The article stated that the company's net earnings represented a 6 percent return on the capital stock purchased. No mention was made that this rate of return was below the 7–10 percent return promised in the AARC's prospectus in 1904. According to the article, the AARC indicated that it "cannot count upon paying this dividend during the current year, as there are some $7,000 of preliminary and promotion expenses connected with launching the Company, which it is the policy of the Board to write off, say in four years against profits which will leave our net earnings against profits, say 3 percent."[5] The article noted that

> the Company has met stubborn and vicious opposition ever since incorporation and such opposition is not founded upon any just grounds of complaints either as to the management of their affairs or the purpose of its officers; the management has been scrupulously honest; their purpose as we have stated before is high and fundamentally beneficent. The accusations aimed at the Company are traceable on the one hand to the somewhat

natural jealousy of successful conduct of affairs, and on the other hand, and to the rumor which early got abroad, that the Company increased the rent of every house over which it got control.[6]

The article then noted that the AARC's annual report contained a response to this accusation:

> We think that all will concede that if the Company buys or leases a dilapidated house or flat, and spends necessary money to put the property in tenantable condition, that it is entitled to a fair return on the money so invested. Then, too, the Company owes it to its stockholders in its operations to rent its properties to the best possible advantage. It is commonly said that colored people pay more rent for the same accommodations than do white people. Assuming this to be a fact, we promise you that when the $500,000 worth of stock of this Company is all subscribed to, it will no longer be possible to truthfully say this. It is the ultimate intention of this Company, realizing and recognizing the fact that our people in this city do not have the same opportunities for making money as do white people, to rent its properties as low as is consistent with keeping them in good repair and on a fair earning basis.[7]

This text was most likely written by Philip Payton, the AARC's president. While he explained why rents in buildings that he assumed control of and renovated would be higher than they were before the renovation, he did not explain how the purchasing of the remainder of the available AARC stock would eliminate the practice of black people paying higher rents. He asserted that his goal was to provide a fair rent and implied that even though the rents the company charged to black people might be higher than the previous white tenants paid, this circumstance was due to the AARC's investments in the buildings, and that the resulting rents were fair. This explanation implies that all buildings controlled by the company were substantially renovated before being rented to black tenants, something that is highly unlikely, given the modest capital available to the AARC.

The rest of the article featured brief profiles, along with photographs of key directors, including Fred R. Moore, publisher of the *Colored American Magazine*, and staff of the company. It concluded with an endorsement of the AARC that reminded the reader that the company was a race enterprise, intent on advancing the goals of black people in New York and eventually the nation:

> The trial of the Realty Company is the trial of the New York Afro-American; the outcome of such trial will be recorded under the Afro-American's name. It's [sic] failure, then, to make a permanent place in the life of the city, then the nation, would be in a powerful proportion, the failure of the Afro-American people. On the other hand, the Company cannot make such a fight, as it would like to make, and as must be fought, unless those for whom it was founded, rally resolutely to its support.... The men who are behind the Company are men who have never failed.[8]

In the course of fifteen pages, the article was a full-throated promotion piece for the AARC as the final instructions to the reader made clear: "This report should be widely circulated, not only among New York Afro-Americans, but among all classes of citizens everywhere. It tells a good story, tells it in figures, and figures do not pervert the truth."[9]

In March, a month after the article appeared, Philip Payton handled the sale of five properties in various areas of Harlem for a range of clients. Neither Payton nor the AARC had purchases or sales in April, but the company did sign a five-year lease for 248 and 250 West 62nd Street during the month. In May Payton sold two properties on 135th Street on behalf of a client.[10] The year 1906 was proceeding to be a banner year for Philip Payton and the company. By the end of June the twelve transactions handled by Payton or the AARC had already exceeded the number of transactions for each of the company's previous three years (eight each in 1903 and 1904, five in 1905), suggesting that the AARC's national ambitions stated in the *New York Age* advertisement and the *Colored American Magazine* article might be a reasonable goal. Renting to black tenants in buildings previously occupied exclusively by white tenants, along with Payton's aggressive advertising and promotional rhetoric, may have been appealing to prospective black tenants, but for many white Harlem residents, the prospect of black neighbors was frightening. Although New York did not have strict residential segregation practices, and blacks and whites lived interspersed in some neighborhoods and buildings, by the latter decades of the 1800s, as New York's black population increased due to migration from the South and the Caribbean, white hostility to the presence of black people also grew, following the pattern being played out in the South, where concerns about the free movement of emancipated African Americans and the potential of them seeking "social equality" resulted in explicit racial segregation laws being enacted in the 1880s and 1890s. While northern cities did not adopt segregation laws, as the urban black presence grew, many cities, including New York, developed more restrictive segregation practices in public transportation, restaurants, and housing. The justification for these practices was supported by social scientists' articles and speeches claiming a link between blackness and criminality, and diseases such as tuberculosis. The real estate field, just becoming professionalized at the turn of the twentieth century, followed this trend. Many white brokers equated the presence of black residents with a reduction in property values.[11]

The *New York Times* sounded the alarm regarding the threat of black residents in Upper Manhattan in a July 21, 1906, article with the headline "Negro Invasion Threat Angers Flat Dwellers." The article recounted the reaction of the janitor of a fifteen-unit apartment building at 525 West 151st Street, Mrs. P. M. Roth. It explained that she was introduced to Philip Payton by the building's previous owner, Louis Myer, who stated: "'This is Mr. Payton, agent for the new owners of the house here. He's going to get all the white families out and put negro families in their places.' 'What!' shrieked Mrs. Roth. 'Going to put all white people out for blacks? Well, what will the neighbors say?' Then she ran out into the street to tell the news." According to the article, Mrs. Roth refused to install a sign on the building indicating "Choice Four and Five Room Apartments for Colored Tenants Apply Janitor." The article explained that a black man was commandeered to install the sign, but neighbors tore it down and burned it.

Payton had demanded that the white tenants at 525 West 151st Street vacate their apartments by August 1, a little over a week away. In addition to the great inconvenience of this request, the *Times* article emphasized the perceived devastating consequences that the arrival of black residents would have on the block. The writer noted that the building had been built by Herman Raabe's Sons approximately a year earlier and sold to Louis Meyer with an unidentified principal of Herman Raabe's Sons stating that the purchase and the plan to introduce black tenants into the building was "a trick to make us buy them out. We own other property in the same block, and anybody with common sense can see that if negroes move into that apartment building our values will be ruined. It's an outrage—a shame. We'll fight it to a finish." The article provided the white residents with an opportunity to express their anger at being ousted from their homes. Nevertheless, as quoted in the article, Payton continued to frame the AARC's actions as trailblazing: "What we wish to do is stop forced colonization. We are in earnest in this proposition. We intend to have negro families in that apartment house. Of course there is prejudice against them. There was prejudice against the Jews and the Italians. They overcame it and we should be able to do so." Considering that he was ousting the white tenants to create an all-black building, Payton framed colonization on a neighborhood level rather than on a building level and seems to have disregarded the AARC prospectus vision of black and white people living in the same building. Moving black tenants into apartments in the building alongside white ones as apartments became available would have been a true test of his challenge to the color line and may have prevented the negative attention that the *Times* article brought to his actions.

Approximately three weeks later, in an August 8 article in the same paper, the outcome of the apartment controversy was described: "The threatened invasion of the block on 151st Street between Amsterdam and Broadway, by colored tenants has been averted. Neighboring property owners have bought the six-story apartment house at 525 West 151st Street, recently leased to the Afro-American Realty Company, and they say that the tenantry of the house will now stay in keeping with the character of the rest of the houses in that section."[12] The article noted that financial support for the purchase had come from property owners on 150th, 151st, and 152nd Streets between Broadway and Amsterdam Avenue. The buyer of record was Loton Horton, the owner of Sheffield Farms Dairy, who made a payment of $100 and assumed payments on three mortgages on the building totaling $50,000. While there were inaccuracies in some of the facts related by the initial July 21 article, which stated that Meyer had sold the building to the AARC, a July 22 *Times* article accurately noted that Meyer had entered into a five-year lease with Philip Payton, "agent of the Afro-American Realty Company." Assuming that Meyer was aware of the sentiments of the tenants and neighbors before he entered into the lease, what was the advantage for him in leasing his building to Payton? The July 22 article noted that "one rumor had it that Louis Meyer, who bought No. 525 about a year ago, hadn't found it a paying proposition and wanted to sell it back to the persons he bought it from or to other owners of nearby property."[13]

If this report was accurate, for both Meyer and Payton the lease had the potential to be a win-win proposition. If Payton successfully leased the building to African American tenants and adopted the common practice of charging them more because of their limited housing choices, he would benefit from a larger management fee since the fees were usually tied to the rents collected. The remainder of the rent revenue could be used to cover the building's costs, which would benefit Meyer. The potential for increased revenue from an all-black building with higher rents explains why Payton broke from the intrabuilding racial integration vision of his prospectus when he had the responsibility of leasing 525 West 151st Street. Moving black tenants into the building as vacancies arose would have been a slower process than the blanket evictions of white tenants. The presence of white tenants with longer residencies at lower rents would have complicated what was becoming his practice (which he denied) of charging black tenants more than white tenants. The inequity of this policy would have been much more apparent if white and black tenants in the building compared their rent charges. The outcome that occurred for 525 West 151st Street, the sale of the building, was also a win for its former owner Louis Meyer, who was relieved of the obligation of making payments on the three mortgages on the property. Philip Payton benefited since his lease agreement contained a clause providing him with a $1,000 payment (over $28,000 in 2020 dollars) in the event of the sale of the building.[14]

Critics of Payton and the AARC could have used the West 151st Street transaction as evidence of the strategy predicted in the headline of the *Times*'s 1904 editorial criticizing the formation of the AARC: "To Make the Color Line Costly." To maintain the color line on West 151st Street, Loton Horton assumed $50,000 of debt, and Payton was paid $1,000. While Payton framed his actions as those of a race champion fighting "negro colonization," the *Times* suggested that the West 151st Street transaction was part of a citywide movement: "Wide discussion has been caused by several cases where a [N]egro agent told of the leasing of a house in the midst of a white settlement, giving wide notice of his intention of moving in negroes. The [N]egroes, it is said, never moved in."[15] Several decades later, such actions would be described as blockbusting. In 1906 Payton's intentions were not entirely clear. What is clear is that he had quickly abandoned his vision of white and black tenants living together in the same buildings. In the West 151st Street incident, he seemed committed to playing on the fears of white

BATTLES IN THE STREETS AND THE COURTROOM

neighbors to benefit black tenants desperate for good housing and willing to pay more for it than whites or to be paid to go away.

As the summer proceeded, the growing success of Philip and Maggie Payton was noticed nationally, illustrated by an August notice included in the "New York Letter" of the *East Oregonian* newspaper, published in Pendleton, Oregon:

> Clerks of the fashionable stores along Fifth [A]venue, Twenty-third [S]treet and Broadway, know by sight a colored woman who is a frequent visitor in her automobile to the shops where the finest things are to be bought. She makes large purchases. The woman is Mrs. Payton, wife of Philip Payton, Jr., the [N]egro who has made a fortune in real estate, and is back of a plan in Harlem to form a colony of well-to-do colored persons. Her tastes are refined and supported by the credit of her husband's name, and she is able to gratify desires which only the wealthy dare to entertain.

The writer then provided readers with a perspective on Payton's work:

> Payton, as a real estate dealer, is daring, and not afraid to stand by his colored brethren. He it was who evicted all the white tenants from a large and fashionable apartment house in a fashionable neighborhood, and filled the apartments with colored tenants. He is making money by it and is pleasing colored people of means, but he isn't pleasing the rich white people who have to move from flats they had held for some time.[16]

After Payton surrendered his lease to 525 West 151st Street and received $1,000, the real estate transactions of Payton and the AARC continued at the pace set in the first half of 1906. Seven transactions were executed between July and September, ranging from leases to sales of buildings in the area between 119th and 135th Streets.[17]

While Payton's efforts to rent to black tenants in predominantly white neighborhoods had been met with verbal attacks, in late September these challenges were put in perspective when Atlanta exploded into three days of rioting as white residents attacked African Americans and destroyed black businesses and homes. Since the end of the Civil War, Atlanta had positioned itself as the center of the New South, a safe place for northerners to invest. In 1895 Booker T. Washington's speech at the Atlanta Cotton

States Exposition, known as the "Atlanta Compromise," had launched his career as a national leader, primarily because he encouraged blacks in the South to remain in the region as loyal, industrious workers. He also implied that black people would adhere to the racial hierarchy of the South, observing that "in all things purely social we can remain as separate as the fingers, yet, one as the hand in those things essential to mutual progress."[18] In the decade since Washington's speech, Atlanta's black community had grown and some had prospered, but others remained unemployed or underemployed and were of great concern to white residents. In the gubernatorial campaign of 1906, candidates Hoke Smith and Clark Howell competed to offer the most restrictive policies directed at idle black men, who they claimed were likely to commit sexual assaults against white women. As the local newspapers began to publish unsubstantiated accounts of sexual assaults of white women by black men, local whites formed vigilante groups and from September 22 through September 24 responded by attacking black people wherever they could be found. The state militia was eventually called in to quell the rioting, with estimates of those killed ranging from twenty-five to forty black residents and two white residents.[19]

Reinforcing the connection between people of African descent north and south, in the aftermath of the Atlanta riot the September 27 edition of the *New York Age* carried a front-page statement from Booker T. Washington clearly designed to appeal to the white and black constituents over whom he had influence. Under the headline "To Retaliate Fatal— Washington," the paper noted that in a speech recently made by him in Atlanta to the National Negro Business League, Washington "spoke plainly against the crime of assaulting women and of resorting to lynching and mob law as a remedy for any evil," but he cautioned "the colored people in Atlanta and elsewhere to exercise self-control and not make the fatal mistake of attempting to retaliate, but to rely upon the efforts of the proper authorities to bring order and security out of confusion. If they do this they will have the sympathy of good people the world over."

The San Juan Hill riot that New York had experienced in 1905, after which Philip Payton led the grievance organization, was a small skirmish compared to the Atlanta riot, but the idea that a conflagration could occur in New York, like the 1900 Tenderloin riots, was not far from the minds of New York residents in the aftermath of the Atlanta riots. Those feelings may have made Harlem more attractive to black New Yorkers since it was not associated with the violence of the Tenderloin or San Juan Hill districts of Midtown Manhattan.

While the Atlanta riot was a public setback for the race, a month later Philip Payton received a personal and professional blow. He received notice that his business practices were being challenged, not by outside adversaries but by some who had been in his inner circle:

> You are hereby summoned to answer the complaint in this action and to serve copy of your answer on the plaintiff's attorney within twenty days after the service of this summons, exclusive of the day of service, and in case of your failure to appear, or answer, judgment will be taken against you by default for the relief demanded in the complaint.
>
> Dated, October 25, 1906
> Wilford H. Smith, Plaintiff's Attorney
> Post Office Address and Office
> No. 150 Nassau Street, New York City[20]

The summons arrived at the AARC's eleventh-floor offices, then at 47 Maiden Lane. It described a lawsuit filed against the Afro-American Realty Company and Philip A. Payton Jr. by an AARC shareholder, Charles J. Crowder, who claimed to represent forty-one other shareholders. Two years into its existence as a corporation, the AARC had gained some visibility through its purchase and lease of strategic properties on previously all-white blocks in Harlem. Some, like the 151st Street property, were quickly sold. Others were "opened" to black tenants, usually by evicting the white tenants. The visibility of these transactions spurred both stock sales and additional business opportunities as the AARC positioned itself in the public eye as the expert in managing "Colored Tenements." But the actions also created hostility from evicted white tenants and their sympathizers. Now Payton faced a challenge from within his own company.

As Payton reviewed the lawsuit papers, he must have experienced a mix of annoyance and anger—annoyance that the lawsuit had the real potential to generate negative publicity, counteracting all his strategic efforts to use the media to promote the AARC as an enterprise benefiting African Americans, which had borne fruit with the flurry of transactions during the first ten months of the year. For a man always on the move, the suit would require his valuable time, but more significantly, Payton was angered by several levels of betrayal illustrated by the lawsuit: it was filed by his own shareholders, people who he thought supported his vision, and for whom he worked day and night. The lead plaintiff, Charles J. Crowder, was one of the AARC's largest shareholders, owning one hundred shares. The people in the group he claimed to represent owned one to fifty shares. But the source of even greater anger for Payton was the fact that, as the summons indicated, the plaintiff was represented by Wilford Smith, a founding AARC director and the company's attorney until his recent resignation. A year earlier, Smith had even shared office space with the AARC when the company was located at 115 Broadway.[21] The suit claimed that:

- Payton's relationship to the AARC, "ever since its organization has been its general manager, and is now its President and General manager, and the owner of its disposed stock and holder of the majority of its disposed of capital stock";
- Crowder had purchased $1,000 of AARC stock and had been assigned to represent the claims of a group of other stockholders;
- in July 1904 Payton and the AARC had issued a "false and fraudulent prospectus . . . intending to mislead and deceive, and to cheat and defraud the general public, and especially the colored people, most who have little or no experience in business enterprises involving subscription to capital stock of corporations";
- the prospectus made fraudulent representations regarding capital paid in ($100,000) as well as the goals of the corporation;
- Payton had concealed that he fraudulently issued 5,000 shares of stock to himself and his associates, above the 5,000 initial shares, in exchange for ownership interests in properties he owned at 65 and 67 West 134th and 30 and 32 West 135th Streets in Harlem;
- many of the properties listed in the AARC prospectus as debt-free in fact had loans on them; and
- the leases held by the AARC at the time the prospectus was issued contained sixty- and ninety-day cancellation clauses, and most had been canceled at the time the prospectus was published.

The brief then listed the names of several other shareholders represented by Crowder, noting the number of shares each owned. It concluded with a demand for judgment consisting of cancelation and rescission of the stock that had been issued to the plaintiff and the shareholders he represented totaling $4,180 plus interest from AARC, along with $4,180 in damages from Payton.[22]

Payton was defended by Arthur C. Bostwick of the firm of McDonald and Bostwick. A 1901 graduate of New York University Law School,[23] the twenty-six-year-old Bostwick, in an undated response to the summons:

- denied that Payton was the "Chief organizer and general promoter of the defendant, Afro-American Realty Company, and alleges that said Payton was merely one of eleven persons who organized the said corporation";
- acknowledged that Crowder had purchased $1,000 of stock but denied knowledge of Crowder's relationship to the other shareholders listed in the summons;
- denied issuing a fraudulent prospectus;
- denied that that plans outlined in the prospectus were false and fraudulent;
- denied that additional stock had been issued to Payton and concealed; and
- noted that the only knowledge that Payton had of the other shareholders listed in the summons was that they had in fact purchased the amount of stock they claimed to have purchased.[24]

The civil trial took place in November 1906 in New York Supreme Court in Lower Manhattan on Chambers Street, named for John Chambers, a prominent member of Trinity Church, the first Episcopal church established in the city.[25] The design and construction of the Old New York County Courthouse, commonly called the Tweed Court House, at 52 Chambers Street on the eastern end of the street just north of City Hall, was commissioned in 1861. The New York City Democratic Party, often referred to by its Tammany Hall headquarters, was led by William "Boss" Tweed, who used the construction of the building to embezzle funds. The building was eventually the instrument of his undoing, as extreme cost overruns drew attention to his embezzlement and led to his arrest. Tweed's trial in 1873 was held in an unfinished courtroom in the building that was finally completed in 1881.[26]

The trial was presided over by Justice James Fitzgerald, an Irishman who had risen through the Democratic Party's political ranks as state assemblyman, state senator, assistant district attorney, and then a New York City judge. In 1901 he was elected to the Supreme Court, New York's civil and criminal court (in New York State, the Court of Appeals is the highest court). Fitzgerald lived in Upper Manhattan on Hamilton Terrace, a short enclave of a street, lined with townhouses, that ran between 141st and 144th Streets. The area was then called Washington Heights but eventually would be subsumed into the area called Harlem. On November 13, 1906, Arthur Bostwick submitted a response to the plaintiff's filings to Justice Fitzgerald, claiming that "each and every of the said alleged separate and distinct causes of action does not, nor does any one of them, state facts sufficient to constitute a cause of action." The trial was then adjourned.[27]

As 1906 drew to a close, Philip Payton continued to move forward with real estate transactions. The *New York Age* carried weekly advertisements of properties available in "just opened" buildings over the name Philip A. Payton Jr. In spite of the trial, advertisements seeking AARC stock purchases continued to run as well. The composition of the AARC's Board of Directors, as noted in the advertisements, changed during this period, with Payton's younger brother Edward listed as a vice president. New directors—Henry Parker, John Nail, and Stephen A. Bennet—were added. There were several other changes in the AARC advertisement. The office address had changed from 115 Broadway to 334 West 59th Street, in the black San Juan Hill neighborhood, rather than the Lower Manhattan locations in previous listings. While the advertisement's headline remained "The Pride of the Negro Race Is the Half-Million Dollar Afro-American Realty Co," the capital stock noted to have been raised was $150,000, rather than the previous $100,000. The year ended with twenty-two real estate transactions by either the AARC or Philip Payton, exceeding by three orders of magnitude activity of any previous year. But this momentum would be challenged on several fronts in the coming year.[28]

The front page of the first issue of the *New York Age* in 1907, on Thursday, January 3, did not chronicle the New Year's celebrations that had taken place earlier in the week, which were typically a major feature of New York papers. Instead, the *New York Age* presented a New Year's message of pragmatic black accomplishment and expectation through a drawing that spanned four of its six columns and, above the fold, moved down to one-third of the paper's space. Under the title "Abreast of the Times," the drawing featured a black couple with a young daughter looking to the right, as if looking to the future. The couple was dressed to suggest that they were from a rural background, with the man wearing a shirt with the sleeves rolled up and blue jeans held up by suspenders. He held a large-brimmed

BATTLES IN THE STREETS AND THE COURTROOM

hat in his right hand, and he was scratching his head with his left hand, giving him a quizzical expression. His wife stood behind him partially obscured, leaning on his shoulder in a common pose that implied that the man was the protector. She wore a head scarf and a dress that came to her ankles. Neither couple wore shoes. Their daughter, a girl of three or four, stood in front of her father looking to the right, with braids standing up on her head and dressed in a jumper. She was also barefoot. Directly in front of them was a plank fence that one might see bordering a farm, and beyond the fence there was a group of two-story buildings suggesting a farmhouse and outbuildings, with a grazing horse in the middle. This image, drawn as an inset illustration, was bordered on the left and right sides by small signs with captions and illustrations that suggested what the couple was hoping the new year of 1907 would bring them and other black people, as well as what black people had accomplished by the end of 1906. The signs behind the couple, to the left of the drawing, were:

- "Comfortable Homes" under a drawing of a row of one-and-a-half-story frame homes surrounded by a picket fence;
- "Personal and Real Property to the Amount of $1,000,000,000"; and
- "Competent Men in Every Branch of the Industrial Arts."

On the right side of the center illustration were:

- "Prosperous Merchants," with a man at the counter of a store serving a customer;
- "31 Banks Owned and Operated by Our Race," with a man in a bowler hat giving a deposit to a man behind a bank window; and
- "Competent Physicians," with a doctor seated at the bedside of a patient.

As a newspaper closely aligned with Booker T. Washington, the vision of black economic progress reflected through the eyes of the young black rural couple that the *New York Age* offered was a succinct New Year's representation of the elements of black progress emphasized by Washington.[29]

Philip Payton undoubtedly entered 1907 with the expectation of victory in the case that AARC shareholder Charles Crowder had brought against him. A review of the transactions of Payton and of the AARC for 1906 hints at possible areas of conflict, beyond the lack of dividends, that had precipitated the case. Of the twenty-two transactions, some were in the name of Payton, and others were in the name of the AARC. Considering that there were fees associated with these transactions, either broker's fees for sales and leases or management fees for leased properties being managed, whether these fees went to the AARC or to Payton personally had legal and business implications. While 1906 was a banner year for the AARC, legally much of the activity and the fees for the year technically went to Payton personally since he was the broker of record for many of the transactions. In the absence of an agreement indicating that he undertook these transactions as an employee of AARC, something not stated in the documents for the transactions, the fees associated them were Payton's, and he had no obligation to share them with the AARC. While this conundrum was not explicitly stated in the trial papers, this could have been the basis for the initial statement seeking to tie Payton explicitly to the AARC as "chief organizer and manager." The fact that his attorney, Arthur C. Bostwick, indicated that Payton was just another employee and director, in spite of substantial evidence (e.g., Payton's photograph in many advertisements, and his name in all advertisements), suggests that Payton may have kept the fees associated with the transactions he undertook. This would have had dramatic financial implications for the AARC. Actions such as this would have made the company's disgruntled shareholders particularly wary of Payton's integrity and of the likelihood that they would obtain the personal damages of $4,180 from him.

On January 22 Payton was arrested in connection with the case. He was arraigned before Judge Edward B. Amend, where his attorney argued that the arrest was inappropriate for a civil case. Wilford Smith, Crowder's attorney, stated that "Payton is transferring his property in order to defraud his creditors, and is about to leave the State in order to avoid arrest. Payton said that he had no intention of leaving the State, adding 'New York is good enough for me.'" Interviewed by the *New York Age*, Payton explained:

> The whole affair is a spite action brought against me by the former counsel of our company and several dissatisfied stockholders. . . . I had planned to buy up the stock of all dissatisfied stockholders and pay 6 per cent on it, but of course that is off now. Wilford H. Smith, the counsel for the plaintiff was our legal advisor up to June, 1906, and gave his advice upon all our actions.

He tried to get control of the company, and when he saw he could not, resigned. All the charges of fraud against me are absolutely absurd, as our records show.[30]

Payton was released from custody, and both sides were instructed to submit briefs within a week. The briefs are no longer a part of the New York County Court records, but there is no evidence that he was rearrested. His unusual arrest for a civil case suggests someone among his adversaries with influence in Manhattan's Police Department or District Attorney's Office.

In an effort to control the narrative regarding the Afro-American Realty Company, following his release Payton wrote a letter to the editor of the *Real Estate Record and Builders Guide* that appeared in the February 2 edition under the title "Mr. Payton's Defence." In the letter he took aim at Wilford Smith, who had a critical role in the formation of the AARC and was

FIGURE 4.1 Philip A. Payton Jr. real estate advertisement. *Source: Real Estate Record and Builders Guide,* January 1907.

leading the lawsuit against him and the AARC as "representing less than five percent of the stockholders." "This action was instituted at the behest of Wilford H. Smith, who was the sole legal advisor for the company from its incorporation until a few months past, when he severed his connection with the company after failing to secure for himself and his friends control." Payton concluded the letter by refuting the lawsuit's implication that the AARC was unprofitable and that he was an erratic manager:

> That the Afro-American Realty Company is not a detriment to the investor is proven by its printed annual statement, prepared by a certified public accountant, showing a net earning of 15 percent on its entire outstanding capital stock for the past year, a copy of which statement I am sending herewith. The policy of the company is toward conservatism, and the officers have served thus far without compensation or remuneration.[31]

The AARC's net earnings in 1905 were 6 percent on outstanding capital stock of approximately $67,000. The 1906 return of 15 percent, if accurate, reflected the dramatic growth of the company, which undoubtedly raised shareholder expectations that they would receive a share of this success in a dividend.[32]

While Philip Payton resumed his real estate business activities in spite of the Crowder civil case, some white Harlem homeowners organized a defense against his efforts to move African Americans onto all-white blocks. Their efforts went beyond complaints in newspaper articles. On February 13, 1907, the owners of twenty-three properties on West 137th Street between Lenox and Seventh Avenues signed an agreement resolving:

> That neither of the parties hereto, nor his her and their heirs legal representatives successors and assigns shall or will at any time hereafter up to and including the 1st day of January, 1917 permit or cause to be permitted, or suffer or cause to be suffered, either directly or indirectly, the said premises to be used or occupied in whole or in part by any negro mulatto, quadroon or octoroon of either sex whatsoever, or any person popularly known and described as a negro, mullato [sic], quadroon or octoroon of either sex as a tenant, subtenant, guest boarder or in any other way, manner or capacity whatsoever, excepting only that any one family occupying an entire house or an entire flat or an entire apartment, may employ one negress or one

female mulatto, or one female quadroon or one female octoroon as a household servant, performing only the duties ordinarily performed by a household servant—it being understood and agreed that this covenant or restriction shall not be enforced personally for damages or by an action in equity or at common law against either of the parties hereto or his, her or their heirs legal representatives, successor or assigns, unless he, she or they be the owner or owners of the said premises at the time of the violation, attempted violation or threatened violation of this covenant or restriction, but this covenant or restriction may be proceeded on for an injunction and for damages against the party or parties, or person or persons who for the time being own, occupy or are in possession of the said premises, and violating or attempting or threatening to violate this covenant or restriction.[33]

The document was a restrictive covenant, a device perfected in England and introduced into the United States in the nineteenth century, typically used to protect public lands and wealthy residential developments. In urban areas, before the introduction of zoning laws in the twentieth century, the restrictive covenant was used to protect property owners against the introduction of noxious property uses such as tanneries and smoke houses. The covenant was also used to restrict the presence of Jews in residential areas. The Harlem covenant seems to be one of the first uses of the device in an American urban neighborhood experiencing racial changes.[34]

The West 137th covenant was quite explicit in describing its inspiration, recounting that it was motivated by the eviction of white tenants from 106 and 108 West 137th Street and the renting of the apartments in the buildings to African American tenants. In 1905 the buildings went through a succession of owners, reflecting the growing demand for properties in Harlem. In May 1905 they were purchased by Wolf Bomzon for $100 and an assumption of mortgages totaling $40,000. Fifteen months later they changed hands twice in the same day. On October 17, 1906, Bomzon sold the properties to Montgomery Rosenberg for $100 and assumption of mortgages of $53,500, an increase in debt on the property of $13,500. Later on the same day Rosenberg sold both properties to Hanna Theobold for $100 and the assumption of mortgages of $60,000. Theobold seems to have been the one who introduced "tenants of the negro race" into the buildings.[35] There is no evidence that Philip Payton or the AARC was associated with these transactions. The buildings were sold on January 31, 1907, to Jacob

Blauner, who purchased 106 West 137th Street and assumed mortgages of $30,000, and to Rosa Newman, who purchased 108 West 137th Street, assuming mortgages of $30,000. This final transaction seems to have had a motivation similar to the purchase of the building leased by Payton on 151st Street in 1905 that had been purchased to prevent it being leased to black tenants. The 137th Street transactions, with increasing purchase prices, did suggest that that the Payton/AARC method of inspiring the purchase of a building to prevent African American tenancy was being followed by others. The February 1907 covenant explicitly noted this practice in justifying the agreement:

> Various parties have been purchasing different parcels of property in and about One Hundred and thirty-seventh Street and in and about the Borough of Manhattan, City of New York, in neighborhoods theretofore occupied exclusively by white tenants and have leased or rented the same to negro tenants for the purpose of compelling adjoining and neighboring owners to purchase the same to protect their holdings.[36]

The covenant also explained why the agreement had a ten-year term: "The parties hereto believe that the system which brought about this situation and which is referred to above will have run its course within ten years."[37]

While these purchases, sales, and restrictive covenants were unfolding, the case against Payton and the AARC was moving through the courts. As Payton's attorney initially suggested, Payton's arrest in the civil case was an overreach, but the plaintiff Charles Crowder seems to have known Payton quite well. Perhaps spurred by his arrest, on March 12 Payton transferred the ownership of his home at 13 West 131st Street to the Hampden Realty and Construction Company. Hampden promised to assume payments on mortgages on the property totaling $12,000 and also paid "One Dollar and other good and valuable consideration lawful money." While the documents suggest a sale, the fact that Philip and Maggie Payton continued to live in the building, according to the City Directories of 1907 and 1908, suggests a more complicated transaction and relationship. Possibly Hampden leased the sold property back to the Paytons. Since many leases were not recorded, there would be no expectation of a record of such a lease, which Payton would not have wanted to be known publicly. The sales document was notarized by Arthur C. Bostwick, Payton's attorney in the Crowder trial. It is possible that Bostwick had suggested the transaction, as Crowder anticipated, to protect Payton's largest asset if he was found personally liable for damages in the case.[38]

There are also hints that what might have appeared as an arm's-length transaction between the Paytons and Hampden Realty and Construction Company was not one. The name of the company receiving the title to the property provides a clue. Payton grew up in Westfield, Massachusetts, which is in Hampden County, Massachusetts. The company name corresponding with Payton's home county may be a coincidence, but since none of its principals were born in Hampden County, why the name was selected cannot be determined. Hampden Realty and Construction was incorporated in New York State in May 1906 by William Dawley, then residing on 76th Street in Manhattan, Joseph A. Whitehouse of Newark, New Jersey, and Lewis Harris of Hackensack, New Jersey. All three were white men. Dawley and Whitehouse owned three shares each in the company, and Harris owned four shares. The purpose of the company included

> to buy, lease, hire, or otherwise acquire, to hold and own, to sell, mortgage, lease, let or otherwise dispose of, real property of every nature and kind soever, and of every estate and interest in real property and personal property incidental thereto, wherever situated; and to make contracts in connection therewith; to deal in and deal with and to operate in real property; to manage and develop real property owned by it or by any person, firm or corporation.[39]

While the name provides a hint of a connection to Payton, personal ties between him and the principals were not apparent. The transaction was among the list of the week's real estate transactions in the March 16 edition of the *Real Estate Record and Builders Guide*, but it seems to have escaped the notice of the *Crowder v. Afro-American Realty Company* plaintiffs. While Payton's connection to Hampden is not clear, it was a real company with which he had other business dealings. In April the AARC surrendered a lease for 311 West 119th Street to Hampden, and in June it conveyed 24 to 28 West 140th Street to Hampden. Rather than a sale, this transaction may have involved the AARC borrowing from Hampden by placing a mortgage on the property, since AARC continued to maintain an interest in the property, as indicated by a November foreclosure suit associated with the property filed against the company by Morris Levy.[40]

While Payton and Bostwick continued to construct a defense against the Crowder lawsuit, white Harlem residents continued to organize defenses against Payton and the AARC. On May 28 a restrictive covenant was executed by seventeen owners of property on West 140th Street between Seventh and Eighth Avenues, a densely developed block consisting primarily of apartment buildings. In contrast to the February covenant on West 137th Street, the 140th Street covenant had no preamble or other explanation for its existence, and no expiration date.[41]

Despite the lawsuit hovering over it, and perhaps in response to the criticism by Crowder and his cohort of shareholders who claimed that the AARC's prospectus was fraudulent, in June 1907 the AARC announced that a dividend of 7 percent would be issued on August 1 for all those who owned shares as of May 1.[42] The dividend provided another promotional opportunity for the AARC. An ad in *New York Age* in October focused specifically on the investment appeal of the company and of the dividend when compared to bank deposit interest. "Our Mathematics Declares 7 Per Cent Minus 3 1-2 Per Cent is Equal to the 3 1-2 Per Cent That You Are Losing Every Day That You Keep it in the Bank, And Fail to Take Hold of the Proposition of THIS COMPANY."[43] Because no prior dividend had been issued and the Crowder case had raised serious issues regarding the AARC's viability, the dividend was most likely an effort to shore up the company's credibility and continue to obtain capital from new shareholders. The source of the AARC's profits came from management fees on properties it managed, sales proceeds from properties it owned and later sold, and brokerage fees on sales and leases it negotiated. The issuance of one dividend did not necessarily attest to the ongoing profitability of the company, but merely the availability of cash necessary to pay the dividend to the shareholders. While Payton and AARC officers might have argued that in the first years of the company's operations it was essential to reinvest surpluses in the company to spur growth, the absence of a dividend in the three years of the company's operation had undermined the confidence of investors. The most disgruntled had joined Crowder in the lawsuit, which further undermined confidence. It would be difficult for one dividend to surmount these concerns, which were well founded. By the time of the June dividend announcement, the real estate transaction activity of Payton and the AARC for 1907 was a sobering contrast to the activity for the same period in 1906. During the first half of 1906, twelve transactions had been executed by June. In 1907, only five transactions had been completed during the same period.

But Payton and the AARC had to be concerned about larger forces inhibiting real estate activities. In the summer of 1907 the United States experienced a series of business collapses, the result of a tightening of credit markets in England that led to higher interest rates there that reduced the annual flow of gold into the United States. The reduced availability of credit led to U.S. business collapses and reduced confidence in the banking industry. These concerns were magnified in mid-October when the press reported on the failed attempt by investor Auguste Heinze to buy up the stock of the United Copper Company and control the copper market. The exposé revealed Heinze's associations with men who served as directors of a network of interlocking financial institutions, including national banks. As the public became nervous about the stability of the banks, depositors began withdrawing their funds in a series of bank runs that culminated in late October with the collapse of New York's Knickerbocker Trust Company, the third largest trust company in the city. With the already limited access to capital available to black investors, the Panic of 1907 had a devastating effect on the AARC. To purchase many of the buildings that it continued to hold, the company assumed the payments on mortgage loans already on the properties. The common structure of these loans called for interest-only payments, with the principal being paid after a period of five to ten years. Lenders had an option to renew or extend loans, but in a time of reduced credit and business confidence, loans often had clauses allowing for the principal to be called for repayment at the will of the lender before the five- or ten-year term was reached. To respond to such a call, the borrower would have to find another lender—an unlikely possibility for a black borrower in a time of tight credit—or sell the building, hoping that its value had not declined along with the lack of confidence, enabling the sales proceeds to exceed the debt on the property. For Philip Payton and the AARC, there would be no other transactions in 1907 after June.[44]

The front page of the January 1, 1908, edition of the *New York Times* contained the usual descriptions of New Year's revelry, "that wild noise which Dobbs Ferry [a town twenty-five miles north of Manhattan] heard from the South at midnight originated in Broadway from Trinity Church to Times

Square when the electric ball fell on THE TIMES building in accordance with the pre-arranged plan." Readers would have quickly understood that entering a new year had not allowed them to escape the financial challenges of 1907. Three of the page's seven columns were stories related to business problems. The body of twenty-seven-year-old Archibald P. Mitchell was found in his Riverside Drive apartment by his maid on New Year's Day. He had died by suicide, inhaling gas used for lighting after his new cigarette business failed. The federal government announced an antitrust lawsuit to dissolve the Union Pacific and Southern Pacific Railroad, the Harriman System. Another article noted that a Virginia judge would soon be asked to appoint a receiver for Seaboard Air Line Railway after complaints from employees over unpaid wages led to a conflict among the company's shareholders.[45]

Most likely recognizing that the business climate that affected other enterprises across the country would also affect the AARC, at the end of January Hampden Realty and Construction Company transferred the deed to the Paytons' home to Maggie Payton "in consideration of One hundred dollars and other valuable considerations." Although the document was executed on January 28, it noted that "at request of Mrs. M. P. Payton" the document would not be recorded until "May 11, 1909 at 1 o'clock and 30 min P.M."[46] This final sentence is unusual. In most cases legal documents were recorded promptly after they were executed. The document indicating the return of ownership of 13 W. 131st Street to Maggie Payton (but not to Philip), if executed promptly, would have occurred in the middle of the Crowder case, alerting those involved in the case that Payton had indeed been trying to hide assets, and that the motivation for Payton's arrest, whether an overreach or not, had some merit. The instructions to delay the recording of the document to a date more than a year away, perhaps when it was expected that the case would have been resolved, seems to have been a strategic measure by the Paytons to protect their home from the plaintiffs in the case.

In addition to a chilled financial climate, in 1908 there were signs that the racial climate for black people in the North was becoming harsher. In mid-August in Springfield, Illinois, two rumors of sexual assaults on white women by black men led a mob to lynch two black men and then move on in a rampage in which they destroyed the homes and businesses of black residents in the area, displacing two thousand people. That such violence occurred in the state's capital, once the home of Abraham Lincoln, in the centennial year of his birth, presented a stark contrast to the Great Emancipator's image. In response to the most devastating race riot in the North since the New York City Draft Riots of 1863, the September 3 edition of the *Independent* newspaper included an article entitled "The Race War in the North" in which William English Walling, a white journalist who had investigated the Springfield riot, observed that the charged "spirit of the abolitionists, of Lincoln and Lovejoy, must be revived and we must come to treat the negro on a plane of absolute political and social equality." Black and white Progressives began discussions regarding the formation of an organization to combat racial discrimination. Philip Payton's mentor Booker T. Washington was approached to participate in the organization, but he declined when he became aware that some of his critics, such as W. E. B. Du Bois, Ida B. Wells, and Mary White Ovington, were also associated with the effort. The resulting organization, the National Association for the Advancement of Colored People (NAACP), would hold its first meeting in New York City in May 1909.[47]

As the foundation of his life's work shifted under his feet, in mid-October the rock of Payton's life was no more. Philip A. Payton Sr. died in Westfield of a stroke. After a first stroke in 1905, he had moved to his son's home in New York to convalesce. While there he had a mild second stroke, but after several months he had regained sufficient strength so that, after several more months in New York, he and his wife, Annie, had returned to Westfield. In the second week of October 1908, he experienced a third stroke that paralyzed him. He never regained consciousness. In all likelihood Philip and his sister, Susan, had been alerted and traveled to Westfield. On Thursday, October 15, 1908, at 3:10 a.m., Philip A. Payton Sr. died. His entrepreneurial example and encouragement had propelled Payton Jr. to venture out from Westfield to prove that he could make his own mark in the world. Payton Sr. had witnessed the growth of the AARC and had watched with pride as his once wayward son began to drink from the cup of success. He may have commiserated with his son regarding the Crowder lawsuit that was still unresolved at the time of his death. A measure of his enduring status in Westfield was his obituary and photograph in the *Valley Echo* (figure 4.2), the newspaper of the Westfield area. It noted that "For years he had the most prominent [barber]shop in town."[48] The funeral was held at the Payton home at 79 Elm Street, Westfield, and afterward the

FIGURE 4.2 Philip Payton Sr. *Source: Valley Echo*, October 1908.

remains of Philip A. Payton Sr. were interred in the Payton family plot at Pine Hill Cemetery, beside the remains of the Paytons' middle son, James, who had died six years earlier to the day of his father's death. Payton Sr. had traveled a long way, literally and figuratively, from his slave era childhood in Washington, North Carolina.[49]

The journey back to New York must have been a sad one for Philip A. Payton Jr., but he most likely looked forward to seeking a distraction from his grief in his business activities, challenging as they were. One month after Philip returned from burying his father, the November 19, 1908, issue of the *New York Age* announced the outcome of the *Crowder v. Afro-American Realty Company* case with the headline "Victory for Payton." While technically accurate, the headline was more a reflection of the close association of the paper's editor, Fred R. Moore, with Philip Payton and the AARC, for which he served as secretary, than the actual outcome of the trial. A "Finding of Fact" section of the verdict noted:

> That on or about the 1st day of July, 1904, the said defendant corporation, intending to mislead and deceive and to cheat and defraud the general public, and especially colored people, and for the purpose of inducing

subscriptions to its capital stock, printed, published and distributed a false and fraudulent prospectus and circular regarding the condition, prospects and purposes of the said corporation which was calculated to deceive, mislead and induce support from the colored people and which did mislead and deceive the plaintiff and the persons hereinbefore mentioned.[50]

The full text of the prospectus was entered into the trial document, and then Justice Dowling proceeded to identify the areas of the prospectus deemed fraudulent. He noted that at the time of issuance of the prospectus the company had $98,000 of capital paid in rather than the $100,000 claimed. He indicated that the prospectus stated "that the said Company held five-year leases on ten flat houses in New York City" and noted that when the prospectus was issued, the company held leases on only seven flat houses [apartment buildings], and that the five-year leases on these houses all included clauses giving the owners the right to cancel the leases (as was done on West 151st Street). Regarding real estate owned by the AARC, Dowling noted that the four five-story flat houses owned by the company when the prospectus was issued were subject to mortgages, a fact not mentioned in the prospectus, giving the misleading impression that the net value of the buildings was greater than it actually was.

The "Conclusions of Law" section that followed noted that "Philip A. Payton, Jr. is not liable to the plaintiff and that the complaint as to him should be, and hereby is dismissed."[51] If this had been the complete verdict, the *New York Age* headline would have been accurate, since this really was a victory for Payton as an individual. The court concluded that his actions as an officer of the corporation were the actions of the corporation and not of an independent individual. But this sentence was followed by a second point that stated that "the plaintiff is entitled to judgment against the Afro-American Realty Company as follows." As for liability, the page and a half of text detailed that

> the subscriptions and payments to the capital stock of said company by the plaintiff and by James H. Gordon, Richard F. Turner, Charles Toots, Arthur W. Clinton and Joseph Brown, be adjudged null and void and cancelled and rescinded, and that the names of the plaintiff and the said James H. Gordon, Richard F. Turner, Arthur W. Clinton and Joseph Brown, be expunged from the stock book of said Company and that the certificates of

stock issued to the plaintiff and [the other five] be cancelled and rescinded and that the plaintiff and [the five] be relieved from all liability, past or future, as a stockholder in said company; and that the plaintiff

and the other five men "do recover from and have judgment against the defendant, Afro-American Realty Company for the sum of seventeen hundred and ten dollars, which included the initial value of their shares and accrued interest."[52] It is not clear how or why the judge determined that Charles Crowder and the other five shareholders were entitled to relief and not the thirty-five other shareholders who were also parties to the lawsuit. The size of the holdings of the favored shareholders does not seem to have been a factor: Crowder owned stock initially valued at $1,000; James Gordon, $110; Richard F. Turner, $100; Charles Toots, $10; Arthur W. Clinton, $220; and L. Joseph Brown, $70. Others who were not included in the judgment owned stock valued at from $1,000 to $10.[53]

While the judge's motivations for the precise verdict are not clear, the stated motivation of the shareholders for undertaking the lawsuit was frustration from not receiving promised dividends. The reason for the participation of attorney Wilford Smith, the initial plaintiffs' attorney, is not clear, but there are some hints as to why he chose to represent the plaintiffs. Smith had helped prepare the very prospectus that he was challenging, which was a point of embarrassment for the plaintiffs in the case when this was revealed. Smith, an 1883 graduate of Boston University's law school, was a skilled attorney. He had a thriving criminal and civil practice in Texas and in 1901 became Booker T. Washington's personal attorney, secretly assisting him in filing lawsuits challenging Jim Crow laws. Smith moved to New York in the first years of the 1900s and in 1903, in *Giles v. Harris*, became one of the first African American attorneys to argue a case before the U.S. Supreme Court.[54] Smith must have anticipated that his role as legal advisor in the formation of the AARC would be revealed in court. His participation in the Crowder case seems to have been motivated by frustration regarding Payton's management practices. This law school graduate, serving as an officer of the AARC, had been outflanked by Payton, who had not even graduated from high school, revealing a management/shareholder divide. The initial AARC shareholders had paid in $98,000 of their funds to incorporate the company, but they were dependent on Payton's real estate expertise, and his devotion of time, to actually run it. While they may have been interested in redirecting his actions as a manager, because the company was so closely identified with Payton, they may have concluded that since ousting him totally had not been possible, the lawsuit could give him a dose of reality and rein him in while also enabling them to recover their capital, since dividends were unlikely to be forthcoming. In a letter to Emmett Scott a few weeks before the October 1906 summons was issued to Payton, Smith suggested that he had resigned from the AARC and noted that he felt the company would never be successful with its current management. He cryptically told Scott that the reasons for his concerns would soon be revealed. The lawsuit against Payton and the AARC was filed soon afterward. Perhaps with Smith's resignation from the company he had also asked Payton to buy his stock (in 1906 he had 518 votes, suggesting 518 shares of preferred stock that came with voting rights in comparison to the common stock owned by the plaintiffs, with a par value of $5,180). Perhaps Payton could not or would not buy the stock. The lawsuit may have been a way for Smith to recover his capital by a court order since Payton would not comply with his request. The case damaged Payton's reputation, and because the AARC was so dependent on customers' confidence in him, the company's reputation was irreparably weakened. Seeing the handwriting on the wall, Emmett Scott implored Payton in 1908 to make a formal announcement of the closing of the company, which Payton never did. Instead he formed a new company, the Philip A. Payton Jr. Company, and endeavored to reclaim his place in New York City's real estate arena.[55]

Chapter Five

TO LIBERIA AND BACK

In describing New Year's celebrations marking the coming of the year 1909, the *New York Tribune* noted:

> The predominating note was one of revelry. Forget the old! Look not to the new! Live for this night!... Blow the trumpets, ring the bells, sound the cymbals.... This was the spirit that was rampant from the courtyard of Old Trinity in lower Broadway all the way to Harlem, running riot and merging into wild revels in the congested centres.... It must have been a relief to the ears of the palsied Old Man—1908—when he passed over the line, away from the shouting and to him heedless world. The shy, shrinking Infant—1909—must have faltered just the fraction of a second, awed by the tumultuous greeting. But he is here. Vale 1908! Salve 1909!

Following the challenges of the lawsuit that had generated so much negative press for Philip Payton and the Afro-American Realty Company, he surely shared the sentiments of the *Tribune* writer, glad to see 1908 recede into the mists of memory. In the new year Payton sought to regain his footing both at home and abroad by strengthening old relationships and cultivating new opportunities, always carefully using the black press to publicize his activities. In 1909 there were no purchases or sales recorded for Philip Payton or the Philip A. Payton Jr. Company. Payton's activities were confined to the renting of apartments and the modest fees associated with this business, illustrated by the consistent advertisements appearing in the *New York Age* indicating the apartments available for rent in various buildings, mainly in Harlem.[1]

Payton continued to be active in the National Negro Business League and in June attended a public meeting hosted by the New York chapter of the NNBL at the AME Zion Church on 89th Street. At the meeting, speaker after speaker preached the gospel of business as the salvation for the black man, led by Booker T. Washington and joined by many others, including Rev. P. E. Jones, who startled the audience by noting:

> For forty-three years we negroes have been singing "You can have all the world; but give me Jesus." Now we are just beginning to find out that the whites really have the whole world, while we have merely prayed the knees of our trousers out. Since our emancipation forty-three years ago, four theories have been advanced for our elevation. Politics, religion and education were three of these panaceas. But it is through business, the fourth and last theory, that our problem will be solved.[2]

In October Payton was part of an organizing committee that hosted a banquet to honor Matthew Henson, the African American who had accompanied Robert Peary on explorations to the Arctic. "The reception tendered him was such a warm and cordial one that for the evening at least, he forgot all about the [Eskimos], the frozen zone, and igloos and basked in the hospitality of his host[s]." The two hundred men and women who gathered at Tuxedo Hall on Madison Avenue at 59th Street were a "who's who" of black New York. A telegram from Booker T. Washington congratulated the hosts and noted, "Permit me to congratulate you and your co-workers upon the wisdom and generosity manifested in providing the dinner in honor of our distinguished and deserving fellow citizen who has by his achievement lifted the race to a higher level." Robert Peary offered a message in a telegram also linking Henson's achievement to the image of black people as a race: "to the world your great adaptability and the fibre of which you are made. He has added to the moral stature of every intelligent man among you. His is the hard-earned reward of tried loyalty, persistence and endurance. He should be an everlasting example to your young men that these qualities will win whatever object they are directed at."³ Charles W. Anderson, Washington's New York lieutenant, presented Henson with a gold Tiffany watch studded with diamonds. In accepting, Henson reminded the audience of the skepticism that he had faced from some: "When I went to Greenland they said I never would come back. They told me that I could not stand the cold—that no black man could. I said I would die if necessary to show them. I survived all right and here I am."⁴ In 1910 Philip Payton would venture out on an expedition of his own.

The *Sun* and the *New York Tribune* departed from chronicling New Year's Eve activities on their front pages, but the *New York Times*, which had orchestrated the move of the celebrations from Trinity Church to Times Square, continued the tradition, noting:

> New Year's has come to be New York's own day and each year coming in finds a brighter, noisier welcome than the one before. . . . And if the acclamation of the tens of thousands, in Broadway when the moment came, and the great ball studded with it 400 golden lights, suspended till then on the flagpole of the Times Tower, dropped to the bottom, and sent flashing out on all four sides the dazzling figures 1910, may be taken as an indication, New York was glad to welcome the newcomer.⁵

At the end of January Maggie Payton hosted a special dinner party at the Paytons' Harlem townhouse. The *New York Age* noted: "In view of his departure for Liberia, where he goes for a visit to the little Black Republic on the west coast of Africa for the first vacation he has had during a strenuous period of business life Mrs. Philip A. Payton last Sunday evening gave a farewell dinner in honor of her husband Philip A. Payton, Jr. at the family residence, 13 West 131st St."⁶ The dinner was attended by Booker T. Washington and members of the inner circle who had surrounded Philip Payton during his rise in New York's business world. On this winter evening they reconvened as he set out on yet another venture. In addition to the Wizard himself, Washington, the guest list included Emmett Scott, Washington's right-hand man; Fred R. Moore, editor of the *Age*; Charles W. Anderson, federal internal revenue collector for lower Manhattan and Washington's eyes and ears in New York, and his wife Emma; undertaker and former AARC officer James C. Thomas and his wife Ella; and Payton's siblings, Susan and Edward.[7] The evening began with martini cocktails, followed by a seven-course meal that included oyster cocktails, foet of beef, and Waldorf salad. The dinner conversation was most likely marked by the banter of the guests who knew one another well enough to be able to laugh at inside jokes. Over many years they had celebrated triumphs and consoled one another through challenges. On this evening they were acknowledging an important trip, more than a mere vacation, being made by one of their own who needed another success. The *Crowder v. AARC and Payton* lawsuit tarnished Payton's reputation and diminished his attractiveness as a real estate broker to black and white property owners and black renters. For a black American man in 1910, Liberia, dominated by Americo-Liberians, black people of American descent, represented, in the views of some black and white people, the potential for bringing the comparative advantage of American ingenuity to the continent. Perhaps Philip Payton could recapture the allure that the Afro-American Realty Company had conveyed to the public earlier in 1904 by seeking business opportunities grounded in the black culture of the West African nation. But there were skeptics. One person, upon learning of Payton's trip, suggested

FIGURE 5.1 Edward Payton. *Source:* Yale yearbook, 1906.

that the Liberians be forewarned to nail down anything of value before he arrived.[8]

The "little Black Republic," as the *New York Age* writer described Liberia, was struggling in 1910. Carved out of West African territory (some accounts claimed at gunpoint) in the 1820s by the American Colonization Society (ACS) as a place to resettle the formerly enslaved from the United States, Liberia followed Haiti as the second black republic in the world when it declared its independence from the grip of the ACS in 1847. In the years immediately preceding Payton's trip, both France and Britain had encroached on Liberia's territory, using the vise of debt obligations to extract claims on Liberian territory. By 1910 the black descendants of Liberia's founding generation ruled the country through an oligarchy, but indigenous Africans in the region were increasing their demands for inclusion in government and in economic and educational institutions that the Americo-Liberians were creating as they built the black nation.

Given that Liberia was founded by black and white Americans, the United States had maintained close ties to the country throughout its history. At the Berlin conference of 1884–1885, European nations had established rules for trade with and making claims to territory in Africa. While Liberia was not a territory that Europeans could formally claim, the scramble for African colonies endangered the weak republic. In 1909, the second decade of post-Berlin European colonization in Africa, President William H. Taft sent a three-person commission to Liberia to determine what was needed. Plans for the commission had begun during Theodore Roosevelt's term, and Booker T. Washington had originally been proposed as a member. As plans proceeded when Taft was elected president in 1908, the new president indicated that he needed Washington's presence in the United States during the early months of his presidency "as his adviser on black and southern affairs." Emmett Scott, Washington's secretary at the Tuskegee Institute and Payton's good friend and former business partner, was a logical second choice for black representation on the commission. Two white men joined Scott: Roland P. Falkner, former chairman of public education in Puerto Rico, who chaired the commission, and George Sale, superintendent of Baptist mission schools in Puerto Rico and Cuba.[9] The three commissioners spent several months touring Liberia, examining financial records, and interviewing government officials and others. When they returned to the United States they submitted a report with recommendations that U.S. banks provide loans to assume Liberia's international debt, that the United States arrange a firm designation of Liberia's geographic boundaries, that the United States take over the Liberian custom service, and that the U.S. Army retrain the Liberian Frontier Force. The Frontier Force was a militia of five hundred men, established in 1908 to patrol the borders and prevent encroachment by Britain or France. Because the threat of encroachment was continuing, changes in the force were clearly needed. Payton traveled to Liberia the following year in the wake of the American commissioners.[10]

Scott and Washington undoubtedly facilitated Payton's trip. Rather than a vacation, as described by the *New York Age*, or one of informal diplomacy, since Payton had shown no particular interest in international affairs, the journey was most likely a mission to identify business opportunities for Payton and perhaps other members of the National Negro Business League. Since Liberia's founding, many black Americans had viewed the country as a refuge from American racial discrimination. But many also viewed it through the white American cultural lens as part of the "Dark Continent" in need of salvation from heathenism and ignorance through religious missions. Equally important, some black Americans saw the country as a place where they could do well financially by bringing business operations that depended on the natural resources of Liberia and the low-wage labor of indigenous people, as white businessmen were doing throughout Africa during these first decades of European colonization on the continent.[11]

On January 26 Payton traveled to Pier 54, one of the new Chelsea piers on lower Manhattan's West Side, and boarded the Cunard Line steamer *Campania*, headed to Liverpool. The steamer left the dock under clear skies as Philip Payton made his first trip abroad. His two African American traveling companions provided excellent and informative company. Bishop Isaiah B. Scott, missionary bishop of the Methodist Episcopal Church, had been elected bishop of Africa in 1904 and had been based in Liberia from 1904 to 1908. Bishop Alexander Walters had been elected bishop of the African Methodist Episcopal Zion Church in 1892 and, after traveling extensively for the denomination, was making his first trip to Africa. Beyond the church, Walters had also been a founding member of T. Thomas Fortune's Afro-American League. When the league failed, he became president of the Afro-American Council, formed in 1898. With some allegiance to both the Booker T. Washington and W. E. B. Du Bois factions of black activism, in

1908 Walters joined the District of Columbia branch of Du Bois's Niagara Movement, formed to advocate for black equality and to challenge the dominance of the Booker T. Washington machine. Both Walters and Scott were two decades older than Payton, and while they undoubtedly respected his business successes, they were probably aware of some of the challenges he had faced in recent years. Most likely the two older men found many opportunities on the seven-day journey to their transfer point in Liverpool to advise Payton about the issues facing Liberia, black America, and perhaps even his own business activities.[12]

The *Compania*, a steamer that was launched on her maiden voyage in 1893, had a capacity of two thousand passengers—six hundred first class, four hundred second class, and one thousand third class—as well as a crew of four hundred. If Payton, Walters, and Scott had first-class tickets, they would have paid approximately $100 (approximately $2,700 in 2019 dollars). In 1845, as Frederick Douglass traveled the abolition circuit in the United States providing firsthand accounts of his escape from slavery, concern that he might be returned to slavery by slave catchers had convinced him to travel to Liverpool, beyond the reach of the peculiar institution. To reach England, he had traveled on a Cunard ship, where his first-class ticket was not honored because of his race; he was allowed to travel on the ship but in more inferior quarters. When the shipping line owner Samuel Cunard heard of the experience, he stated: "I can assure you that nothing of the kind will again take place on the steamships in which I am connected." Douglass's freedom was purchased by friends while he was abroad. If the Cunard policy of access regardless of race was still in effect in 1910, Philip Payton and his companions would have had access to the *Compania*'s spacious drawing room, music room, and vast dining room, all decorated to the height of Edwardian splendor.[13]

In his memoirs, Walters described the trip: "After a pleasant sail of seven days we reached Liverpool, England. We had to wait over for a week in order to catch a fast steamer for Monrovia. Mr. Payton remained in Liverpool two weeks awaiting the arrival of United States Minister Lyons, who he hoped would join him from America."[14] Walters was referring to Ernest Lyon, a native of Honduras and former professor of church history at Morgan College, a black college in Baltimore, who at the recommendation of Booker T. Washington was appointed U.S. minister and consul general to Liberia in 1903. Lyon did not arrive in Liverpool, and after two weeks there, Payton made his way to Liberia by himself. The fact that he had planned to coordinate his travel with Lyon is another indication that his trip was known at the highest levels of the U.S. diplomatic corps, indicating that it was more than a vacation.[15]

An account of Philip Payton's travel to Liberia from Liverpool has not survived, but it was most likely similar to that left by Bishop Walters. Departing from Liverpool, Bishop Walters and Bishop Scott traveled six days to Las Palmas in the Canary Islands, where they stopped and were able to send mail back to friends and relatives. Next they traveled another six days to Freetown, Sierra Leone. They marveled at the British colonial city of 40,000 in which "all except high government officials were colored." Walters noted:

> I left Sierra Leone on Sunday, the 20th. I was up early Monday morning, February 21, and on deck to get the first sight of Liberia. I did not have to wait very long ere I got a glimpse of the mainland, and soon we were in sight of Monrovia, the Capital of the little Black Republic, founded in 1847, colonized by free Negroes in 1821. We cast anchor about a mile from the shore, fired a signal to inform the Liberians that a vessel was in the harbor. The regular mail-boats do not stop at Monrovia, so we were not expected until the 26th of February. It was but a short while before we saw the little boats coming out to meet us; first, the diving boys, who are experts at seeing money under water and catching it ere it reaches the bottom; next came the government officers, a fine set of young looking Negroes, as gallant looking as any set of officers I ever saw. We with our luggage were placed aboard the boats; we waved a farewell to the officers and fellow passengers of the ship, Dakar, and were off to shore, while the ship started to the far south. A kind of bond of friendship had sprung up between crew and passengers while aboard; hence I was a little sorry to leave them, but at last we waved the final farewell and became interested in our own skilled oarsmen. Why, what master strokes! And now we are at the wharf at Monrovia. A thrill of joy possessed me as I stepped from the boat on to the shores of my fatherland.[16]

There is no record of what Payton did during his four months in Liberia or where he stayed. Considering that he had hoped to travel from Liverpool to Liberia with diplomat Ernest Lyon, it is likely that Payton was embraced by Liberia's Americo-Liberia community, initially in the capital of Monrovia and then in other areas to which he traveled. If Payton had explored rural areas, there was a wealth of options, from agricultural opportunities, timber harvesting, mining, and other activities.

The next time Payton's Liberian trip appeared in the surviving historical record was three months later, in the May 15 edition of the *Liberian Register*: "Philip A. Payton, the New York real estate dealer departed Liberia on Tuesday, May 10th after a visit of four months in Liberia, during which he explored business opportunities. Bishop Isaiah B. Scott, Missionary Bishop of the Methodist Episcopal Church, and Rev. Alexander Walter, bishop of the AME Church accompanied him . . . for Liverpool."[17] As Payton departed "the little Black Republic," he must have reviewed the new experiences he had had and the various ways he could take advantage of the business opportunities he had seen.

Departing from Liberia, Payton traveled to Liverpool, where he was met by his wife, Maggie, who had been seen off from New York by "a large number of friends" as she departed on the steamer *Mauretania* on May 4 (the Cunard line would withdraw the ship from service in 1934 and launch a second ship by the same name in 1938; that ship became known for its service to the military during World War II). From Liverpool, the Paytons embarked on a tour of the Continent. A June *New York Age* article on Harlem real estate brokers noted that Payton "is doing a thriving business and has it in such shape as to be able to leave it in the hands of his assistants without loss of income." A six-month absence from his business does suggest that Payton had very able assistants, but also that, even without publicly recorded property sales in 1909, the business was generating sufficient income from management fees for him to be able to visit Liberia and then vacation with his wife for several weeks in Europe.[18]

As the Paytons traveled through Europe, in a style similar to that of well-to-do white Americans, Jack Johnson, the black heavyweight boxing champion of the world, proved that a black man was worthy of continuing to hold this title when he successfully defended his title against James Jeffries. As a retired former champion who was white, Jeffries had been entreated to come out of his six-year retirement by whites concerned that a black heavyweight champion was upsetting notions of the racial hierarchy in the United States. Jeffries, was nicknamed "the Great White Hope" in "the Fight of the Century," scheduled for July 4, 1910. But the boxer was knocked down twice, and Jefferies's corner threw in the towel in the fifteenth round of the one-sided fight in Reno, Nevada. Many white Americans were humiliated by the fight, and as black Americans celebrated, race riots sparked by whites' anger occurred in many cities across the nation, including New York. It is not known whether Philip Payton followed boxing, but regardless, it is possible that with telegraph communication to Europe that he learned of results of the fight. Considering his confrontations with white people in the real estate field, he would have celebrated Johnson's effort as a victory for the race. In mid-July the *New York Age* noted that the Paytons were in Rome.[19]

In late August Philip and Maggie Payton finally returned to the United States. Before returning to Harlem, in Washington, DC, Philip joined educator Anna Julia Cooper and Josephine F. Lawson on Sunday, August 28, for the christening of Anna Rosetta Lawson, daughter of Dr. and Mrs. James F. Lawson of Plainfield, New Jersey. After visiting friends and family in Massachusetts, by early September the Paytons were back at home on West 131st Street in Harlem.[20] The Harlem that the Paytons returned to in the summer of 1910 differed from the community they had left behind months before. Racial restrictive covenants had gained renewed momentum. Three years after the first Harlem covenant had been recorded for 137th Street in February 1907, in June 1910 ninety-nine owners of properties on West 136th Street between Lenox and Eighth Avenues, two long brownstone blocks, executed the largest such covenant to date. The document explained that it was necessary because "various parties have been purchasing different parcels of property in and about 136th Street, West with the purpose of renting the properties to African Americans in order to compel the adjacent white property owners to purchase the properties."[21]

Payton continued to cultivate his social relationships with the local and national network of black men who were satellites around the Wizard, Booker T. Washington. In the fall of 1910 a key indicator that Philip Payton had maintained his position as one of Washington's key men in New York City was his participation as part of an organizing committee for a welcome home "magnificent banquet" at the end of October at the Park Place Trades Club for the Wizard following Washington's return from "a tour of Europe where he had been entertained by royalty and by the most distinguished persons on the Continent." The planning committee of thirteen men, chaired by Charles W. Anderson, included New Yorkers such as

Fred R. Moore, as well as Robert H. Terrell of Washington, D.C., and Washington's old friend Dr. Samuel Courtney of Boston.[22]

In Payton's business life, the 136th Street restrictive covenant, signed in June, opened another phase in the covenant movement. By December, thirteen owners of properties on West 135th Street between Seventh and Eighth Avenues entered into a covenant. There was a substantial growth in the black population in Harlem when compared to the traditional Midtown black enclaves. By 1910 almost half of Manhattan's African American community lived in eight assembly districts above 86th Street compared to 20 percent in 1900. The absolute number of blacks in Manhattan increased from 36,000 in 1900 to 60,000 in 1910. The restrictive covenants were responses to this very visible increase in black residents who were moving beyond the Midtown enclaves and attempting to move beyond the boundaries of the Little Africa 135th Street enclave in Harlem.[23]

While Philip Payton looked for ways to do business in New York by navigating the potential land mines that the covenants represented for his business, which was so dependent on black residential buildings, the Paytons continued to move in New York black society, cultivating social and business relationships. By 1910 the couple was regularly hosting dinner parties in their West 131st Street home for friends, business colleagues and others. These parties served a number of purposes. With options for entertaining at area restaurants or banquet rooms declining as the New York City color line hardened, home entertaining was an attractive option to avoid the potential embarrassment of discriminatory public treatment observed by all present. The home dinner parties provided the Paytons with an opportunity to tailor the menus to the tastes of their guests and the goals of the dinners, such as simple enjoyment or seeking to impress. The parties were an important tool for maintaining social ties with old friends and cultivating social and business ties with acquaintances. The way the table was set, the menu selection, and the manner in which the food was served all became evidence for those in attendance of the prosperity and class status of the Paytons and the strength of Payton's business. Maggie Payton may have drawn on her experience as a young woman working as a domestic for Abiah Strong, the elite white woman in Payton's hometown of Westfield, to plan elaborate menus, table settings, and other dinner logistics. It is not clear whether the meals were cooked by Clara Wright, the Paytons' twenty-year-old black servant, or whether Maggie played an active role in meal preparations, but the dinners, and the publicity of the gatherings, orchestrated by Philip, would play a substantial role in keeping Philip Payton in the public eye in the new decade.

In early December Maggie Payton opened their home to Margaret Murray Washington, wife of Booker T. Washington, and Nellie Griswold Francis, a Minnesota churchwoman and suffragist. Over several days the trio attended a concert by Enrico Caruso, a performance of *Macbeth*, and a performance by Sarah Bernhardt.[24] On December 12 a reception for the visitors at the home of Mrs. M. L. Hunter on Canal Street in Manhattan included a performance by violinist David Martin, former director of Harlem's Music Settlement for Colored Children. A week later, on December 19, the Paytons hosted a dinner for twelve at Henry's Empire, a Harlem restaurant. Guests included Nellie Francis, Mr. and Mrs. Charles W. Anderson, architect Vertner Tandy, and New York City assistant district attorney Cornelius McDougald. The joking nature of the article describing it alluded to McDougald's possible engagement (he married educator Elise Johnson in 1911): "At the close of the dinner—it was not a farewell bachelor dinner at all—the party got to writing souvenir cards. On one sent south, was this: 'A dinner given through Mr. Payton by Mr. McDougald in aid of hopes, desires, ambitions, and designs. May the Lord bless him. Henry's Empire, December 19, '10.'"[25] On December 23 the Paytons hosted a banquet in honor of Booker T. Washington, Mrs. Washington, and Mrs. Francis at their home. Described by the *New York Age* in a front-page article as a "brilliant social function," the "reception brought out many of the leading people of Greater New York and New Jersey.... A delightful light repast was served in the dining room by sections, the last group sitting with Dr. and Mrs. Washington and Mrs. Francis. Afterwards Mr. Harry Williams was persuaded to sing and he rendered three solos with his old time grace and effect. Master Eugene Martin, the child violinist, delighted the company with several selections."[26] Black newspapers in other parts of the country also carried the story. Julius F. Taylor, editor of the *Broad Ax*, based in Washington, D.C., with the motto, "Democratic in politics, advocating the immortal principles of Jefferson and Jackson,"[27] described the function and used the lavishness of the reception to critique Booker T. Washington: "No doubt some of the money the great wizard of Tuskegee begs for educational purpose is used to enable him to pull off many of his social stunts and come to think of it beggars have no right to shine in first class society."[28]

The *New York Age* was an important resource in Philip Payton's media machine. Its reports of his social activities reinforced an image of personal prosperity commensurate with that of a successful businessman. As 1910, a year in which Payton had spent over six months abroad, came to a close, the newspaper left its readers with an admiring account of Payton's publicity strategies:

> Philip Payton, the real estate wonder, and the typical New York business man, has set the town to talking by his advertising methods. Nothing that Mr. Payton has done, gets beyond those clocks he had made for his customers not to mention the diaries. Every colored man in New York feels like a real man when he looks up in the street car, elevated car, and subway cars of the city and sees "P. A. P" [the company's logo placed on Payton-managed buildings], written everywhere in red. Don't stop to explain anything, Phil, but move on and swing out. The people will judge for themselves. Take that from *The Age*.[29]

As in 1910, the shift of New Year's Eve celebrations to Times Square and the implicit publicity given to the *New York Times* with every mention of the location of the revelry seemed to have confined to the *Times* the practice of devoting a portion of the front page of the January 1 edition of the daily paper to New Year's Eve coverage. But early in the new year the *New York Age* sought to give its readers a perspective on how they were viewed by white southerners. Its January 10 issue contained a reprint of a January 6 editorial from the *Roanoke* [Virginia] *Times*. Entitled "Negroes and Negroes," the Roanoke editorial sought to reinforce the popular trope that blacks in the South were contented in their poverty, and that northern blacks advocating for equality were maladjusted: "At the North is a class of Negroes who seem to always be in a passion, always sour and quarrelsome, and anxious to make discord. They are in sharp contrast to the majority of our Southern Negroes who almost always are in good humor, ready to laugh at the first opportunity and always among the first and foremost to enjoy whatever may be going on." The Roanoke editorial writer attributed the supposed distemper of black northerners to their disappointment at not being accepted socially by white people: "Being turned down, they turn bitter and proceed and try to make everybody else so." Even the Wizard, for all his shape-shifting machinations, did not escape the writer's scrutiny: "Booker T.

Washington is a citizen we have under observation. He seems almost too good to be true, and we never have got quite ready to endorse him fully. Yet, so long as he seems to be trying to do good and help his race, we are glad to do all we can to encourage and help him." The writer complained of the Negroes who had the audacity to criticize Washington and to publicize their critiques in Europe. He provided a common recommendation to black complainers: "Why, feeling as they do, they refuse to leave and go back to Africa and join themselves to those Negroes there who are supposed to be free and happy under their own association and management, we do not know."[30] For readers of the *New York Age*, the only surprising element of the reprinted *Roanoke Times* editorial was that the "n" in Negro was capitalized, two decades before the *New York Times* acceded to this convention. By the time the editorial was written, the National Association for the Advancement of Colored People was a little more than a year old, having grown out of a collaboration between the Niagara Movement led by W. E. B. Du Bois and a group of white progressives, for the purpose of advocating for racial equality. They had invited Washington to join, but he had declined, undoubtedly not wanting to be seen as exemplifying the adage, "if you can't beat them, join them." But even though not affiliated with this group, according to the Roanoke writer, Washington was not quite fully seen as a Good Negro but instead as one requiring constant observation. Philip Payton's allegiance to the Wizard would have prevented Payton from joining the NAACP, but his actions of moving black people into previously white blocks in Harlem demonstrated his belief in racial equality. In the eyes of the *Roanoke Times* writer, Payton's actions would have surely qualified him as a surly northerner. He had recently returned from Africa with no clear plans to settle there, in spite of the writer's recommendation, perhaps because while there he had received a clear perspective of the various ways that European intrigue was crippling Liberia.[31]

Rather than seeking to socialize with white people, as the *Roanoke Times* writer suggested was the goal of all northern blacks, in less than a decade in New York, the Paytons had become expert at socializing with a wide black social circle. Maggie Payton began 1911 entertaining. On Sunday, January 22, she hosted a dinner at the Payton home on West 131st Street for friends: Mrs. Cole K. Nelson, Mrs. Baldwin, Mrs. R. P. Wilson, Edwin F. and Edna Scottron Horne, and Edwin F. Horne Jr. Mrs. Horne was from the prominent Scottron family of Brooklyn. Her grandfather, Samuel, had been a successful merchant and had served on the Brooklyn Board of Education in the 1890s, before that city was subsumed as part of Greater New York in 1898. The Hornes' daughter, Lena, would be born in 1917 and would become a famous singer and actress.[32]

While the Paytons continued to use their home as a base for entertaining black New Yorkers, they remained the black exceptions on their block, which remained entirely white, even though it was not covered by one of the recent racial restrictive covenants. According to the 1910 census taker, even the Paytons had one foot in the realm of whiteness. The census taker identified them and their niece Bessie Hobby and nephew Duke Hobby as "mulatto." The only black person on the block, as identified by the census taker, was the Paytons' servant Clara Wright. To the west of the Payton block, across Lenox Avenue, in the previous half-decade, several groups of white homeowners were continuing to organize to execute racial restrictive covenants in a move to stem the tide of black movement into Harlem.[33]

In Baltimore, homeowners were also organizing to challenge black movement beyond their traditional residential boundaries. The result was "An Ordinance for Preserving Peace, Preventing Conflict and Ill-Feelings Between the White and Colored Races, and Promoting the General Welfare of the City of Baltimore." Behind this long name was an effort to maintain Baltimore's racially segregated neighborhoods by prohibiting movement of African Americans to white neighborhoods and white residents to African American neighborhoods. In early February news came down that the law had been thrown out because its title was invalid. Baltimore state's attorney agreed noting that the ordinance violated the city charter because "the subject embraced is invalid." The sponsor of the ordinance, Councilman Samuel West, vowed to have another ordinance drafted.[34]

In Harlem, on February 4, 1911, forty-two owners on the 200 block of West 132nd Street, between Seventh and Eighth Avenues, signed a covenant. Considering that the momentum of the covenant movement may have curtailed purchase and lease opportunities for Philip Payton in Harlem, he broadened the geographical range of his work. On February 24 his real estate ventures returned to the public record (after a year's absence) when he sold a six-story tenement at 235 East 81st Street on behalf of Alfred and Benjamin Oppenheim. Negotiating the sale of a building in this German enclave in Manhattan was a strategic move for Payton to keep his business alive in the face of competition from other black brokers and the barriers to entry on restrictive covenant blocks. There is no indication that the East 81st building would be occupied by African Americans, suggesting that Payton was developing general market transactions to complement the race transactions for which he had made his name.[35]

On March 28 Philip Payton reunited with his Liberia traveling companion Bishop Alexander Walters, attending the annual musicale for the African Society of Redemption hosted by Walters's wife Lelia at their home at 208 West 134th Street, one block from Payton's office. Musical presentations were offered by sopranos Annie Harper and Jessie Laguin, contralto Daisy Tapley, pianists Edith McKinney, and Mrs. E. A. Johnson. As part of the program, Payton and Walters spoke about their travels in Liberia.[36]

In December another large covenant was signed by sixty-six owners of properties in the 100 blocks of West 129th, West 130th, and West 131st Streets (between Seventh and Lenox Avenues). The signatures of the three most recent covenants signed in June and December 1910 and February 1911 were all witnessed by the same person, John G. Taylor. He would become a prime adversary for Philip Payton and serve as the voice of Harlem residents hostile to black movement to Harlem.[37] Taylor was a retired police officer who in 1903 had moved with his wife Agnes from a Greenwich Village apartment building they operated as a rooming house to a brownstone on West 136th Street in Harlem, one block east of the Little Africa settlement. Taylor probably believed that the location of his new home, west of Lenox Avenue, then seen as the dividing line between blacks and whites, protected it from black "invasion." The Waverly Place block from which he had moved in Greenwich Village was white on the end of the block on which he lived and black on the other end. The move to Harlem was a move up in class and status. His home was now a large single-family home, and his neighbors were clerks, accountants, and other professionals. But the next year, 1904, the failed eviction attempt by the Hudson Realty Company in the 135th Street area had unleashed an organized response that inspired the rise of Philip Payton and the Afro-American Realty Company.

Although by 1911 the Afro-American Realty Company was just a memory, Philip Payton and the Philip A. Payton Jr. Company were quite present. And Payton's efforts had inspired other black real estate brokers to enter the field. John Nail, once employed by Payton, had joined with Henry Parker to form Nail and Parker Real Estate. In 1910, working on behalf of

St. Philip's Episcopal Church, the oldest black Episcopal congregation in the nation, the firm orchestrated the sale of the church's West 25th Street building and adjacent apartment buildings owned by the congregation. In 1911 the firm brokered the purchase by St. Philip's of a row of ten apartment buildings on West 135th Street and facilitated the transfer to the congregation of property on West 134th Street that St. Philip's rector Hutchens Bishop had purchased surreptitiously for the construction of a new church. Another prominent black real estate broker was John Royall, a native of Virginia. With an office on 134th, John Royall Real Estate regularly ran advertisements for properties adjacent to Payton Company advertisements.[38] There were also a number of lesser-known black brokers, such as Julia Liggan, Maybelle McAdoo, and Charles Hutchinson. In his return to the United States after his Liberia trip in 1910, Payton was now competing with black colleagues in a market for buildings occupied by black people that he had helped to establish.

Philip Payton would face new business and family challenges in 1912. His brother Edward, six years younger, who had joined the Afro-American Realty Company after his graduation from Yale in 1906, had spent time away from the company in 1908 learning new business techniques, and by 1911 was listed as vice president of the company. He was by Payton's side through the many ups and downs of his business. In all likelihood Edward's stewardship of the business had made it possible for Payton to travel abroad for six months in 1910. Edward lived at 63 West 134th Street, next door to the building that housed Payton's real estate office.[39]

In 1906, the year of Edward Payton's college graduation, Paul Laurence Dunbar, the poet laureate of Negro America, succumbed to tuberculosis, a high-profile victim of a malady that disproportionately afflicted African Americans at the time. Some observers, swept up in the growing racism of the era, attributed the health disparities experienced by black people to racial weakness rather than the often overcrowded, poorly maintained conditions in which they lived and the poor nutrition, overwork, and continuous stress that characterized many of their lives. While Edward Payton lived a life of privilege relative to most black New Yorkers, he lived in Harlem, an area that was becoming overcrowded as black migration to New York continued and segregation practices steered and attracted black arrivals to the dense collection of buildings in the community. In August 1911 Edward began to exhibit symptoms indicating that tubercle bacillus had entered his lungs, most likely fever, lethargy, and swelling of the throat and lymphatic glands. He was diagnosed with tuberculosis, a disease for which no successful medicine had yet been developed. In January 1912 he suffered through a bout of pneumonia. In the ensuing months, as his symptoms continued, his privilege did give him the option of trying the one treatment that in 1912 had a record of some success, the rest cure. The standard rest cure treatment at the time called for an alleviation of stress by placing patients in a setting where they could rest in spaces with substantial light and fresh outdoor air. This regimen had been developed by Dr. Paul Trudeau, who had been cured of tuberculosis after spending time in the 1870s in the Adirondack mountain town of Saranac Lake in upstate New York, where days of bed rest had been punctuated by being rowed across the lake periodically. After regaining his health, and with donations from patrons, Trudeau began building the first cure cottages, homes often with screened porches, in Saranac Lake. He adopted the cottage approach in an effort to limit the airborne transmission of tuberculosis that could occur in larger congregant settings. This practice was affirmed by Dr. Robert Koch, who in 1882 identified the bacteria responsible for tuberculosis and became an advocate of the cure cottage regimen.[40]

In March 1912, as his symptoms continued unabated, Edward Payton traveled to Saranac Lake. By then the town was almost completely devoted to a network of tuberculosis cure cottages. Because of his symptoms, and some understanding of the contagious nature of tuberculosis, Philip and Maggie Payton probably drove Edward on the three-hundred-mile journey through the Adirondacks to Saranac Lake in their automobile, which they had owned since the early years of Philip's success. In Saranac Lake, Edward moved into one of the smallest cure homes, a bungalow (smaller than a cottage) in the village, at 62 Margaret Street. He had the entire house, which was owned by Burton and Ollie (Olivia) Moody. Burton Moodys' ancestor Jacob Moody was known as the first white settler in the Adirondack region. The Moodys had begun operating cure cottages soon after their marriage. Most cure cottages were managed by women, and Olivia Moody managed the Margaret Street bungalow, making sure that Edward received nutritious meals, that he did not exert himself, and that his doctor, David C. Twichell, scheduled regular visits.[41]

Because tuberculosis patients were required to severely limit physical activity until their health passed certain benchmarks, Edward most likely spent his days either in bed or perhaps reclining on an Adirondack chair, the chaise lounge that had been designed specifically for tuberculosis patients. Because most were produced in Saranac Lake, the name of the region had been attached to them. Many long-term single patients with improving health were able to take in the fresh air through walks. In Saranac Lake, the culture of invalids developed a courting practice in which couples referred to each other as "cousins." Few African Americans had the means to cease work for months at a time, and fewer had the means to travel to Saranac Lake and rent lodgings for long periods of time as Edward Payton was able to do; therefore there were very few black patients in Saranac Lake. Edward appears to have been one of the first. If his health improved, the color line would have prevented him from cousining with white women living in cure cottages, but Saranac Lake had a small but thriving black community that may have interacted with Edward. The rest cure was not successful for everyone, and unfortunately this was the case for Edward, who died on June 23 in Saranac Lake at the age of twenty-nine. He was buried a few days later in the Payton family plot in Westfield. Within a decade Susan and Philip Payton, the two elder Payton siblings, had lost their younger brothers. For Philip, the emotional blow was exacerbated by the fact that for him, someone concerned about his legacy, the death of a brother whom he had mentored in his real estate business for six years must have created a feeling of uncertainty for the future.[42]

Returning to New York, the Paytons resumed their social obligations. In mid-July their Harlem church, St. Mark's Methodist Episcopal, was overflowing for the funeral of Mollie Roberts, who had died at the age of thirty-four after a lingering illness of two years. The wife of Dr. Eugene P. Roberts, a Harlem physician and civic leader, Mrs. Roberts was held in high regard, a sign of the which was the quartet of officiating ministers at her funeral: Dr. W. H. Brooks, pastor of St. Mark's, Rev. Hutchens C. Bishop (St. Philips Episcopal Church), Rev. Horace G. Miller (Mt. Tabor Presbyterian Church), and Rev. W. R. Lawton (St. James Presbyterian Church). Philip and Maggie Payton were among more than fifty people who sent floral tributes.[43]

A few weeks after Mollie Roberts's funeral, in mid-August the Paytons observed the annual ritual of the growing black middle class in the Northeast and traveled to the shore for vacation. Philip, his mother, Annie, and Susan Payton journeyed to Asbury Park, New Jersey, where they vacationed at the Whitehead Cottage, a summer retreat operated by Mrs. L. B.

Whitehead. Philip's wife Maggie was not listed among the guests. Since the 1890s Mrs. Whitehead had served as host for a small but growing group of the black middle class who could afford to take time off from earning a living and also had enough resources to both travel and pay for food, lodging, and entertainment for a period from several days to several weeks at a resort. For several days the Paytons enjoyed meals provided by Mrs. Whitehead and the conversation and company of more than twenty-five other guests from New York, Washington, D.C., Philadelphia, and New Jersey. In all likelihood Philip Payton drove his automobile to facilitate excursions to the beach, approximately eight blocks from the Whitehead Cottage.[44]

By the end of the month, Philip was back at work. Under the title "[N]egro Co. Buys Mt. Vernon Dwelling," the August 27 edition of the *Sun* noted: "The Revenue Realty Company, represented by Philip A. Payton, the negro realty operator has purchased from Mrs. Margaret P. Hicks her residence at 121 North Terrace avenue, Mount Vernon, a three story structure, on plot 60 x 100 [feet]. The M. Morganthau Jr. Company negotiated the sale."[45] Although the property, in a suburb of thirty thousand people ten miles north of Harlem, seemed innocuous, the *Sun* article title identifying that the purchase was made by a black-controlled company indicated that such a purchase was unusual. The Revenue Realty Company seems to have represented Payton's attempt to diversify even while remaining in the real estate field. The Philip A. Payton Jr. Company, created in the wake of the 1907 lawsuit, was a primary and visible vehicle for Payton's business operations, but as his name became widely known, with positive and negative connotations associated with it, Payton seems to have joined in the creation of Revenue Realty, of which he was president, to operate in a more generic manner. While Revenue Realty had a generic ring to it, it did not provide a shield of anonymity to Payton. The *Sun* had been able to determine that the company was African American–controlled. The Mount Vernon purchase most likely also represented Payton's recognition that in order to survive and eventually thrive, he might have to move beyond the proving ground of Harlem that he had cultivated but which was becoming populated by many black business competitors. An irony of the Mount Vernon transaction is that the sale was negotiated by the M. Morganthau Jr. Company, whose principal, Maximilian Morganthau Jr., was the son of the principal of the Hudson Realty Company. Payton and his colleagues had blocked the effort of Morganthau Sr. to gain control of properties in the 135th Street area by evicting black tenants of properties, and the effort had launched Payton on a trajectory that had led to national acclaim in the black community. That the Mount Vernon transaction, although identifying Payton's race, was reported as a routine transaction may have been an example proving Payton's prediction, made at the National Negro Business League's annual meeting less than a decade earlier, that the "better class" of white people would look past race to transact business in which they made a reasonable profit. There may also have been a generational aspect to the differences on matters of race from Morganthau the father, born in 1847, to the son, born in 1878, who was therefore a contemporary of Payton, born in 1876.[46]

As 1912 came to a close, the *New York Age* began a series on the status of New York black businesses. The December 5 article focused on the real estate industry, with the unnamed reporter visiting "several of the Negro real estate agents whose offices are located in the Harlem section." Philip Payton was the first agent profiled, befitting his status as "pioneer Negro real estate agent in New York." After recounting how he started in the business, Payton reflected on his achievements: "By opening for colored tenants, first a house in one block and then a house in another I have finally succeeded in securing for the colored people of New York over two hundred and fifty first class flats and dwellings conveniently located as to transportation facilities, etc." He also noted a case in which owners of buildings adjacent to his reduced their rents in order to retain their long-term white tenants. Payton then reflected on the various sections of Upper Manhattan that had been opened to African Americans by black real estate brokers, such as 119th Street between Eighth and Manhattan Avenues and 99th Street between Central Park West and Columbus Avenue. The rest of the article, profiling other Black Harlem real estate agents, competitors of Payton, confirmed why Payton was expanding his focus beyond Harlem. The activities of C. E. Hutchinson, located at 5 West 134th Street, the same block as Payton's office, were noted. Described by the *Age* as the second black person to enter the real estate field, Hutchinson had six employees. The ten employees at Nail & Parker Real Estate, at 145 West 135th Street, were led by John "Jack" Nail, a former Payton employee, and Henry Parker. With a slight air of defensiveness Parker explained that "the Negro real estate agent is not understood by the people. He is fighting the Negro's battles every day and is always striving hard to break down the prejudice that exists against the Negro as a tenant." In describing the disparity between the rents of white tenants and black tenants, the *Age* explained: "It was claimed by Mr. Parker that the Negro tenant pays more rent proportionately than the white tenant, not because his rent is higher, but because there is greater demand for Negro tenement property and they are filled while the white tenement is vacant." The final sentence of the article mentioned a firm, L. C. Whitfield, that had been in business for seven years with seven employees.[47]

The comments made by Philip Payton and Henry Parker regarding the different rents paid by black and white tenants shone a light on the segregated real estate market in Harlem that Payton had nurtured and those real estate agents who followed him had reinforced as the black population in the Harlem had grown. As Payton had proposed in his Afro-American Realty Company prospectus in 1904, he and the black real estate agents who joined him had made the color line costly to white property owners committed to maintaining white segregated buildings and willing to pay black real estate agents for buildings on the verge of turning black, in order to keep black tenants out, thereby holding back the tide of black housing demand. But as Henry Parker's defensiveness suggested, the cost of the color line was being more commonly borne by the hundreds of black tenants being attracted to Harlem by black real estate agents like Payton and Parker. Their black renters were introduced to a dual, segregated housing market in which their rents went higher and higher, while landlords, as both Payton and Parker explained to the *Age*'s reporter, often lowered the rents of white residents in an effort to retain those who chose to remain rather than flee. In its article on black real estate agents, the *Age* presented the brokers' views without judgment.

In 1913 black tenants in Harlem would challenge the notion that black real estate brokers were "fighting their battles." With some assistance from the *Age*, black tenants would organize a campaign, built on their complaints of exploitation, targeting black real estate brokers.

Chapter Six

FIFTY YEARS OF FREEDOM NATIONAL

Celebrations marking the New Year of 1913 had special meaning for African Americans. Fifty years earlier, on January 1, 1863, Abraham Lincoln had signed the Emancipation Proclamation declaring enslaved people in the territories then in rebellion "forever free." During the first week of January 1913, standard New Year's celebrations were supplemented in black communities nationwide by programs commemorating the signing of the proclamation. Harlemites gathered at Young's Casino at Park Avenue and 134th Street in New York City on Thursday evening, January 2, 1913, to celebrate. Those in the audience who could remember that New Year's Day fifty years earlier undoubtedly reflected on the excitement that had filled black Americans when they heard that Abraham Lincoln had signed the document. In the midst of the Civil War, when the possibility of the proclamation had been announced in September 1862, there had been some doubt that it would actually be signed. But the Confederate states' failure to return to the Union, as the Preliminary Proclamation had required, gave Lincoln, seeking to undermine the institution of slavery and therefore the strength of the Confederate Army, the political justification to sign the document that would forever link his name with freedom as the Great Emancipator. On that January 1 in 1863, black Americans and their allies had celebrated what they viewed as the manifestation of the Biblical Jubilee, a year of freedom. Those celebrations had primarily been in the North, since the

Confederates did everything possible to prevent the news of the proclamation by the president of their enemy, the United States of America, from reaching the ears of the enslaved. Nevertheless, intrepid black and white people carried the news to many places in the South through the informal word-of-mouth communication network that existed there, leading to a wave of freedom seekers, some of whom took advantage of the provision of the proclamation indicating that black men could be considered for army service. They joined the Union Army, and as U.S. Colored Troops they would help to shift the momentum of the Civil War toward a Union victory.[1]

The commemoration of the fiftieth anniversary of the signing of the proclamation was a time of both celebration and assessment for African Americans. How far had they moved beyond their previous condition as enslaved people? Some people, black and white, who believed that slavery had degraded the morals and behavior of the enslaved, argued that black people would not be treated equally until they adopted the behaviors of the American middle class. In assessing progress of the race, they emphasized behavior as a sign of progress.[2]

The year 1913 also marked the tenth anniversary of Philip Payton's formation of the Afro-American Realty Company partnership and his concerted move into the real estate field. But ten years into his journey, he was stalled. He had to determine how to respond to changed conditions in the real estate market that now had several black competitors, and he had to develop a strategy to overcome racial restrictive covenants inspired by his and others' highly publicize moves to "open" Harlem blocks to black residents. While determining his next move, he continued to project a public image of prosperity and success even when the reality was more challenging. White Americans also celebrated the anniversary of the Emancipation Proclamation, but in assessing black progress, they were often inclined to use the popular phrase "the Negro Problem," observing the position of the race with a critical eye, focusing on the deficits that continued to burden black people and interpreting them as signs of weakness. Black Americans for the most part celebrated five decades of achievement in freedom.

Philip Payton had been scheduled to speak at the Young's Casino program, but newspaper accounts of the occasion did not refer to his presence on the program, which was full of reflection, celebration, and commemoration. Following music provided by the Abyssinian Military Band,

Mrs. M. C. Lawton, chair of the Brooklyn-based Conference of Workers Among Girls, "represented the women and told of their progress and development during the last fifty years ... paying high tribute to their work on behalf of neglected womanhood." Then attorney James L. Curtis, the main speaker, reviewed "minutely the progress of the race from abolition of slavery down to the present." Philip Payton's former business partner, Fred R. Moore, editor of the *New York Age*, offered remarks looking to the future and "pointed out how the race could further develop by cooperation and unity of purpose."[3]

Philip Payton's mentor, Booker T. Washington, was a featured speaker the following Sunday evening at an Emancipation Proclamation program at the Church of the Messiah, at Park Avenue and 34th Street in Manhattan. True to form, Washington first presented the evidence of black economic progress over fifty years: twenty million acres of land under cultivation, real estate ownership valued at $600 million, ownership of 10,000 stores, and 57 banks and 33,000 black churches. But Washington also offered a call to action that was uncharacteristic but reflective of the increase in hostilities that African Americans were experiencing in 1913 as a white supremacist backlash to black progress was unleashed: "But all has not been accomplished ... so long as a prominent official of a State can advocate in the public press the abuse of a race of people, and so long as lynchings and burnings are prevalent and the same law does not apply to all peoples[,] there remains something to be done."[4] Washington's comments were motivated by the reign of terror inflicted on black people in the South, but northern cities were also becoming increasingly hostile places for African Americans as their numbers increased in metropolitan areas. In 1913 Philip Payton, whose actions since 1903 had been a catalyst for black movement to Harlem, a phenomenon that had also led to a white backlash, would continue to be a central figure in what was becoming a racial war for territorial control in Harlem.

A little more than a month after the Emancipation Proclamation commemorations, the Equity Congress, a black men's group of which Payton was an early member, agreed to enter the field of battle for control of territory in Harlem. On Sunday, February 9, at its weekly meeting at 89 West 134th Street, real estate broker J. B. Wood introduced the following resolution for consideration by members of the Equity Congress: "In view of the fact that there is a certain institution known as the Harlem Home Protective

Association, its object being to advise white property owners to sign a petition restricting colored people from living in certain sections or occupying certain properties in New York City or in Harlem." The resolution noted that several (actually ninety-one) residents had signed a February 1911 petition, and that the Equity Congress questioned the constitutionality of the petition.[5] The resolution then called for the appointment of a committee of the Equity Congress to obtain a copy of the petition from the New York City Hall of Records and concluded: "Be it resolved that the committee shall have the right to make all necessary arrangements for the purpose of procuring means to pay all legal expenses which will occur in having said petition removed."[6] The resolution passed unanimously. The petition referred to in the resolution was the largest racial restrictive covenant to date of Harlem properties. More than an expression of solidarity among homeowners, the covenant was a legal document that attached the restriction against selling to black people or allowing them to occupy the properties, to the deeds of the properties of the owners who signed the document. But what made the document even more powerful was that the restrictions remained on the properties for all future owners.[7]

J. B. Wood, the broker who introduced the Equity Congress resolution, was an up-and-coming broker. The congress, of which he was a member, was formed by undertaker James C. Thomas, vaudevillian Bert Williams, Philip Payton, and others in 1911, the year that the covenant in question was filed. The organization's goals were to increase opportunities for black New Yorkers in public and professional life in New York City. Before moving to Harlem, the congress held its Sunday meetings at Thomas's undertaking parlor in the Tenderloin area of Midtown Manhattan. In Harlem they met at 89 West 134th Street, following Thomas when he moved his business to that location. Wood's resolution passed unanimously, and with it the Equity Congress made a commitment to directly confront the restrictive covenant movement. The timing of the first racial restrictive covenants in Harlem, 1906, following Payton's attempt to evict white residents of 525 West 151st Street and "open" the building to black tenants and a similar effort by a white owner, Hannah Theobold, on West 137th Street, suggests that the covenants were defensive measures by worried white Harlem property owners. While brokers such as Philip Payton, John Royall, John Nail, and Henry Parker had higher public profiles, the lesser-known broker J. B. Wood took the initiative to propose confronting the covenants directly.[8]

The Harlem Home Protective Association, identified in the Equity Congress resolution as the organization behind the February 1911 covenant, is most likely the Property Owners Protective Association. Formed in 1900 for the purposes of community improvement at a time when the miniscule presence of black people in Harlem, primarily in the Little Africa enclave at 133rd, 134th, and 135th Streets, was not a threat, the association shifted its focus from general community improvement to racial defense as substantial numbers of black people moved beyond Little Africa after 1904. The Protective Association then focused on protecting its members from the threat of encroaching blackness in Harlem. The racial covenant became an important tool of defense for concerned white property owners, and because it required the organizing of substantial numbers of owners living in close proximity, organization and coordination was critical to successfully obtaining the required signatures, then believed to be at least a majority of the owners in an area, in order to be credible.[9]

Philip Payton's social calendar kept him in the news in 1913, and on the evening of Friday, March 14, he attended the annual fundraising program of the Lucy Laney League at Young's Casino. The league was formed by supporters of the Haines Normal and Industrial Institute of Augusta, Georgia, and named for its headmistress. The reception was one of the major social events of the year. At the event a three-act play, *A Kentucky Belle*, was presented by a cast of twenty-five, followed by dancing to the music of the New Amsterdam Orchestra. The *New York Age* noted that among those in attendance, "many handsome and beautiful gowns were displayed." The article then provided a sample list of over twenty couples or individuals in attendance, with Philip Payton's name listed first, concluding that "a splendid audience was present and the financial benefit accruing to the school as a result of this effort will be ample."[10]

At the end of March, Erduin von der Horst Koch, chairman of the Harlem Board of Commerce, hosted a private meeting at his home at 290 Lenox Avenue near 122nd Street for a group of black property owners and a special committee of the board. The purpose of the meeting was an attempt to resolve the growing tensions between longtime white Harlem property owners and the increasing numbers of black newcomers. A *New York Times* article on the meeting noted that several "well-known Harlem [N]egroes were present" but mentioned only broker John Nail by name. While Payton was not mentioned, it is very likely that he was in attendance. Responding to white residents' concerns regarding the dramatic increase in the presence of black residents in Harlem, Nail, unable to imagine the flood of black migrants that would soon come north as part of the Great Migration beginning with World War I, indicated that the current black property ownership in Harlem was sufficient to meet the demand over the next five years without expanding their holdings into new areas of Harlem.

John G. Taylor, leader of the Property Owners Protective Association, was excluded from the meeting but told the *Times* reporter that he believed that its real purpose was to placate black residents in order to obtain their votes. E. H. Koch denied any political motive and in closing the meeting reiterated that its purpose was to gain a better understanding between Harlem property owners and the African Americans who had moved into the 135th Street district. He made an observation that was consistent with Philip Payton's vision conveyed in his Afro-American Realty Company prospectus in 1904, something that was particularly remarkable considering the hostility to the black presence in Harlem that had grown in the ensuing nine years since Payton had first expressed it: "The [N]egroes have a right to live and the privilege of going on Fifth Avenue or Riverside Drive if they can pay for it." Perhaps thinking of the racial violence witnessed in New York in 1900 and 1905, Atlanta in 1906, and Springfield, Illinois, in 1908, he added that "many obnoxious things have arisen from the antagonism stirred up between the races.[11]

As the year proceeded, Philip Payton remained moderately active in the real estate market. At the end of May he purchased four apartment houses at 335–341 West 59th Street between Eighth and Ninth Avenues from Matilda Minck, a forty-five-year-old German American widow with her own income who lived on West 100th Street in Manhattan. The Minck transaction provides a window on race and real estate in New York City in the second decade of the twentieth century and the role that Payton was continuing to play in transactions involving buildings occupied by black New Yorkers. Minck had purchased the two buildings on April 29, 1902, buying 335 West 59th Street from Rosina Vollhart for $1 and assuming mortgages of $30,000. On the same day she also purchased 341 West 59th from Rosina Vollhart for $3 and assumed a mortgage of $26,000. At the time of the sale to Payton, Minck lived at the Apthorp, a residential hotel on Broadway at 79th Street. In 1900 the West 59th Street buildings purchased by Minck had been occupied by a diverse mix of eighty-one white residents in thirty-one households. The tenants were born in places such as Germany, Connecticut, New York, Ohio, and Kentucky. They earned their livings in working-class and middle-class jobs of the day: coachman, salesman, saleswoman, and telegraph operator. Most likely this was the residential mix two years later when Minck bought the buildings.[12]

By 1913, when Payton purchased the buildings from Minck, their residential mix had changed dramatically from all white to all black. Although Harlem had by then become the area of choice for many black New Yorkers, apartment buildings located in the San Juan Hill district, the northern portion of the Midtown black enclave, still retained a substantial black residential base as new migrants to New York continued to arrive to an area long associated with black residence and culture. In 1910 the black tenants of 335 and 341 West 59th Street were housed more densely than their white predecessors, with 145 people living in the two buildings in 39 households. While some tenants were born in New York, a majority were born elsewhere, including Virginia, South Carolina, and Pennsylvania, with a substantial number from the West Indies. In 1900, when the residents were all white, the buildings had included only two "boarders," but reflecting the pressure to meet the higher rents usually charged in all-black buildings, by 1910 the buildings included thirty-four "lodgers." The Minck buildings were twenty-seven blocks from where Philip Payton's first real estate office had been located thirteen years before. While he may not have been responsible for the shift in the racial makeup of the buildings' tenants, a building densely populated with black residents was an ideal fit for his business model as a specialist in "colored tenements," since maximum rents could be extracted from tenants who had a limited range of other housing choices.[13]

While Payton was concluding the Minck transactions, the Equity Congress experienced a breakthrough on its years of advocacy to the state government for a black National Guard regiment. Some black New Yorkers undoubtedly would have preferred that black and white guardsmen serve side by side, but the demand for racial segregation by many white National Guard officers led African Americans to conclude that a segregated regiment would be better than no service opportunity at all. With military service seen as one of the important criteria of citizenship and of masculinity, African American men had historically used their military service as a bargaining chip for fair treatment. In the first years of the 1900s, as the fitness for citizenship and the manhood of black men were being routinely challenged, the opportunity for National Guard service would provide black men in New York State with an opportunity to raise their status. This goal was in alignment with the mission of the Equity Congress. For Philip Payton, an early member of the organization and one who had been advocating for full participation of black people in the housing market in New York City, pushing for the National Guard service, even in a segregated unit, aligned well with his beliefs.

The bill to establish the regiment passed in the New York State Assembly on May 2 and in the state Senate on May 8. Because in past years several previous governors, state legislators, and National Guard officers had not followed through on promises to make the legislation a reality, members of the Equity Congress and many African Americans throughout the state accepted the black vernacular caution "don't shout too soon" and awaited Governor William Sulzer's actual signing of the bill into law before celebrating. The Equity Congress marked the achievement of one of its major goals on June 2. In the waning minutes of the legislative session, Governor Sulzer signed the legislation providing for the formation of a black regiment. Sulzer, a Democrat who stressed his independence from the Tammany machine, in office less than a year, did what his predecessors could not or would not do. At the end of June, on a Wednesday evening, the first company of the provisional black regiment that had been formed in September 1912 in anticipation of the law becoming effective marched through the streets of Harlem accompanied by a sixteen-piece drum corps. They then assembled at Odd Fellows Hall on West 138th Street and presented an exhibition drill. Regiment advocates began planning for the organization of a second company.[14] The work of Philip Payton and his fellow members of the Equity Congress had become a reality.

While the National Guard advocates were experiencing success, in the Harlem real estate field Payton and his fellow real estate agents were beginning to experience a backlash to their rental and management practices from black tenants and their advocates. In January 1913 the League of Urban Conditions Among Negroes had established a Housing Bureau in Harlem. The *New York Age* explained the problem that the bureau planned to address: "For some time colored tenants of the city have complained strenuously to the fact that persons moving into new apartments, have no guarantee that their neighbors will be found quiet and orderly. In fact, frequently these tenants and their families are brought in contact with immoral and debased associations which have a most deterrent effect upon efforts for family upbuilding." The article noted that the roots of the idea for the bureau could be traced to a 1911 conference at St. Philip's Episcopal Church in which numerous "irregularities" experienced by tenants in "Negro districts" were related. The result was the formation of a committee chaired by Rev. Adam Clayton Powell Sr., pastor of Abyssinian Baptist Church, to "devise means whereby the evils might be corrected." While the "evils" were not directly articulated, other accounts of the period note that the struggle to meet exorbitant rents often led black renters to take in roomers in order to supplement their incomes. These unrelated people were seen as threats to the stability of black family life, raising the potential of marital infidelity, exposing children to wayward influences, and sexual abuse. The bureau was the result. Its initial task would be to develop a list of "reliable, first-class apartments" with reasonable rents and "respectable environments."[15] In 1911 the League of Urban Conditions Among Negroes in New York City was newly formed from the merger of three biracial, young New York progressive organizations, the League for Protection of Colored Women, the Committee for Improving the Industrial Conditions Among Negroes, and the Committee on Urban Conditions Among Negroes. Each organization was formed to address the different aspects of the challenges faced by black people in New York as their numbers increased with new migrants to the city. The merged organization, which would soon be popularly known as the Urban League, "held that the Negro needed not alms, but opportunity."[16]

By June the Housing Bureau, led by John T. Clark, an African American native of Louisville, had moved beyond compiling lists of respectable apartments to challenging apartment owners and managers such as Philip Payton for a failure to screen out disreputable tenants. The *New York Age* interviewed several black broker/managers on their perspectives on the work the bureau was undertaking. One agent, who was one of "the largest operators" in Harlem, declined to have his name used but noted that property managers were already working very hard to keep undesirable tenants out of their buildings. John Royall, one of the most active black broker/managers, was decidedly against the idea and was quoted at length. The *Age* reported that Royall believed that

> it was regarded as a meddler, and the sooner it was discontinued the better it would be. Owing possibly to lack of knowledge on the part of the operators

its efforts seem to be misspent. It is trying to handle a proposition that has been given up by other committees as untenable. The bureau is bothering the agent with complaints and questions which the agent is already doing his utmost to correct and answer, and which should be directed to the Tenement House Department [a city agency], or directed to the tenants themselves.

John E. Nail, former employee of Philip Payton and by then a partner in the real estate firm of Nail and Parker, responded to the *Age*'s questions about the bureau with a letter in which he observed that he "believe[d] such efforts as were being put forth by the bureau to be a waste of energy. His experience had been that such movements seldom amounted to anything or accomplished any tangible good." The article also noted that Nail believed energies would be better spent encouraging black people to become property owners.[17]

Philip Payton's view of the bureau was different than that of his colleagues. The *Age* noted that Payton indicated that he "knew nothing of the object and the intent of the bureau and was not in a position to express an opinion. He had received requests from the bureau to attend meetings but had been unable to do so. However, said he, there is an opportunity for good work by the bureau if it is gone at in the right way."[18] Compared to the critical comments by his real estate colleagues, Payton's strikingly different, cautiously optimistic view of the Housing Bureau's potential may have been a sign that, even almost a decade after he publicly announced the formation of the Afro-American Realty Company as a corporation that would be a race champion, he still recognized the need to improve the living conditions of black New Yorkers. The fact that he thought that an intermediary, the Housing Bureau, could play a productive role, "if it is gone about in the right way," was perhaps a recognition, after a decade as a New York real estate operator, that the Philip A. Payton Jr. Company and its competitors, all with profit as their first priority, could not meet the housing needs of all black New Yorkers without some assistance from an entity with other priorities.

In September 1913 a group of "representative and influential citizens" met at Thomas Hall, James C. Thomas's undertaking parlor at 89 West 134th Street, to form a new citywide organization, the Civic League, to "conduct a campaign to secure Negro representation in administration of the city's affairs." The impetus for the organization was an attempt to gain a black nominee for the Progressive Party candidacy for alderman for the Twenty-first District in Harlem. With boundaries ranging from 127th Street on the south to 141st Street on the north, Fifth Avenue on the east, and the Hudson River on the west, the district covered the majority of the area of Harlem where black residents had settled over the previous decade. The Progressive Party had denied black Harlemites efforts to get a nominee on its ticket, so they decided to identify an independent candidate. Those attending the Civic League meeting considered their host James C. Thomas, Philip Payton, and his real estate rival John Royall as potential nominees. Over the next few weeks the league settled on Royall as their nominee. In October Payton was among the signers of a letter of support for Royall developed by area ministers. Payton continued to support Royall's campaign, and when the campaign proved unsuccessful in the November election, he served on the committee of arrangements for a December Civic League dinner honoring Royall's effort.[19]

Black New York entered 1914 with messages of earnestness and protest. The front page of the January 1 edition of the *New York Age* included an editorial cartoon with an unmistakable message. With a subheading "WHAT THE NEGRO SHOULD STRIVE FOR IN 1914," a black man, back to the reader, with shirt-sleeves rolled up and holding an unfurled scroll containing the word "TOILER," viewed a stone monument over twice his height that contained the words:

MORE
SUCCESSES
MORE AND
BETTER HOMES
MORE
FARM LANDS
MORE
BUSINESS
ENTERPRISES
MORE
RACE CONFIDENCE
MORE
EDUCATION

MORE
CHARACTER[20]

On the same page was a reprint of "The Crime Against the Negro," a recent *San Francisco Examiner* article by Rev. Charles F. Aked, former pastor of New York's Fifth Avenue Baptist Church, in which he stated: "The crime against the Negro continues, North as well as South, equally with West, hangs, shoots, and essentially roasts its Negroes by order of Judge Lynch. State after State disfranchises its Negroes; the 'Jim Crow' car is still running; the Wilson administration discriminates against the Negro clerk or employee at Washington—and nobody seems to mind."

In a New Year's sermon entitled "Going Forward," Rev. Adam Clayton Powell, pastor of the Abyssinian Baptist Church on 40th Street in the Tenderloin, encouraged black New Yorkers to change their ways in 1914. He asserted:

> The Negro race is dancing itself to death. We could not even celebrate our fifty years of progress without advertising "dancing every afternoon." . . . Our young people are too frivolous because they feed on too much trash. . . . You can see the effect of the Tango, the Chicago, the Turkey Trot, the Texas Tommy, and ragtime music not only in their conversations but in the movement of their bodies about the home and on the street. Grace and modesty are becoming rare virtues.

Instead of dancing, Rev. Powell suggested that there "should be a more general movement of support for our business and professional men." He encouraged support of black businesses in all lines of work. Reacting to the hardening of the color line in New York and other cities, he noted that "The white man has forced us into separate lodges, [C]hristian associations, churches and even in large American cities. Now, we should force him out of the money-making business among us and force ourselves to patronize our own enterprises and strong race men."[21]

But the Paytons were Methodists and unlikely to have been in the congregation at Abyssinian Baptist Church to hear Rev. Powell's admonitions. Perhaps they read the article about his sermon, but nevertheless, on Friday, January 2, members of their family entered the new year dancing. A debutante party was held for their eighteen-year-old niece Bessie Hobby, whom Philip and Maggie Payton had raised along with her brother Duke after the death of their mother, Maggie's sister Julia, in North Carolina. The coming-out party took place in the Bronx, at the home of Leonard and Eva Payne, a couple in their late twenties. Maggie Payton was present to usher her niece into black society, as was architect Vertner Tandy and his wife, Sadie, and more than a dozen other New Yorkers, including young women friends of Bessie, as well as guests from Washington, D.C. (including Bessie's future brother-in-law George Lattimore) and Boston. Neither Philip Payton nor his sister Susan were present for this party, which marked a milestone in Bessie's life as a black New Yorker.[22] Regardless, Bessie undoubtedly enjoyed herself, and "the evening was spent in dancing followed by a substantial and palatable repast."[23] Such debutante parties were "among the most notable social occasions in the homes of the black upper class."[24] The fact that Bessie's party was not held in the Paytons' Harlem home, the site of so many parties honoring Booker T. Washington and others, as well as the absence of Philip and Susan, suggests that the Paytons may have been entering the year with challenges ahead even as they continued to present an optimistic face in public accounts.

In February Philip Payton's public profile was raised when he wrote a letter to New York Republican senator Elihu Root protesting the Smith-Lever Act, legislation proposed by Senator Hoke Smith of Georgia and Senator Asbury Lever of South Carolina. The act proposed to provide funding to encourage land-grant colleges to develop and provide divisions that would offer agricultural and home economics education to residents of their states. The purpose seemed commendable, but Payton's protest was based on the fact that most of the original 1862 land-grant colleges were white institutions. The 1890 land-grant act did include a few black colleges, such as Tuskegee Institute.[25] In Payton's letter, published in the *New York Age*, he noted, "You will notice, I hope, that under this bill the Negro people of the South, who constitute nearly one-half of the population, will share in none of the benefits whatever of this proposed legislat[ion]." Using the example of Georgia State College for Negroes, he suggested that rather than use state funds to support black colleges they had created, states were using land-grant funds, which were limited, for this purpose. He concluded:

> As one of your Negro constituents in New York, I most earnestly urge that the benefit of your scrutiny be given this proposed legislation.... It does seem that the Negroes, who are an integ[ral] part of the government, should,

since they are denied the right to vote, be permitted to profit by such agricultural instruction as the government may appropriate the funds for. Certainly there should be no such discriminations as have been and are practiced in the South under the present Moral [Morrill] Act.[26]

In all likelihood, Payton's ties to Booker T. Washington and Tuskegee Institute, one of the few 1890 black land-grant colleges, inspired him to write the letter. His misspelling of the Morrill Act, the 1862 legislation that created the initial land-grant colleges, as the "Moral Act" was perhaps a Freudian slip, since his letter appealed to the fair play of the legislators. Payton's candid reference to the exclusion of black southerners from voting was perhaps an effort to shame Senator Root for not living up to the American creed.

In early March Payton joined with one hundred friends celebrating the birthday of Rev. Richard Manuel Bolden, pastor of First Emmanuel Baptist Church. The program at Bolden's home on West 146th Street featured solos and remarks by a number of people, including Payton. Birthday gifts included a brass bookstand from Payton and his sister, Susan. A contemporary of Payton, Bolden was born in Maryland in 1878. He was a graduate of Livingstone College, the Salisbury, North Carolina, college where Payton had attended high school for one year in 1893–1894. It is possible that this common tie had solidified their friendship. Bolden was active in community affairs and would run unsuccessfully for alderman in 1915.[27]

On March 11 fire swept through four apartment buildings at 128, 130, and 132 West 134th Street, a block from Payton's office. Seventy-three families were left without homes and were assisted by relief benefit performances at the Lafayette, Franklin, and Lincoln Theaters. Temporary housing was provided at St. Philip's Parish House on West 134th Street and the Music School Settlement for Colored Children on West 131st Street. A Citizen's Relief Committee was formed that was chaired by Payton's real estate colleague John Nail, with broker John Royall serving as treasurer. Other members included ministers Hutchens Bishop of St. Philip's Episcopal Church and Rev. Adam Clayton Powell of Abyssinian Baptist Church. No mention was made of Payton's participation.[28]

On March 13 Payton attended the ninth annual reception of the Lucy Laney League. The ambitious program, held at the Manhattan Casino, included a children's comedy skit, "The Children's Graduation," and "Don't

Blame It on Broadway," a musical production. The large audience included lawyer J. Frank Wheaton, performer Ada Overton Walker, and activist Cyril Briggs. The event was described as a "success financially, histrionically, and musically." The stage productions were followed by dancing to music furnished by the New Amsterdam Orchestra.[29]

In mid-March, in an attempt to resolve rising racial tensions inspired by the increased black presence in Harlem, John Nail and Henry Parker hosted a meeting between "a number of colored citizens" and Meyer Jarmulowsky, who represented the Property Owner's Improvement Corporation. The organization's previous leader, John G. Taylor, who had organized several restrictive covenants in Harlem and had been excluded from the 1913 meeting hosted by the Harlem Board of Commerce with a similar purpose, had died in February 1914, just as tension related to race and real estate in Harlem was at its height.[30] At the March meeting at the office of Nail and Parker at 145 West 135th Street, Jarmulowsky, leader of a Lower East Side family bank, "extended an invitation to colored property owners of Harlem to join with the white owners in a movement to protect each other's interests against the depreciation of property, which also includes a plan to provide better housing conditions for Negroes." Although Jarmulowsky would "not say why property had depreciated in value in certain sections of Harlem," he claimed that the efforts of the Improvement Corporation were "not actuated by race prejudice." Contrary to this assertion, he then presented a list of reasons for the real estate "problems" that pointed quite directly to race prejudice. He claimed that property values had recently declined by $100 million. He noted that "there are 35,000 Negroes [in Harlem] at the present time and more expected," but rather than conclude that the demand for housing from this increased number would result in higher rents and therefore an appreciation in property values, Jarmulowsky claimed that most of the current and future black residents were "unable to pay rents necessary to maintain values." He then claimed that properties occupied by African Americans in Harlem were "not marketable," that mortgages on the buildings "are constantly being called and it is difficult to replace them," and that "general business in Harlem has been seriously injured due to the changed character of the population." He lamented the movement of African Americans to streets south of West 125th Street, the primary commercial thoroughfare, and proposed that, instead, the Improvement Corporation had a plan to "place at the disposal of Negroes, buildings arranged for their special use, so that they may be able to pay rents and will not find it necessary to overspread the district."[31]

In the discussion that followed "the real estate dealers present confessed that since the promiscuous opening of houses to Negroes in the Harlem section many flats were constantly vacant, occasioned by the inclination of Negroes, as a rule, to move about from place to place at frequent intervals. The consensus of opinion was that supply of houses in Harlem was greater than the demand." The meeting concluded with a unanimous decision to "organize a colored committee of fifteen to meet and take up the question of housing conditions in Harlem with the white committee, and [appointed] John Nail to name the members of this committee."[32] Those present were:

- Rev. Hutchens C. Bishop, rector of St. Philip's Church on West 134th Street. Since 1910, the church had owned of a row of apartment buildings on West 135th Street that included Nail and Parker's office, where the meeting was held. The firm had orchestrated the sale of St. Philip's West 25th Street church and apartment buildings in the area, and the purchase of the Harlem properties that had been front page news, and a symbol of the arrival of black ownership in Harlem.
- Fred R. Moore, editor of the *New York Age* and former officer with Philip Payton in the Afro-American Realty Company
- James Garner, owner of a home maintenance and repair company and a former partner in the AARC
- Gilchrist Stewart, an attorney, businessman, and chairman of the Vigilance Committee of the New York NAACP[33]
- J. B. Wood, Harlem-based broker who had put forward the Equity Congress resolution to counter raise funds to challenge racial restrictive covenants
- Edward A. Warren, editor of the *New York Amsterdam News*[34]
- George W. Harris, editor of the *New York News*[35]
- Paul G. Prayer, a local businessman
- Dr. J. S. Williams, D. P. Agard, S. Bailey, T. J. Clark, and Rufus Herbert

Although the meeting was hosted by his protégé John Nail, Philip Payton was notably absent from this list of attendees, suggesting that he was no longer considered a principal in the battle for Harlem real estate.

At the meeting Meyer Jarmulowsky claimed that the proposal of the Improvement Corporation to create racially segregated districts in Harlem was not motivated by racial prejudice, but the depreciation in real estate prices that he described, if accurate, could be accounted for only by racial prejudice. In the absence of race prejudice, the movement of large numbers of black people to Harlem, who were typically charged higher rents than white tenants, should have increased the value of the properties they occupied, since those properties were generating more income for their owners. The only explanation for a decline in the value of income-generating properties occupied by black people was race prejudice. In addition to income generation, the value of a property was also determined by the views of the market—the general public. If the general public believed that buildings occupied by black people were of less value than those occupied by white people, this assumption could prevail regardless of the income that all-black buildings generated. By 1914 the national real estate industry had crafted and disseminated its theory, affirmed by social scientists studying black urban neighborhoods, that black residents "destabilized" neighborhoods and lowered property values. As the real estate industry had professionalized following the formation of the National Association of Real Estate Boards in 1908, the organization excluded black brokers from its membership and prohibited them from calling themselves realtors. Given these policies, which exemplified the members' belief in the inferiority of black people, it is quite likely that appraisers of Harlem real estate assessing properties occupied by black people valued those properties well below the value that the higher income they generated would have otherwise called for. The NAREB theory became self-fulfilling and was reified by mortgage holders calling due mortgages on some properties when occupied by black tenants, ostensibly in an effort to protect their collateral, an action resulting in further destabilization of the buildings since their owners were no longer able to obtain conventional financing for purchase or renovations.[36]

In mid-June Philip Payton hosted a dinner for John Lewis Morris, secretary of the treasury for Liberia, who was spending several weeks in the United States to "protect its interest in the customs and other revenues pledged to guarantee the $1,700,000 American loan."[37] Morris was married to Maude Lyon, the daughter of Ernest Lyon, the U.S. minister to Liberia whom Payton had tried to connect with in England on his way to Liberia in 1910. Most likely they had met during the weeks that Payton spent in

Liberia. The dinner for Lyon's son-in-law was an opportunity for Payton to renew his connections with the little Black Republic, with which he still hoped to do business.[38]

On June 29 newspapers carried the news that on the previous day Archduke Franz Ferdinand, emperor of Austria-Hungary, and his wife, Sophie, duchess of Hohenberg, had been assassinated by a Serbian nationalist during a visit to Sarajevo. Earlier on the same day the archduke had deflected a bomb thrown at their car, but after continuing on to a reception in their honor, they were then on their way to the hospital to visit those injured in the previous attack. It was then that Gavrilo Princip, nineteen years old, ran to their open car and fired two shots that proved fatal.[39] In the following weeks the interlocking defense alliances that European countries had secretly entered into would lead to declarations of war between most European nations, resulting in what became known as the Great War. Even though most people in the United States viewed the European war as "over there" and not a matter for American involvement, the years-long advocacy of black men in Harlem for a National Guard regiment gained new relevance with the prospect of war. In early July the governing board of the 15th Regiment was reorganized, with Philip Payton named to the new board, which included attorney Charles Toney, songwriter Richard C. McPherson (a.k.a. Cecil Mack), Caribbean immigrant Samuel A. Duncan, and Alpha Physical Club cofounder Conrad Norman.[40] The regiment threatened to go to court using the mandamus procedure to compel the adjutant general of the National Guard "to commission the officers and muster in" the Negro regiment.[41]

As the summer of 1914 proceeded, front pages of New York City newspapers shifted from coverage of local incidents, such as a high-society murder trial and the twists and turns of Mexican rebels' incursions along the southern border of the United States, to the war in Europe. While Americans were concerned about the battles in Europe, they maintained a distant interest. Susan Payton spent the month of July vacationing in Hampton, Virginia, and Atlantic City. But the war did have an impact on the United States. At the end of July the New York Stock Exchange and other local exchanges were closed due to instability brought on by the withdrawal of substantial amounts of gold by European countries. By August newspaper front pages were primarily about the war.[42]

With the coming of fall, Philip Payton continued his support of Harlem organizations, serving on the Advisory Committee for the Autumn Exposition and Amusement Festival at Manhattan Casino at 155th Street and Eighth Avenue. An advertisement described the five-day event, from Monday, September 28, through Friday, October 2, as "the most stupendous affair of its kind ever offered to and by colored people." The program included daily screenings of "moving pictures" of the more than 120 exhibits featured at the exposition as well as film of the visitors who had attended on the previous day. The Wednesday evening activities featured the "Greatest Dance Night in New York's History" most likely to the dismay of Rev. Adam Clayton Powell, followed by a "Composer's and Reminiscent Night" on Thursday. Children were the focus of the final day on Friday, with a "Mother Goose Night." The exposition also featured the photographs of "the Chosen Fifteen," the black women from across the country selected as winners of a beauty contest sponsored by the *New York Age*. Winners were primarily women from large cities, such as New York, Boston, and Philadelphia, but women from the smaller locales of Sheridan, Wyoming, and Oakland, California, were also represented.[43]

In October Payton demonstrated his support of Harlem youth by sponsoring a children's block party on 134th Street between Fifth and Lenox Avenues, the block where his office was located. The Saturday afternoon event came together after

> fifty written and as many verbal invitations were issued to the children of 134th street ... and nearly one hundred of the little ones participated in the festivities. The afternoon went pleasantly with music, recitations, and games. Refreshments consisting of sandwiches, ice cream and cake, candies and soda were served. At the close, the awarding to each child of a variety of wrapped favors by numbers, created intense interest. Miss Susan Payton, assisted by Mrs. P. L. Denney and Miss Carman St. Clair, looked after the entertainment of the little ones.[44]

The ability to send personal invitations to the children who attended the block party reflects the fact that Philip Payton was clearly a neighborhood fixture. With his office on 134th Street for over a decade, he undoubtedly knew the parents of the children, and these parents may have made their children aware of the man whose activities were still occasionally chronicled in the local newspapers.

In November Payton and other black real estate dealers who may have been prevented from purchasing properties because of racial restrictive covenants had a reason for optimism when the Advisory Council of Real Estate Interests announced the formation of a special committee to investigate "the question of restrictive covenants as they apply to real estate in New York City," which the committee stated are a "source of annoyance to all real estate men." Unfortunately for the black brokers, the committee's focus was specifically on covenants that prohibited certain types of properties from being built, such as apartment buildings in areas of lower-density homes, or prevented certain business uses in particular properties. The committee made no mention of an interest in racial restrictive covenants that restricted who could own or occupy a property.[45]

At the beginning of December the National League for Urban Conditions Among Negroes held its second public meeting at Bethel A.M.E. Church at 132nd Street in Harlem. The keynote speaker, scholar Felix Adler, focused his remarks on the war in Europe and noted that the "deep underlying cause of this war is that all these nations in Europe are contending together to determine which shall have the power to rule the black and yellow races of Asia and Africa." Using the Philippines as an example, he recommended that these nations should be prepared for self-government. Philip Payton does not seem to have been in attendance at this meeting, but several people who were in Booker T. Washington's circle were. Major Robert Russa Moton, an administrator at Hampton Institute, the Wizard's alma mater, provided remarks encouraging the "cooperation between the best elements of both races in dealing with the problems of Negroes in cities." To affirm this optimistic message he sang "Jacob's Ladder," which includes the lyric "every round goes higher, higher." The league's associate director, Eugene Kinckle Jones noted the progress the league had made since 1910, with its annual budget growing from $2,000 to $20,000 and with headquarters in New York, a housing bureau in Harlem, and a branch in Brooklyn. One of the local programs he highlighted was the organization of public porters, elevator men, chauffeurs, and mechanics into "associations which can better deal with their own interests and which tend to raise the standards of their members."[46]

In the coming years Philip Payton would face new challenges from black entrepreneurs traveling the real estate paths he had blazed a decade earlier. White resistance to the growing black population would continue, but Payton would continue to use the media to shape his personal and professional images, and this strategy would result in tangible benefits for him as the nation entered the years of the Great War.

Chapter Seven

THE LAST BIG DEAL

The Great War was on the mind of many as New Yorkers gathered on New Year's Eve to celebrate the coming of 1915. Nevertheless celebrations proceeded, although many included symbols related to the conflict. The writer of the *New York Times* account of the celebrations could not resist generous allusions to the war: "The influence of war was apparent in the souvenirs that were distributed at hotels and restaurants. Besides iron crosses, miniature submarines, airships and similar warlike decorations, there were military paper hats, which crowned most of the homeward bound bacchanalians." As had been the case since 1906, "Times Square and the district just north of it were centres of revelry. Not that there were no cafes elsewhere which kept open till daybreak, but most of the all-nighters buzzed about from one to another of the cafes in the central zone of the hostilities."[1] The *Times* reported on the front page of its January 1 edition the midnight assumption of duties by the state's new governor, Charles S. Whitman, former district attorney of New York County. An account of fighting on the Eastern and Western Fronts indicated a "belligerent Europe, after five months of war, fighting as sternly as at the beginning, but seemingly without prospects of immediate big victories." More than a year before the United States would enter the war as an adversary to Germany, Kaiser Wilhelm telegraphed to President Woodrow Wilson, his "wishes for a happy New Year." As 1914 came to a close, the U.S. Senate had voted 47 to 12 to retain a literary test provision in a bill restricting immigration, and 29 to 25 to add "black or African race" to the list of persons excluded from the country under an immigration bill tightening entry, a response to the Great War.[2]

A view of the advertisements in a January 7 edition of Philip Payton's paper of record, the *New York Age*, provided some indication of where Payton and his firm were positioned in the real estate firmament as 1915 began. The one-column, one-inch advertisement for Philip Payton Jr. Co. "Real Estate & Insurance" listed one apartment at 30 West 135th Street, "Hot Water Supply," "6 Rooms, Rent $23." By 1915 Payton's past successes in the real estate field had inspired a cadre of black and some white competitors. The rise of Payton's protégés John Nail and Henry Parker could be seen in a two-column, two-inch ad for Nail & Parker, Agents, listing an apartment on West 98th Street and five in Harlem, as well as a private home for rent on West 133rd Street. A two-column, one-inch advertisement by Robert Ladson and Ralph Langston's firm Ladson & Langston listed a five-room apartment on 132nd Street as well as "private houses for sale or rent." Clarence Hutchinson's firm, C. E. Hutchinson, had a two-column, three-inch advertisement listing five Harlem apartments for rent as well as "Private Houses—Rent, Lease or for Sale." In addition to the agents with properties in Harlem, others used the *New York Age* to bring their properties in other parts of Manhattan to the attention of black readers, as Philip Payton sometimes did. C. M. Folsom pushed three apartments at 674 Third Avenue, near 43rd Street, for "refined colored tenants of good references and character" in a one-column, two-inch advertisement. Four-room apartments at 329 West 39th Street in the old Tenderloin black community were offered by Joseph Levy & Sons in a two-column, one-inch advertisement.[3] While Philip Payton remained on the real estate scene, he was clearly just one player, with a relatively modest profile now, among an array of new and old firms, some of which were larger than his. But with a flourish, he would show that he was still a force to be reckoned with by announcing the largest deal of his career.

By 1915 Philip and Maggie Payton were maintaining separate households. Maggie remained at the townhouse at 13 West 131st Street the couple had purchased in 1903, in a household that included her eighteen-year-old niece Bessie Hobby and her seventeen-year-old nephew Duke Hobby. As was common with many Harlem residents grappling with covering the high cost of housing during the World War I years, they were joined by African American

THE LAST BIG DEAL

FIGURE 7.1 Philip A. Payton Jr. *Source*: Photographs and Prints Division, Schomburg Center for Research in Black Culture, New York Public Library.

lodgers Henry Karney, a thirty-three-year-old railroad messenger, and his wife, Lula, a registered nurse. Marion Woodson, a thirty-year-old real estate clerk (possibly employed by Payton) was listed as the head of a separate household, suggesting that he may have occupied a separate apartment in the home. Three blocks away, Philip Payton had established a separate household in the apartment building where his office was located at 67 West 134th Street. There he lived with his, mother Anna, then seventy-one, who spent part of the year in New York, and his sister, Susan, who had left her teaching job and was then working as a bookkeeper, possibly for Payton.[4]

From August 18 through 20, 1915, the National Negro Business League returned to Boston, the site of its founding meeting in 1900, for its annual meeting. The report of the meeting proceedings illustrated the importance of the league as a vehicle to make manifest the core philosophies of its founder and leader, Booker T. Washington:

> Think of it. Within the comparatively brief period of fifteen years, under the wise leadership of this great man, Dr. Booker T. Washington, acting through the medium of the National Negro Business League and its numerous local branches, ten thousand Negro business missionaries have been peacefully mobilized and commissioned to preach, in their respective communities, by example as well as by precept, the Race-redeeming and respect-commanding doctrine of economy, thrift, home and farm ownership, industrial and business enterprise.[5]

In the fifteen year since its founding, the NNBL had grown to a network of six hundred chapters in cities and towns across the nation. In the meeting's opening session on the evening of Wednesday, August 18, at Boston's Symphony Hall before "a mixed audience of about five thousand people," following Washington's opening remarks on the organization's achievement, Charles H. Moore, national organizer of local leagues, reflected on the climate of the nation:

> I regret that since our last meeting the number of lynchings in this country for a given six months' period has increased rather than decreased. Strikingly suggestive is the fact that while the number of black people lynched has decreased, the number of white people lynched has increased. But no matter what the color of the man may be who is lynched, we as American citizens and as business men will not perform our duty until we exercise every iota of power and influence that is ours against the lynching of human beings for any cause.[6]

The proceedings on August 19 were devoted to presentations by industry category of the National Negro Funeral Directors' Association, the National Negro Insurance Association, the National Negro Press Association, and the National Bar Association. Black real estate professionals were not then represented by a national organization. Instead, Frank Howard and George E. Beckett made remarks on their real estate activities in Providence, Rhode Island. Emmett Scott, who was chairing the session, thanked the men for their remarks and then noted that "we have with us this morning three young men hailing from three of the leading cities of this country who operate as real estate dealers or brokers just exactly as white men do, on the largest possible scale." He then asked Watt Terry of Brockton, Massachusetts, E. C. Brown of Philadelphia, and Philip Payton of New York to come forward and offer remarks. Surveying the audience, and perhaps thinking back to how far he and the organization had come since their initial meeting in Boston in 1900, Payton, a life member of the NNBL, stated:

> I have often thought and still believe that probably in years to come when our honored President and perhaps the rest of us, shall have gone hence, the organization of the National Negro Business League and the good which has followed in its train, will be considered as Dr. Washington's greatest work. I am sure that any number of young men during the past fifteen or sixteen years have received inspiration from this League and its numerous branch local leagues, which has started them out in various lines of business endeavor and many of them have made and are making an enviable record of success and winning a name for themselves as well as for our race. It is from the small beginning that the large result frequently comes.[7]

The progress of businesses in the fifteen years since the first meeting, which coincided with the professional career of Philip Payton, was surveyed in the Report of the Committee of Resolutions and Declarations:

In 1900, when the National Negro Business League was organized there were approximately 20,000 Negro business enterprises,—now there are over 45,000.
In 1900, there were two Negro Banks now there are 51.
In 1900, Negroes were operating 250 Drug Stores, now they have 695.
In 1900, there were 450 Undertaking Establishments run by Negroes, now they have about 1,000.
In 1900, there were 149 Negro Merchants engaged in wholesale business, now there are 240.
Fifteen years ago, there were only 10,000 Negro Retail Merchants, now there are 25,000.[8]

For Payton, rather than a steady upward trajectory, the fifteen-year period since 1900 had been a roller-coaster ride. He had arrived in New York in 1899 with not much more than most black men coming to the city had. He had worked menial jobs and, then after a relatively short period, began his work in the real estate field and experienced quick and steady success on an upward trajectory for a few years, until the lawsuit from his investors stalled his progress and led to a downward slide that he was still on even as he had reflected on the NNBL's years of progress. After the meeting he returned to New York, a city in which in 1915 he had recorded not even one purchase or sale of property so far.

On November 15, 1915, Americans awakened to the stunning news that Booker T. Washington was dead. Washington and his wife, Margaret Murray Washington, had traveled to New York several weeks earlier, where he received treatment for arterial sclerosis at the Rockefeller Institute before being transferred to St. Luke's Hospital. There he had rallied briefly but then begun to decline. When the doctors delivered the news that he would not recover, on Friday, November 13, Washington, Margaret, and his physician, Dr. John Kenney, boarded a train for his final trip from New York to Tuskegee, arriving at 12:30 a.m. on Sunday morning, November 15, where the party was met by a car that transported them to the grounds of Tuskegee Institute. It was there, in his bed, on the campus that he had begun to build more than thirty years earlier, in the South that he had celebrated as the best choice for black Americans, that Washington died four hours after arriving at his home. He was fifty-nine years old.

The *New York Age* account of Washington's death reminded readers of his common statement, "I was born in the South, and expect to die and be buried in the South." For the person who in his 1895 speech at the Atlanta Cotton Exchange Exposition had encouraged black people to remain in the South by popularizing the phrase "cast down your buckets where you are," the account of his journey to return home to the South to die burnished his legend one last time. In the days after his death, encomiums for Washington were expressed by black and white people from across the country. Steel baron Andrew Carnegie, who had created a $600,000 fund at Tuskegee, the interest of which was to be used specifically to support Washington, noted, "Booker Washington is the combined Moses and Joshua of his people. History is to tell of two Washingtons, the white and the black. One was the father of his country, the other the leader of his race."[9] For Philip Payton, who had been in Washington's orbit for fifteen years, the death represented the extinguishing of the sun, the light that had energized his career for fifteen years, through good and bad times. Washington never cast Payton out, even after the 1908 lawsuit against the Afro-American Realty Company that made clear that Payton had not lived up to the expectations of frugality and straight dealing that Washington promoted for black people. Like the father of the Prodigal Son, after the lawsuit Washington welcomed Payton back to the fold of the men who remained in the Wizard's orbit. In turn, during happier times Philip and Maggie Payton had entertained Washington regularly in the home they once shared, and Payton had frequently joined with his colleagues in hosting public receptions for the Wizard during his sojourns in New York. All this was now in the past. The shadow of Washington's death descended as Payton's public profile was already receding and his fortunes declining.

Funeral services for Washington took place on November 17 at the Tuskegee Institute Chapel and were attended by nearly eight thousand people "of both races and coming from every section of the country." Six pallbearers represented the teachers, alumni, and students of the institute. Over twenty men served as honorary pallbearers, including Washington's right-hand man Emmett Scott, former Louisiana politician P. B. S. Pinchback, Bostonian Dr. Samuel Courtney, friend of Washington from their youth, and insurance magnate Alonzo Herndon of Atlanta. Philip Payton was not included in the list, although in all likelihood he was present for the services. The funeral, "marked by simplicity" began with the Tuskegee choir singing "We Shall Walk Through the Valley and the Shadow of Death," followed by scripture reading, a prayer, two musical selections, announcements by Trustee William G. Wilcox and Tuskegee treasurer Emmett Scott, and concluded with the choir presenting "Still, Still With Thee" by Harriet Beecher Stowe. Washington's remains were interred in a sealed vault of brick constructed by Tuskegee students on a mound adjacent to the institute's chapel.[10]

The year that had begun with commemorations of the fiftieth anniversary of the Civil War victory ended with a business transaction for Philip Payton. He served as broker representing businesswoman Estelle Wilson in the sale of her five-story double flat at 151 West 133rd Street to Dr. Frank Caffey. A resident of Montgomery, Alabama, Caffey was as a physician to boxer Jack Johnson and had trained him for his April 1915 fight against Jess Willard, which had ended in a Johnson loss. It was noted that the purchase of the West 133rd building added to the New York holdings of Dr. Caffey, a black man who spent part of each year in New York. In other matters, Payton's modest philanthropy continued. As the year came to an end, he made a $5.00 donation to the Hope Day Nursery to support its move to 33 West 133rd Street, as noted in the *New York Age*.[11]

The Manhattan celebrations welcoming 1916 were larger than usual, as reported in the *New York Times*:

> New York welcomed the New Year with a celebration which for noise and boisterousness outdid all former efforts. From 10 o'clock last night until early this morning hotels, restaurants, and streets were filled with a record breaking throng.... The coming of the New Year was announced to the throngs in Times Square when a ball, ablaze with electric lights was dropped from the flagpole of the Times building and [lights] in the Times building were turned on.[12]

The account of New Year's revelry was overshadowed, however, by front-page news of the Great War in Europe, which continued unabated. Canada announced an increase in the number of men eligible for overseas service, from 250,000 to 500,000. The British cruiser *Natal* sank in an unnamed port following an "internal explosion" that was reported to have killed up to three hundred of the seven hundred men onboard the ship. In London, King George telegraphed New Year's greetings to French president Raymond Poincare, assuring him that they would ultimately be victorious. Detailed articles outlined negotiations with Austria-Hungary over the sinking of the *Lusitania* passenger ship in 1915 and the November 15 sinking of the Italian liner *Ancona* in the Mediterranean. A brief announcement noted that Kaiser Wilhelm of Germany had called "a great war council" to meet in Berlin on his birthday, January 27.[13]

On the evening of Wednesday, January 12, Philip and Susan Payton and their mother, Annie, spent a pleasant evening attending a program at a neighborhood church. They arrived home to the 134th Street apartment they shared shortly after 11:00 p.m., when Mrs. Payton complained of numbness in her hand and foot. The numbness grew worse, and Mrs. Payton suggested that the symptoms were signs of a stroke. Within half an hour she lost consciousness, which she never regained. Annie Payton died at 7:40 a.m. on January 13. Following the death of Philip Payton Sr., she had spent most of the year in New York living with Philip Jr., although she had maintained her Westfield home, to which she traveled periodically. In New York she had attended St. Mark's Methodist Episcopal Church. On January 15 a prayer service was held for Mrs. Payton at the undertaker J. C. Thomas's chapel at 89 West 134th Street, on the same block where she had lived in New York. On January 17 a service was held at the Westfield Methodist Church. Born in Baltimore during the era of slavery, with her husband Annie had experienced financial success in life and had lived to see her oldest son share in some of those successes, as well as work to overcome many challenges. Her remains were interred in the family plot in Pine Hill cemetery in Westfield, adjacent to those of her sons Edward and James and her husband, Philip Sr.[14] Susan and Philip, the two oldest and the only remaining children of Philip and Annie Payton, returned to the household they shared on West 134th Street and were able to comfort each other through their grief. The generation of their parents was no more, but the lessons they had gained from Philip A. Payton Sr. and Annie M. Ryans Payton, by their examples of perseverance, ambition, and hard work, and their explicit teachings, would remain with the two siblings as a legacy of their parents' lives.

As the year moved into February, there were signs that Philip Payton's business was picking up. In midmonth, serving again as the broker for the investor Estelle Wilson, he sold a five-story apartment building at 28 West 134th Street. At the same time he also sold a five-story apartment building at 672 West End Avenue, between 92nd and 93rd Streets, on behalf of Mrs. A. K. Wright. The February 19 issue of the *Real Estate Record and Builders Guide* provides some indication regarding the breadth of Philip Payton's business activities in 1916 and also hints at financial challenges, as seen in the list of "Mechanic's Liens" filed by craftsmen against property owners for delinquent payment. Six of the seven liens reported listed Philip Payton as the agent for the owners. The owners ranged from Estelle Wilson, for a property at 314 East 34th Street, to Dickie F. Caffey, for a property at 151 West 133rd Street that had been purchased at the end of 1915, and Matilda Minck, whom Payton had represented in a 1913 sale of Tenderloin property, for a property at 33–37 West 138th Street. The mechanic filing the liens was Wolf Cohn, and the lien amounts ranged from $18.25 to $55.00.[15]

Later in February Payton attended a meeting at St. Mark's Methodist Episcopal Church to discuss fundraising for the Booker T. Washington Memorial Fund. Following Washington's death in November 1915, Tuskegee trustees and other Washington supporters had begun an effort to raise

$2 million, with the goal of earmarking $250,000 for a memorial to be placed on the Tuskegee campus, with the balance of the funds to be used for Tuskegee's operations. The African American community was asked to focus on the $250,000 fund by forming state and local fundraising committees. At the St. Mark's meeting, a New York committee was formed, with Rev. Adam Clayton Powell serving as the chairman and James Weldon Johnson as vice chairman. Payton was named to the executive committee of twenty-eight, which included Washington's lieutenant Charles W. Anderson, the Urban League's Eugene Kinckle Jones, real estate brokers John Nail and John Royall, actress Rose McClendon, and Marie C. Lawton, president of the Empire State Federation of Women's Clubs.[16]

Payton continued to be active in the real estate field. In mid-March he obtained a $40,000 mortgage from real estate investor Lizzie W. Wright on a building at 101 East 128th Street, west of Third Avenue. He soon sold the building, and on the same day he sold 6 West 19th Street.[17] In March he attended a dinner for track-and-field champion Howard Drew at the Hof Brau House in Brooklyn. Then competing on the University of Southern California track team, Drew had been a sprinter at the 1912 Olympics in Stockholm, Sweden, but had to withdraw from competition after pulling a muscle in a preliminary heat. It is likely that Payton became acquainted with him through their common Massachusetts links. Born in 1890, Drew grew up in Springfield, ten miles from Payton's hometown of Westfield.[18]

In April another Massachusetts link brought Philip and Susan Payton to the home of Bishop Alexander Walters to attend a reception for newlyweds Dr. H. G. and Eva McKerrow. The couple had been married in the home of Mrs. McKerrow in Boston and were spending their honeymoon in New York before returning to make their home in Worcester, where Dr. McKerrow had a thriving practice. In 1913, at a meeting in Boston of the New England chapter of the National Medical Association, the organization of black physicians, McKerrow had reported on his experiments to cure tuberculosis, possibly another link to Payton, whose brother Edward had died of the disease in 1912. A number of local physicians, other professionals, and their wives were present to honor the newlyweds.[19]

Payton's social calendar remained full in May, with his attendance at a testimonial dinner hosted by the Citizens Club for the vaudeville performer Bert Williams at the Hof Brau House in Brooklyn. Payton most likely came to know Williams through their membership in the Manhattan-based

Equity Congress, the black men's organization that met weekly and was responsible for advocating for, among other things, the appointment of Samuel Battle, the first black police officer in New York City. The Citizens Club, formed in 1914, was a corollary of the Equity Congress, also with a goal of advocating for the equal rights of black people.[20] The impetus for the dinner may have been to provide moral support and to celebrate a new chapter in Williams's life after a time of transition. His longtime performing partner George Walker had died in 1911 after retiring in 1909 due to illness. In 1910 Williams, unable to develop material of interest to producers without his longtime partner, and observing a shift in interest away from black musicals, had signed on as a performer with the Ziegfield Follies, the only black performer in the famous review. At the Brooklyn dinner, attended by over fifty people, Payton was among a who's who of black New York. Speakers included bandleader James Reese Europe, attorney Gilchrist Stewart, and Charles W. Anderson. "Mr. Williams responded in a short address thanking the club and incidentally getting off a few of his inimitable jokes."[21]

A few weeks after the Williams dinner, Philip Payton served on the Reception Committee receiving New York governor Charles Whitman, the keynote speaker at a Manhattan Casino event celebrating Booker T. Washington Day in New York. The event was part of the drive to raise funds for the Booker T. Washington Memorial. In his remarks, to a predominantly black audience, the governor acknowledged the citizenship of African Americans in a way that, if made manifest, would have retired W. E. B. Du Bois's concept of the double-consciousness of a typical black American, who he observed experienced life as "an American, a Negro; two warring ideals in one dark body, whose dogged strength alone keeps it from being torn asunder".[22] "The old dream of a Negro government in another land was a foolish dream . . . you are here, you are part and parcel of America, and there can be no progress in which you are not considered."[23] But even with this optimistic outlook, Governor Whitman acknowledged the "race problem had not been solved, but if the problem had not been solved, Booker T. Washington had made clear the one clear solution, by encouraging the Negro to higher self development."[24]

In addition to acknowledging Washington at the Manhattan Casino event, Governor Whitman announced that he had just issued an order authorizing the long-sought organization of a black regiment of the National Guard. A few weeks later, in July, Philip Payton's nephew, Duke Hobby joined the unit. He was mustered into the 15th Regiment, along with 172 other men comprising Companies B, C, and D, one evening at Lafayette Hall, at 132nd Street and Seventh Avenue. The initial mustering seemed to be for a part-time commitment. An article describing the men noted that the driving force behind the regiment, Colonel William Hayward, stated "that as many of the men already enlisted are employed at irregular hours, he will arrange drills for their convenience."[25]

In mid-November Philip Payton was part of a "representative gathering" of over thirty-five black men who hosted a dinner in honor of Dr. Robert Russa Moton, the new principal of Tuskegee Institute, at the Libya Club on West 131st Street in Harlem. *New York Age* editor Fred Moore served as toastmaster. Washington's former lieutenant Charles W. Anderson and Tuskegee secretary Emmett Scott also made brief remarks. A year after the death of Booker T. Washington, Moton, who had previously been on the faculty at Tuskegee, used the dinner to manage expectations associated with his new position. In brief remarks, he explained that while he looked forward to leading Tuskegee, with the support of its loyal faculty and black and white people across the country, he had no expectation of attempting to occupy Washington's other role as "leader of the Negro race." Those in attendance included musicians J. Rosamond Johnson and James Reese Europe, educators W. S. Scarborough and W. L. Bulkley, real estate broker Henry Parker and his partner John E. Nail, former Afro-American Realty Company attorney Wilford Smith, and minister R. M. Bolden.[26]

As World War I contributed to material shortages and inflation, Harlem rents increased and black tenants responded. At the end of December a front-page *New York Age* article noted:

> The women who reside in the block on West 143rd Street between Seventh and Eighth avenues have made a strong and consistent campaign against exorbitant and unnecessary rentals charged by Harlem real estate agents, not only on that particular block, but throughout the whole neighborhood. Mrs. Daniel J. Rice and Mrs. C. R. Leonard from West 143rd Street, and Mrs. C. DaSilva from West 137th street, all of whom are sufferers from the intolerable high rents, were prime movers in the campaign.

The article described the third of a series of public meetings hosted by the campaign organizers at St. James Presbyterian Church, West 138th Street.

After an opening discussion regarding the crisis by St. James's pastor Rev. Frank Hyder, J. M. Green, and A. M. Robinson, Harlem broker John Royall interjected a harsh critique of the meeting and the campaign, noting that "he had never heard of bettering the conditions of the renting class by providing lower rents for them. Characterizing the whole thing as a foolish idea, he demanded to know why a movement was not started to lower the high cost of living instead of rents, saying that when the high cost of living is reduced, the rent problem will be solved." Royall became increasingly agitated as he denounced the rationale for the meeting, and whether the Presbytery approved of it being held at St. James. "He attributed a political purpose to the movement, declaring it was nothing but a socialistic idea or grafting scheme." Several people challenged him and defended Dr. Hyder and the women campaign organizers. They also admonished Royall for side remarks and laughter about their comments that disrupted the meeting. Philip Payton was not present at the meeting, but in comments submitted in response to a National Urban League Housing Bureau request to brokers for explanations for the rent increases, his perspective compared to Royall's was laconic but practical:

> If misery likes company, the colored people get plenty of it, because rents are being raised all over the city; cause, increased taxes, increased costs of materials and increased cost of coal; the tenants being the party who must pay the cost of upkeep, naturally these increases mean more money from the tenants; remedy is electing to office men who will give an economical government of the city; self-preservation gives owner and agent no alternative but to raise rents when cost of upkeep increases so largely.

The meeting at St. James concluded with the establishment of a committee of nine men and five women "to formulate suggestions to be presented at a future meeting." In spite of his vocal criticism, John Royall was appointed to the committee.[27]

As 1916 came to a close, Philip Payton welcomed a new member to the family. On December 30 his sister, Susan Ann Wesley Payton, married William Hilmon Wortham in the Payton apartment at 67 West 134th Street. Susan was thirty-five, well into what would have been considered "old maid territory" in the 1910s. For her, marriage to William Wortham may have represented an unexpected opportunity for love and companionship, even if their pairing was somewhat unconventional for the time. Wortham, a twenty-nine year-old widower, was six years younger than Susan. A native of Raleigh, North Carolina, he had spent part of his childhood living at the Oxford Orphan Asylum in Fishing Creek Township, North Carolina, but later attended the Bordentown Academy School, a black boarding school in Bordentown, New Jersey, where Susan had once taught. This common link may have led to their acquaintance, but it is also possible that they met on the job. At the time of their marriage, both were working in Payton's real estate office. The wedding was officiated by Rev. William H. Brooks, pastor of St. Mark's Methodist Episcopal Church, then on West 53rd Street, which the Paytons attended. There is no existing newspaper article on the wedding, suggesting that it may have been a low-key affair. While Philip may have been protective of his sister, who was one year older than him, with both of his brothers dead, no biological children, and his niece and nephew living with his estranged wife, Maggie, it is quite possible that he saw in William Wortham a possibility to extend his business to a younger generation in the absence of offspring of his own.[28]

The day after the wedding, New Year's Eve witnessed celebrations welcoming the coming of 1917 that were much more subdued than in previous years. New Year's Eve was on a Sunday, and some people questioned the appropriateness of drinking and celebrating on that day. In addition, "the Anti-Saloon League and others had insisted that they would 'keep a lid on' celebrations."[29] Bars were traditionally not open on Sundays, but on New Year's Eve drinks could be purchased at hotels with a meal. That evening the crowds at Times Square were smaller than in the past, but they rallied before midnight with the dropping of the ball of incandescent lights at the New York Times building and the flashing of lights indicating "1917" to welcome in the New Year.

The Payton family began the New Year with a second wedding in less than a month. On January 11 the Paytons' niece Mary Elizabeth (Bessie) Hobby married Robert Pinkerton Lattimore. In the first decade of the 1900s, Lattimore had been a member of the Smart Set basketball team based in Brooklyn, whose members were described as coming from "a tight knit clique of well-educated, affluent, old-money" African Americans. Lattimore was an attorney, but old money or not, in employment he faced the same barriers that his new brother-in-law, Philip, had faced when he arrived in

New York in 1899. At the time of his marriage, the twenty-eight-year old Lattimore was working as a porter at the Colonial Theater in Brooklyn. One of Payton's initial jobs had been as a porter in a real estate office. But true to his Smart Set roots, Lattimore was ambitious. By 1920 he would be working as an attorney in his own private practice. At the time of the wedding, Bessie, twenty-one years old, was living with Maggie in the Paytons' West 131st Street town house, while Philip Payton lived in the 134th Street apartment, in the same building where his office was located. Although Bessie was Maggie's blood relation, Philip had helped to raise her for almost ten years. The wedding was held at Payton's apartment, and in all likelihood the Paytons set aside whatever differences had led to their separation so that Maggie could launch her niece into married life. The wedding was officiated by Rev. George F. Miller, rector of St. Augustine's Episcopal Church in Brooklyn, possibly a sign of Lattimore's Brooklyn ties. They would make their home on Tompkins Street in that borough.[30]

Philip Payton's charitable and business activities continued to be chronicled in local newspapers. In a February letter to the editor of the *New York Age* describing the increasing popularity of the books on Black culture that he sold, George Young, owner of Young's Book Exchange on West 135th Street in Harlem, highlighted Payton, along with John Nail, as two who "head the list of our friends and well-wishers."[31] In mid-April Payton joined with Freidus & Co., a real estate firm based on Broadway near 149th Street, to broker the sale of 110 West 143rd Street, a six-story apartment building owned by real estate investor Millie Rosenberg. The property was purchased by Aaron Coleman, a real estate investor from South Islip, New York, who traded a five-story loft building at 128 West 26th Street as partial payment.[32]

In May Payton served as a team captain in a citywide campaign in which he joined with a large cohort of prominent black New Yorkers to raise money for Brooklyn's Howard Orphanage. Begun in 1866 by Sarah A. Tillman, the Howard Orphan Asylum was established out of the ashes of Manhattan's Colored Orphan Asylum. Operated by Quaker women, the orphanage had been burned to the ground during the Draft Riots of 1863, the violence directed at black people in response to the drafting of white men during the Civil War. After the riot, with no building, Mrs. Tillman took twenty of the children into her home on 13th Street in Manhattan. On the advice of Freedmen's Bureau head General Oliver Howard, she moved the orphanage to Weeksville, the black community in Brooklyn that had been established in the 1840s. There the orphanage grew with the volunteerism of black women and the contributions from black and white New Yorkers. At the time of the 1917 fundraising campaign, the orphanage had experienced a transition. Its financial challenges had resulted in the ousting of most of the black women who had led the organization. They were replaced by a predominantly white board of managers. The fundraising campaign was very ambitious, with Harlem and Brooklyn teams who met nightly, except on Saturday, to tabulate results. In each area a large flag was awarded to the team that had obtained the highest number of donations that day, and a smaller flag was awarded to the team that had obtained the largest number of pledges.[33] Although he had grown up with two parents, in a stable household of relative privilege, after almost twenty years in New York Philip Payton knew all too well how precarious life could be for a child in the city without parents, or with one parent lacking the means to provide child care. He and Maggie had stepped in to rescue his niece and nephew Bessie and Duke Hobby from such a fate, and he undoubtedly was aware of the role that a home in the Oxford Orphanage in North Carolina had played in the life of his sister's husband, William Wortham.

Philanthropic reports about Payton continued in June with a note of his donation of a large box of Lifebuoy soap to the Women's Auxiliary of the 15th Regiment, the black National Guard regiment that Payton had been instrumental in getting established. The regiment was celebrating its one-year anniversary, and the Women's Auxiliary was hard at work with a series of events that raised cash and in-kind contributions, which the organization used to supplement the support the regiment received from New York State. Payton was in good company. His donation of soap was accompanied by a donation of tobacco and magazines by John B. Nail, the father of real estate broker John E. Nail, a large box of tooth powder and stationery from Fred Moore, editor of the *New York Age*, over seven hundred pencils from the YMCA, and one thousand washcloths from the Lincoln Hospital Alumni Association. The range of donations and the fact that they were needed suggests either that state support for the regiment, even in time of war, was limited or that Harlem residents were anxious to show their support for the regiment they had fought so hard to get formed by supplementing whatever help it did receive from the state.[34]

THE LAST BIG DEAL

War in Europe continued to dominate the front pages of New York's newspapers in the summer of 1917. But the war had led to a cessation in housing production, exacerbating the shortages in apartments that had been a problem in many neighborhoods even before the war began. Black people, who had increasingly limited choices before the war, felt this shortage severely. In late July the *Sun* reported on a major housing development in Harlem:

> While well-meaning white folks, philanthropists, real estate men and others are planning and talking about improving the housing conditions of [N]egroes in this city, the [N]egro himself has set out to solve his own housing problem. He took the first step in this direction last week when he amazed those who have been working in his interest by the purchase of six fine apartment houses on One Hundred and Forty-First and One Hundred and Forty-second streets between Lenox and Seventh avenue[s] ... Mr. Payton, [N]egro real estate man, organized the Philton Realty Company to buy the One Hundred and [Forty-]First and One Hundred and [Forty-]Second-street apartments.[35]

A month later, in a *New York Age* advertisement that spanned two-thirds of a page on August 16, the six-story buildings were pictured on the tree-lined street under the headline, "The World's Finest Housing Proposition" (fig. 7.2). Below was the notation, "Catering Exclusively to Refined Colored Tenants." The bold-faced print of the last three words added special emphasis. On the left side was a photograph of three large Harlem apartment buildings with their names underneath: "Toussaint Court"..."Attucks Court"..."Wheatley Court." On the right side was another large photograph of three more buildings: "Dunbar Court"..."Douglass Court"... "Washington Court." In the center of the advertisement were comments about the buildings from six of the New York daily papers as well as the weekly *Real Estate Record and Guide*, whose reporter wrote: "Most important deal not only on account of the size and cost of the properties involved, but also because it indicates the unusual growth of the Negro section in Harlem."[36] The names of the buildings, drawn from the names of black icons, emphasized that African Americans were the target market for the buildings: Wheatley Court for the Revolutionary-era poet Phillis Wheatley, Toussaint Court for Haitian liberator Toussaint L'Ouverture; Washington

FIGURE 7.2 Payton apartments. Source: New York Age, July 1917.

Court for Booker T. Washington; Dunbar Court for writer Paul Laurence Dunbar; Douglass Court for Frederick Douglass; and Attucks Court for Revolutionary War era martyr Crispus Attucks. The foyer of each building would have a portrait of the person for whom the building was named. Payton's advertisement also used the notion of premium pricing to create an aura of exclusivity: "Only People Able to Furnish Satisfactory Reference as to Character and Standing are Invited to Inspect these Houses as it is Intended that a Tenancy in these Houses shall be Almost Equivalent to a Certificate of Character and a Recommendation as to Responsibility."[37] The *Sun* article in July had contrasted the apartments with earlier charitable housing efforts that white and black reformers had developed to meet the limited incomes of most black New Yorkers: "But there were other families in the [N]egro section who wanted better homes than these houses would provide. They wanted dwelling places as fine as the whites, since they were able to afford them." The article linked these desires with the goals of Philip Payton and his colleagues undertaking the venture:

> They are colored folks, however as far as can be learned, who have entered the company not out of philanthropy, but on a purely commercial basis, that is, to make money. They know to what extent the colored man has profited by the prosperity waves which have been sweeping over the United States for the last few years. Apparently [N]egroes have met these waves, for they are willing to pay in the new apartment houses a rental of $10 a room, which means that a four-room flat will cost them $40 a month. The larger apartments will cost them from $60 to $70 a month to rent.[38]

With over three hundred apartments in the six buildings, the complex would make a significant contribution to meeting the demand for quality rental housing. It was Philip Payton's largest deal. His ambitious vision of housing black and white people in quality housing, articulated thirteen years earlier with the launch of the Afro-American Realty Company, by 1917 was just a memory, long overtaken by the scramble to house increasing numbers of black arrivals in New York City, particularly in Harlem. Segregated housing was the custom. Challenging segregated housing and forgoing the high rents that could be charged to black tenants in segregated buildings would have been honorable, but Payton was clearly more committed to maximizing his profits. The half-page advertisement for the Payton apartments continued to run in the *New York Age*, and an August article detailed the apartments and their homage to African American icons. The ambitious scale of the development, its location well outside the concentration of black residency in the streets numbered in the 130s, and its exclusivity kept Philip Payton in the public eye with a deal that represented his return to leadership of the Harlem real estate scene.

Following the pattern of many middle- and upper-middle-class people in the Northeast, Payton spent the summer of 1917 at the Jersey shore in Allenhurst, a community of Victorian homes on tree-lined streets along the Atlantic Ocean. In all likelihood Susan and her husband joined him there, and perhaps Bessie and her husband visited periodically. Since his separation from Maggie continued, she did not visit. As the summer came to a close, the August 30 edition of the *New York Age* carried a brief notice: "Philip A.

Payton is under the care of a doctor and nurse at his summer home at Allenhurst, N.J., and will not be able to be out for at least two weeks."[39]

But by the time the notice appeared, Philip Payton was dead. He had died the day before, on August 29. When the information reached the black community, the reaction was one of shock mixed with grief, particularly given the somewhat hopeful tone of the *Age* notice. In reality, as he had for the previous fifteen years, Payton had skillfully managed his image to the end. The symptoms of the liver cancer that took his life most likely appeared months before he died. Even as he assembled what would become his last big deal, the apartments on West 141st and West 142nd Streets, he was probably already experiencing some of the symptoms: loss of appetite and weight, abdominal pain, nausea and vomiting, dark urine, and weakness and fatigue. The majority of people diagnosed with liver cancer at that time died within a year, suggesting that during much of 1917 Payton may have known that he was ill. But there may have been limits to what he knew. In the early twentieth century it was common practice for physicians to withhold information on the terminal nature of diseases from their patients, assuming that the knowledge would inspire a mental state in the patient that would accelerate their demise. While Payton's physician may have diagnosed the liver cancer, surgery to remove cancerous portions of the liver were at an experimental stage in 1917, with unpromising results. The treatment offered to Payton most likely focused on limiting the discomfort from his symptoms. Susan Payton Wortham informed his good friend Emmett Scott, traveling in Chicago in late August, that "it is going to be some time before he [Payton] is up and about." In the same letter she hinted at the severity of Philip's illness. "He is completely out of commission—stomach, liver, kidneys, nerves."[40]

On the evening of Wednesday, August 29, Susan was at Philip's bedside. As it became apparent that the end was near, Payton attempted to sing "Nearer My God to Thee" but was too weak to continue. Susan, supporting her brother to the end, stepped in and sang a few lines from the hymn. With the reality of the imminent death of her last sibling on her mind, her voice quivered as she sang "Nearer my God to thee, nearer to thee, even though it be a cross that raiseth me."[41] Comparing her singing to that of the Australian operatic soprano Nellie Melba, then at the height of her fame, Philip Payton's last words reflected the humor that he shared with his older sister, from whom he was separated in age by only one year. Even as he faced death, he joked, "Darling, you'll never be a Melba." With that statement, the life of Philip Anthony Payton Jr., forty-one years old, son of Westfield, Massachusetts, founder of the Afro-American Realty Company, Father of Black Harlem, who had made good in New York City, came to an end.[42]

EPILOGUE

Upon the news of Philip Payton's death, tributes came from all parts of the country by telegraph, mail, and letters to editors of black newspapers. The common message honored the pioneering nature of Payton's perseverance to provide housing to black New Yorkers in areas where they had previously been unwelcome, and to the very end his ability to weather setbacks and regroup to win another day.

Payton's funeral took place in New York on Sunday, September 2, at 12:30 p.m., immediately following morning worship services at St. Mark's Methodist Church on West 53rd Street. The description of the funeral in the *New York Age* identified the core element of Payton's fame: "The church was thronged with friends and acquaintances to pay their last respects to the man who made it possible for colored people to rent modern flats in the Harlem section." Civic League members served as pallbearers: William H. Willis, John Earle, J. W. Rose, E. A. Johnson, Charles H. Payne, and attorney Louis Leavelle. Over fifteen men from across the country served as honorary pallbearers, including Payton's good friend Emmett Scott, Brockton, Massachusetts, realtor Watt Terry, and Professor George E. Haynes. The eulogy by St. Mark's pastor Dr. W. H. Brooks reflected a continuation in the shaping of Payton's legacy:

> In 1900 he commenced a business career in this city, being a pioneer in real estate, without experience and without funds, as I heard him relate that he

EPILOGUE

would often walk home from downtown because he did not have the fare and refused to borrow it. He passed away controlling over a quarter of a million [dollars in property]. The story of these seventeen years if put in book form would be as thrilling as "Uncle Tom's Cabin," "Up From Slavery," or Paul Laurence Dunbar's "Lyrics of Lowly Life."

Dr. Brooks reflected on Payton's perseverance, his practice of omitting sentiment from business decisions, his charity, his commitment to his family, and his love of literature. Regarding Payton's faith, Brooks described an afternoon on which he met with Payton and tried to "lead him to an open confession of Christ." He noted that Payton candidly stated he believed in "our Savior, but I have never felt what other Christian people say they feel." To assuage any skeptics in the congregation, Brooks added that Payton always "tried to do right by all." Regarding Payton's work in the world, the pastor did not sidestep the ups and downs that Payton had experienced in his career.

> This man, like the ships, was sometimes high up on the crest of the waves and then seemingly engulfed; there were headwinds and choppy seas and it was necessary to tack but when the tempest lulled he was seen to ride the waves and driving with propelling power of a mighty will towards the object of pursuit. He would not be defeated. He would not be mastered by circumstances. In his pathway there were no Alps. If he could not scale or circumvent them he bore through. He might have said with Paul, "This one thing I do, forgetting the things which are before, 'I press toward the mark.'"[1]

After the service at St. Mark's, Payton's remains were transported to his hometown of Westfield, Massachusetts. The next morning on Monday, September 3, Labor Day, following a service attended by friends from New York, Massachusetts, and other parts of the country, Payton's remains were buried in the family plot in the Pine Hill Cemetery in Westfield, beside those of his parents and his younger brothers, James and Edward.

The *New York Age* account of Payton's funeral noted that his business would continue under the management of the Philip A. Payton Jr. Company. In February 1918 Susan Payton Wortham filed a petition to have Payton's will, executed in 1910, probated. In the petition Maggie Payton renounced her appointment as administrator of the estate, which she had

EPILOGUE

received before being made aware of the will. The two people named in the will as executors, Edward Payton and David I. Reynolds, predeceased Payton; therefore Susan was appointed executor. The probate petition noted that, at his death, Philip Payton owned $25,000 of personal property. Information on real property owned was not noted in the document. The inventory of assets was missing from the probate records. Philip Payton had executed a will on January 25, 1910, before he left on his Liberia trip, most likely aware that some Americans, such as minister Henry Highland Garnet, had died of tropical diseases soon after they arrived in the little Black Republic. Payton's will did not identify his assets in 1910 but instead detailed how his estate was to be distributed. It called for the income from the estate to be distributed annually, with Maggie receiving one-half, his mother receiving one-fourth, and Edward and Susan receiving one-eighth each. The will included contingencies in the case of deaths prior to the will being probated. While income from the estate was provided to Maggie, no contingency would have resulted in her receiving the assets of the estate, perhaps reflecting the tension between the couple that would later become public when they began living apart. The will called for the assets of the estate to ultimately be divided between Duke and Bessie Hobby and Edward and Susan Payton.[2]

Rather than the Philip A. Payton Jr. Company, the Massachusetts real estate broker Watt Terry took over the marketing of the six buildings on West 141st and West 142nd Streets following Payton's death, offering advertisements with the headlines of "Only a Few More Left!" and "Rents Reduced," perhaps addressing potential tenants' concerns regarding the rents. As I noted in *Race and Real Estate: Conflict and Cooperation in Harlem, 1890 to 1920*:

> Although the advertisements by both Payton and Terry suggested that they had purchased the buildings, during the time from 1917 into 1918, when their advertisements were promoting the buildings for African Americans, the buildings were actually owned by 135 Holding Corporation, a company formed in 1915. The principals of the corporation were five white men—Cyril H. Burdett, Frank L. Cooke, Gerhard Kuehne, Floyd W. Davis, and Leo Schloss— who lived in Manhattan, Brooklyn, and New Jersey.... Three of the men were senior officials with New York Title and Mortgage Company.[3]

EPILOGUE

The news articles in the spring and summer of 1917 that had announced Payton's purchase of the buildings indicate that he understood the power of the Payton brand in Harlem, and that he was depending on the average person not consulting the public record to determine the actual owner of the buildings, which became known as the Payton Apartments even when Terry assumed management of the buildings. "This [Payton] 'brand' recognition would have been important to the 135 Broadway Holding Corporation in leasing the six buildings to blacks at relatively high rents (Payton's advertisements listed apartments of three rooms to six rooms with monthly rents from $26 to $52)."[4] In the same August 1917 issue of the *New York Age* that advertised the Payton apartments, John Royall advertised five-room apartments at 38 West 136th Street for $28 and $29 per month and four-, five-, and six-room apartments at 240 West 143rd Street for $24 to $34 per month. "While 135 Broadway Holding Corporation would likely have been viewed by many potential African American tenants as white exploiters, Payton's advertisements emphasized the opening of deluxe housing for the first time to blacks who had previously been deprived of these accommodations."[5] In October 1918 the Payton name was formally affiliated with the Payton Apartments and black owners when the buildings were purchased by the Payton Apartments Corporation, led by E. C. Brown, a black real estate investor and banker from Philadelphia, and Andrew F. Stevens, also of Philadelphia, where he was Brown's partner in the firm Brown and Stevens. The men had recently expanded their investment purview to New York. Neither William Wortham nor the Philip A. Payton Jr. Company was among the initial shareholders of the Apartments Corporation.[6]

In reviving the Payton Apartments deal as an exclusive residence for black tenants, Terry, Brown, and Stevens were following what was by then a well-trod path for Harlem real estate dealers, blazed by Philip Payton, for navigating the trail of racial capitalism. Because of their race, these black real estate dealers had a limited selection of routes to pursue, but Payton had demonstrated that the one leading to segregated housing for black residents, while not risk-free, had the potential for maximizing their profits in an environment of scarce choices and limited capital opportunities. In theory they and Philip Payton could have pursued another path. Consider the possible outcomes that could have unfolded if Payton had executed his 1904 vision of black and white people living in the same buildings. In the first Harlem buildings that he gained control of after announcing the incorporation of the Afro-American Realty Company, he would have rented apartments in the same buildings to black and to white people at comparable rents. The following are some possible outcomes:

- Scenario 1: White and black tenants would have lived in these buildings, with black residents attracted by the rents that would have been lower than in other buildings in Harlem then available to them. Because of the lower rents he was charging, Payton's company would have had a lower profit margin than the margins of white-owned buildings in which black residents were segregated (there were no comparable black competitors in Harlem in 1904). Over the long run, because of this lower profit margin, Payton may have had more problems attracting investors because of his inability to provide competitive dividends (something he actually experienced even with his segregated buildings), and the fact that his potential investors would likely be limited to black people, a group with limited wealth. Because of a lack of capital, he would not have been able to grow his business at the same rate as his competitors, who would have more accumulated capital because of their higher profits.
- Scenario 2: It is also possible that the demand from black renters for apartments at competitive rents in his buildings with black and white tenants could have made it possible for Payton to rent more buildings and, through volume, match the net revenue of his competitors.
- Scenario 3: While white tenants did occasionally live in the same buildings as black tenants in Harlem before 1904, when the numbers of black residents in Harlem was small, it is possible that if Philip Payton had intentionally adopted this practice, as the number of black residents in Harlem grew over the next decade and the hostility against black residents increased, white tenants who had not been hostile to blacks before may have been influenced by their white peers and the press to become hostile, and therefore uncomfortable with living with black residents in the same buildings. This is the process of differentiation within capitalism described by Gargi Bhatcharyya in *Rethinking Racial Capitalism: Questions of Reproduction and Survival* as a characteristic of racial capitalism. In the buildings where black and white people lived together before 1904, the white residents and black residents minimized the differences between one another and lived in the same buildings, and in some cases the same apartments. After 1904 in Harlem there was a concerted campaign, initially spurred by the Hudson Realty Company and taken up by the white media and some white Harlem residents, to portray black people as vectors of crime and disease and threats to property values. Under this

EPILOGUE

scenario, even if Payton wanted to rent to both white and black tenants, white tenants viewing themselves as fundamentally different from and superior to black tenants would have been uninterested in remaining in these buildings or even on blocks with all-black buildings.[7]

Because scenario 3 describes the outcome that resulted in the segregated Harlem with which we are familiar, this outcome might be considered foreordained. A Harlem with buildings occupied by black and white people would have required Payton to pursue a different business model. Creation of the Afro-American Realty Company was a strategy he followed to use race pride as a business model for attracting investors and then customers, at a time when blackness was not considered a positive attribute by many people, black or white. This race pride allowed Payton to attract the attention of black investors and the black press and to be accepted into the inner circle of Booker T. Washington, the man recognized by many as the leader of black people in 1904. In the AARC prospectus, Payton's reference in the Afro-American Realty Company prospectus and in later public statements to working to facilitate black and white people living in the same building is an admirable, and for that time even visionary, goal, but it was framed as an outcome to benefit the black people who would have access to the quality housing that had only previously been available to white residents. The benefit of hindsight allows one to recognize that Payton could have instead positioned his company as one that would benefit black and white people. By promoting a model of housing in which black and white people lived together, the disruption that white Harlem residents experienced as the Afro-American Realty Company prospered and they were evicted from buildings that Payton "opened" to black tenants would have been avoided. It is possible that the restrictive covenant movement, a backlash to Payton's evictions of white tenants and to the creation of all-black buildings, may not have been able to generate sufficient momentum, driven in part by the anger of evicted white tenants. For white tenants to remain in buildings as black tenants were introduced, Payton would have needed to counter the negative media images of black people with a campaign of his own, perhaps promoting the class status of black renters as he did in his last big deal, or instead highlight the affordability of his buildings to potential black renters and perhaps the progressive aspects of multiracial living to current or potential white renters. Such a plan seems within the realm of possibility to such a media master as Philip Payton. To undertake this strategy, a race-neutral company name, such as the Harlem Realty Company, would have been necessary. It is not surprising that Payton did not pursue this strategy. It would have been a high-risk choice at a time when there was no evidence that it would succeed and many examples that the less risky, dependable profits available by promoting segregated housing to black residents could.

Race enterprises such as the Afro-American Realty Company have been and can be successful, but because their very existence often depends on the exploitation of the fact of racial inequality, providing services to people whom the market has ignored or underserved, these successful businesses exist as islands in the floodwaters of capitalism. They often succeed as long as the market's levees of racial difference that made serving their customers an unattractive or unrecognized proposition are maintained. But sometimes white business owners compete with race enterprises by creating the illusion that they are black-owned and use the advantage of greater access to capital to outcompete race enterprises. Sometimes the illusion is not necessary and white-owned companies, to attract black customers, rely on the legacy of the racial hierarchy exemplified by the black folk saying that "the white man's ice is colder" and the desirability of whiteness that cannot help but be internalized by black people living in a society in which whiteness is supreme. When the levees that protect race enterprises from white competitors are breached, sometimes ironically by the victories against racial inequality, such as during the era of civil rights desegregation that occurred fifty years after Payton's death, the floodwaters of the market overflow the islands of race enterprises and they are subsumed in the flood of capitalism. Philip Payton was long dead when this process unfolded for the black real estate industry in Harlem in the 2000s. Downtown real estate brokers opened Harlem offices, white development companies competed to acquire scarce remaining vacant land, New York pushed through a rezoning plan to shepherd in high-rise developments on 125th Street, the main commercial thoroughfare in the neighborhood, and rising housing prices pushed out some longtime black residents.[8]

In the decades following Payton's death, the townhouse at 13 West 131st Street, which he and Maggie had purchased in 1903, and the block on which it was located, between Lenox and Fifth Avenues, went through transformations illustrative of the changes taking place in Black Harlem. Maggie sold the building in 1919, after which it changed hands several times. West 131st Street was a few blocks away from many of the entertainment venues of the Harlem Renaissance, the arts movement of the 1920s that would not have been centered in Harlem without the thousands of black people concentrated there, in some measure due to Philip Payton's work two decades before. During the renaissance, the former Payton home was just across Harlem from Niggerati Manor, the brownstone hangout of Langston Hughes, Richard Bruce Nugent, Zora Neale Hurston, and Wallace Thurman chronicled in Thurman's 1932 roman à clef novel *Infants of the Spring*. By the time the novel appeared, Harlem was in the midst of the Great Depression. In 1927, 13 West 131st Street appeared in the news when four trunks of stolen fur coats and dresses were found in its basement, having been mailed to the address from Boston. Resident Anna Pendleton and Melissa Clark, owner of a beauty parlor on West 143rd Street, were arrested.[9] As Harlem residents navigated the economic nadir of the Depression, during which unemployment in the community rose to 50 percent, most owners of the townhouses on the street either took in roomers or renovated their buildings into rooming houses. The apartment houses in the block were densely occupied, as low-paid or unemployed residents doubled up and tripled up to make their wages stretch.

Harlem and the nation emerged from the Depression only through the economic demands that came with mobilization for World War II. While the increase in employment opportunities was welcome, the next wave of migration of black people to New York, steered to racially segregated Harlem, led to a new wave of overcrowding and problems, punctuated by a race riot in 1943 on Eighth Avenue and 125th Street, sparked by a confrontation between a white police officer and a black soldier. In *Notes of a Native Son*, James Baldwin described the aftermath he surveyed as the funeral procession for his father, who had died on the day of the riot, moved through the streets of Harlem: "On the morning of August 3rd we drove my father to the graveyard through a wilderness of smashed plate glass. . . . As we drove him to the graveyard, the spoils of injustice, anarchy, discontent, and hatred were all around us."[10]

During the 1950s and 1960s, as black residents agitated first for integrated schools and then for community control of schools, many middle-class black Harlem residents took advantage of the civil rights victories and moved out of Harlem either to the Bronx, to Westchester County, or to New Jersey. The Arab oil embargo of the 1970s led to massive housing abandonment in New York. Like thousands of buildings across the city, many of the buildings on West 131st Street were abandoned, including 13 West 131st Street. Although most of these buildings became the property of the city under a law that allowed it to take over ownership of tax- and/or utility-payment-delinquent buildings after several years, 13 West 131st, though empty, was purchased in the 1980s by Robert Pugh, the owner of a monument company. In the 1990s the Abyssinian Development Corporation, an affiliate of the Abyssinian Baptist Church, centered several of its first real estate developments on West 131st Street, including a new one-hundred-unit senior citizens building, renovation of an apartment building and two adjacent brownstones into moderate-income condominiums, and renovation of five brownstones on the south side of the street and an apartment building at 28–30 West 131st Street into low-income rental apartments. Pugh had hoped to renovate the Payton townhouse and move there from the large apartment in the Bronx that he shared with his wife. As he entered his late sixties, however, his wife was wary of this plan, so the building remained vacant until it was purchased in the early 2000s. As Harlem became more attractive to higher-income blacks and whites in the late 1990s and early 2000s, private investment in the area was seen on many of the blocks and avenues of the community. Payton's former home was part of this trend and was fully renovated into several apartments.[11]

In 1920, after Maggie Payton sold 13 West 131st Street, she rented an apartment at 2184 Fifth Avenue near 135th Street, which she shared with two roomers, Louis Patterson, a hotel cook, and Harold Peace, a clerk. In 1930 Maggie and Duke Hobby were living in a home valued at $5,000 in Clarkstown, Rockland County, New York, twenty-eight miles north of their previous home. Maggie operated a laundry, and Duke worked as a laborer. Duke was no longer living with Maggie in Clarkstown in 1940, but James L. Kingsland, a postal clerk, was a lodger in the home. Sometime after 1940 he and Maggie seem to have married, and Maggie left behind the diminutive of her first name that she had used since her birth and adopted the more matronly name of Margaret. By 1950 Margaret Kingsland had restored her household, joined by her niece Bessie Hobby Lattimore, Bessie's daughter Evelyn Forster, and her grandchildren Cecil and Sandra Forster. Margaret Payton Kingsland died in 1956.[12]

After Philip Payton's death in 1917, his brother-in-law, William H. Wortham, assumed leadership of the Philip A. Payton Jr. Company and soon became a business leader in Harlem. He and Susan moved to an apartment at 130 West 142nd Street in one of the six buildings that had been part of Philip Payton's last big deal. By 1920 they were joined by Susan's two-year-old cousin, Philip A. Payton of North Carolina, and William's twelve-year old niece, Sadie Wortham. As Harlem weathered the Depression, marked by the 1935 civil disturbance on 125th Street that was sparked by the detention of a young shoplifter in a department store, Wortham continued to lead the Payton Company and to serve on the boards of directors of several other black enterprises, including Congamond Holding Company and the Supreme Liberty Life Insurance Company of Chicago. Susan Payton Wortham died in 1953 and was lauded for her civic work and her participation in various organizations of St Mark's Methodist Church, which in 1926 had built an impressive building in Harlem at Edgecombe and West 137th Street. Her remains were interred in the family plot in Westfield, completing the reassembling of the remains of the nuclear family of Philip A. Payton Sr. and Annie Ryans Payton.[13]

William Wortham, who survived Susan, became the keeper of the Payton legacy. When he died in 1958, he was also buried in the Payton family plot. For anyone seeking the final resting place of the remains of Philip Payton, the Payton family plot is easy to find in the Pine Hill Cemetery in Westfield, Massachusetts. The cemetery is in the middle of the town. Its curving roadways and shade trees serve as a testament to the nineteenth-century belief that cemeteries could be enjoyed as parks for the living as well as monuments to the dead. Not far into the cemetery, near a curve in the road, is the large family plot that reunited in death the remains of Philip Anthony Payton Jr. and those of his siblings, parents, and brother-in-law. Individual six-by-twelve-inch stones lie along the ground, marking the exact location of the individual graves, with "Mother and "Father" designating the parents and the names of each child designating the location of their

EPILOGUE

FIGURE E.1 Payton gravesite monument. *Source:* Author's collection.

remains. William Wortham's grave is not similarly marked, which is ironic since he was most likely responsible for the addition of a large monument in the center of the plot that leaves no doubt regarding the achievements of those buried there. Approximately eight feet wide and three feet high, the stone contains more complete information on the names and birth and death dates of all the Paytons. The middle of the stone has a pediment that rises a foot higher than the wings on both sides. Near its top are the initials P * A* P, the logo of the Philip A. Payton Jr. Company that graced the buildings managed by the company. Beneath the Payton logo, under an engraving of a classical valance, is the initial W. On the left side of the monument, under the name Wortham, the birth and death dates of Susan Payton Wortham, June 15, 1875–January 6, 1953, are listed. On the reverse side of the monument are the names of James Warren Payton, July 30, 1877–October 15, 1902, and Edward Payton, September 19, 1882–June 23, 1912. As evidence of the importance of their college educations to the family, under their names are their college graduation years, Yale 1900, Yale 1906. With the words of Payton's contemporary Paul Laurence Dunbar, the base of the stone provides a final testament to the seventeen-year flurry of business activity that marked the short but remarkable life of Philip Anthony Payton Jr.: "Beyond the years the soul shall find the endless peace for which it pined."[14]

EPILOGUE

BEYOND THE YEARS[15]

Paul Laurence Dunbar—1872–1906

I

Beyond the years the answer lies,
Beyond where brood the grieving skies
    And Night drops tears.
Where Faith rod-chastened smiles to rise
    And doff its fears,
And carping Sorrow pines and dies—
    Beyond the years.

II

Beyond the years the prayer for rest
Shall beat no more within the breast;
    The darkness clears,
And Morn perched on the mountain's crest
    Her form uprears—
The day that is to come is best,
    Beyond the years.

III

Beyond the years the soul shall find
That endless peace for which it pined,
    For light appears,
And to the eyes that still were blind
    With blood and tears,
Their sight shall come all unconfined
    Beyond the years.

NOTES

INTRODUCTION

1. Booker T. Washington, *The Negro in Business* (Chicago: Hertel & Jenkins, 1907), 197–205.
2. Afro-American Realty Company, Prospectus, July 1904, 3–4.
3. "Negro Invasion Threat Angers Flat Dwellers," *New York Times*, July 27, 1906; John H. Hewitt, Jr., *Protest and Progress: New York's First Black Episcopal Church Fights Racism* (2000; New York: Routledge, 2018), 138–40.
4. Gargi Bhatcharyya, *Rethinking Racial Capitalism: Questions of Reproduction and Survival* (New York: Rowman and Littlefield, 2018), ix–16.
5. Washington, *The Negro in Business*, 205.
6. James Weldon Johnson, *Black Manhattan* (1930; Cambridge, Mass.: DeCapo Press, 1991); Gilbert Osofsky, *Harlem, the Making of a Ghetto: Negro New York, 1890–1930* (1966; Chicago: Ivan R. Dee, 1996), 92–104.
7. Kevin McGruder, *Race and Real Estate: Conflict and Cooperation in Harlem, 1890–1920* (New York: Columbia University Press, 2015); Shannon King, *Whose Harlem Is This, Anyway? Community Politics and Grassroots Activism During the New Negro Era* (New York: New York University Press, 2015); Brian Goldstein, *The Roots of Urban Renaissance: Gentrification and the Struggle Over Harlem* (Cambridge, Mass.: Harvard University Press, 2017).
8. Shennette Garret-Scott, *Banking on Freedom: Black Women in U.S. Finance Before the New Deal* (New York: Columbia University Press, 2019), 5.
9. Brandon K. Winford, *John Hervey Wheeler, Black Banking, and the Economic Struggle for Civil Rights* (Lexington: University Press of Kentucky, 2020).
10. David Freund, *Colored Property: State Policy and White Racial Politics in Suburban America* (Chicago: University of Chicago Press, 2007); Keeanga-Yamahtta Taylor,

INTRODUCTION

Race for Profit: How Banks and the Real Estate Industry Undermined Black Homeownership (Chapel Hill: University of North Carolina Press, 2019).
11. "Father of Harlem," *New York Age*, September 6, 1917; "Chief Points of Interest in Upper Manhattan," Automobile Club of Rochester, N.Y., 1920; Jonathan Gill, *Harlem: The Four Hundred Year History from Dutch Village to Capital of Black America* (New York: Grove Press, 2011), 1–130; McGruder, *Race and Real Estate*, 35–39.
12. David Levering Lewis, *When Harlem Was in Vogue* (New York: Penguin, 1997), 119–55.
13. Afro-American Realty Company, Prospectus, 5.

1. THE PAYTONS BEFORE AND IN WESTFIELD

1. Booker T. Washington, *The Negro in Business* (Chicago: Hertel & Jenkins, 1907), 197–205.
2. Louis Van Camp, *Washington, North Carolina* (Mt. Pleasant, S.C.: Arcadia, 2000), 7; U.S. State Department, *Compendium of the Enumeration of Inhabitants and Statistics of the United States as Obtained at the Department of State from the Returns of the Sixth Census* (Washington, D.C.: Department of State, 1841), 40–42.
3. Donald Richard Deskins, Hanes Walton, and Sherman C. Puckett, *Presidential Elections, 1789–2008: County, State, and National Mapping of Election Data* (Ann Arbor: University of Michigan Press, 2010), 174; Steven A. Channing, *Crisis of Fear: Secession in South Carolina* (New York: Norton, 1974), 284.
4. John G. Barrett, *The Civil War in North Carolina* (Chapel Hill: University of North Carolina Press, 1995), 3–4, 395; John Hope Franklin, *The Free Negro in North Carolina, 1790–1860* (Chapel Hill: University of North Carolina Press, 2000), 17–18.
5. Barrett, *The Civil War in North Carolina*, 6.
6. Douglas J. Butler, *North Carolina Civil War Monuments: An Illustrated History* (Jefferson, N.C.: McFarland, 2013), 74; Jeffrey W. McClurken, *Take Care of the Living: Reconstructing Confederate Veteran Families in Virginia* (Charlottesville: University of Virginia Press, 2009), 11; Charles Manfred Thompson, *History of the United States: Political, Industrial, Social* (Boston: Benjamin H. Sanborn, 1917), 294.
7. Barrett, *The Civil War in North Carolina*, 10–29.
8. *History of The Connecticut Valley in Massachusetts*, vol. 1 (Philadelphia: Louis H. Everts, 1879) 146–47; Michael P. Zatarga, *The Battle of Roanoke Island: Burnside and the Fight for North Carolina* (Mt. Pleasant, S.C.: History Press, 2015), 63–72.
9. David Eicher, *The Longest Night: A Military History of the Civil War* (New York: Simon and Schuster, 2002), 199.
10. Janette Thomas Greenwood, *First Fruits of Freedom: The Migration of Former Slaves and Their Search for Equality in Worcester, Massachusetts, 1862–1900* (Chapel Hill: University of North Carolina Press, 2009), 31–42.
11. Robert B. Outland, III, *Tapping the Pines: The Naval Stores Industry in the American South* (Baton Rouge: Lousiana State University Press, 2004), 54.
12. Greenwood, *First Fruits of Freedom*, 43–47; *History of the Connecticut Valley in Masssachusetts*, 2:149–50.

13. *Annual Catalogue Virginia Union University* (Richmond, Va.: Clemmitt & Jones, 1922), 2; Raymond Pierre Hilton, *Virginia Union University* (Mt. Pleasant, S.C.: Arcadia Press, 2014); Audrey Elisa Kerr, *The Paper Bag Principle: Class, Colorism, and Rumor and the Case of Black Washington*, part 3 (Knoxville: University of Tennessee Press, 2006), 105. In 1899 Weyland Seminary merged with the Richmond Theological Institute, resulting in Virginia Union Institute (now University), based in Richmond.
14. Map of the City of New York Showing Its Political Divisions and Subdivisions, November 1870, https://upload.wikimedia.org/wikipedia/commons/f/f7/1870_Hardy_Map_of_Manhattan%2C_New_York_City_-_Geographicus_-_Political Divisions-hardy-1870.jpg; U.S. Department of Commerce and Labor, *Ninth Census of the United States*, 1870, County of New York, State of New York, Schedule I, p. 15; Marriages Registered in the Town of Westfield in the Year Eighteen Seventy-four, *Massachusetts Marriage Records, 1840–1915*, 412.
15. U.S. Department of Commerce and Labor, "Population of Civil Divisions Less Than Counties," *Ninth Census of the United States* (Washington, D.C.: U.S. Department of Commerce, 1870), 166.
16. *Atlas of Hampden County, Massachusetts* (New York: Beers, Ellis, and Soule, 1870).
17. Joanne E. Moller, "1876: Local Observance of the Centennial," *Historical Journal of Western Massachusetts* 5, no. 1 (Spring 1976): 32–33.
18. Gennifer Fabre and Robert O'Meally, eds., *History and Memory in African American Culture* (New York: Oxford University Press, 1994), 80; W. E. B. Du Bois, *Black Reconstruction* (New York: Atheneum, 1992), 580–636.
19. Map of the City of New York, 1870; *Ninth Census of the United States*, 1870, County of New York, 15; Marriages Registered in the Town of Westfield, 412.
20. *Westfield Directory* (Westfield, Mass.: Ridley's, 1874), 35; *Westfield Directory* (Albany, N.Y.: R. S. Dillon, 1881), 76; *Westfield Directory* (Albany, N.Y: R. S. Dillon, 1885), 19.
21. Moller, "1876: Local Observance of the Centennial," 32–33.
22. U.S. Department of Commerce and Labor, *Tenth Census of the United States*, 1880, Schedule I, Westfield, Mass., Hampden County, 36.
23. *Tenth Census of the United States*, 1880, Schedule I, Supervisor's District 60, Enumeration District 295, 37–39.
24. *Tenth Census of the United States*, 1880, Schedule I, Supervisor's District 60, Enumeration District 295, 41; Writers' Program (Mass.), *The State Teacher's College at Westfield* (Boston: Jerome Press, 1941), 41–42.
25. Hampden County Registry of Deeds, Book 399, 11; Westfield Directory (Albany, N.Y.: R. S. Dillon, 1888), 37; Westfield Athenaeum, *Westfield: Images of America* (Charleston, S.C.: Arcadia, 1996), 49; "Green Street District School, 1892," http://lostnewengland.com/category/massachusetts/westfield-massachusetts/.
26. Washington, *The Negro in Business*, 200; Edgar Wallace Knight, *Public School Education in North Carolina* (New York: Houghton Mifflin, 1916), 140–45, 235.
27. Knight, *Public School Education in North Carolina*, 140–45, 235; Sharon Gayle Pierson, *Laboratory of Learning: HBCU Laboratory Schools and Alabama State College Lab High in the Era of Jim Crow* (Bern, Switz.: Peter Lang, 2015), 1–6.
28. National Center for Education Statistics, *120 Years of American Education: A Statistical Portrait* (Darby, Pa.: Diane, 1993), 64.

1. THE PAYTONS BEFORE AND IN WESTFIELD

29. Helen G. Edmonds, *The Negro and Fusion Politics in North Carolina* (Chapel Hill: University of North Carolina Press, 2015), 189.
30. North Carolina History Project, "Rowan County," *Encyclopedia of the Old North State*, http://northcarolinahistory.org/encyclopedia/rowan-county-1753/.
31. Willliam J. Simmons and Henry McNeal Turner, *Men of Mark: Eminent, Progressive, and Rising* (Cleveland: George M. Rewell, 1887), 754–58.
32. D. Lawrence Bivins, *North Carolina: The State of Minds* (Encino, Calif.: Cherbo, 2004), 112.
33. Livingstone College, Commencement Program, May 16, 1888, J. C. Price Papers, Livingstone College Archives.
34. *Sketch Book of Livingstone College and East Tennessee Industrial School* (Salisbury, N.C., 1903), 34.
35. W. E. B. Du Bois, *Black Reconstruction in America, 1860–1880* (New York: Atheneum, 1992), 687–708.
36. "J. C. Price Dead," *Western Sentinel* (Winston-Salem, N.C.), November 2, 1893.
37. Washington, *The Negro in Business*, 200.
38. Louise M. Rountree, *Blue Bear Trax: Highlights of the Livingstone College Blue Bear Football Record and Gridiron Greats, and a Documented Scoreboard 1892–1966* (Salisbury, N.C.: Livingstone College, 1967), 4–5.
39. Washington, *The Negro in Business*, 200.
40. "Westfield," *Springfield* (Mass.) *Republican*, November 23, 1896.
41. Payton Family Records, Westfield Athaeneum.
42. "Our Story," Westfield State University, 4:32–34.
43. Edith Armstrong Talbot, *Samuel Chapman Armstrong: A Biographical Sketch* (Doubleday, Page, 1904), 5; "Our Story," 32–34.
44. "Our Story," 32–34.
45. Washington, *The Negro in Business*, 201.

2. THE PROVINCIAL IN NEW YORK CITY

1. Paul Laurence Dunbar, *The Sport of the Gods* (New York: Dodd, Mead, 1902), 81.
2. Jim Harter, *World Railroads of the Nineteenth Century: A Pictorial History in Victorian Engravings* (Baltimore: Johns Hopkins University Press, 2005), 274.
3. Dunbar, *The Sport of the Gods*, 82.
4. "Ending War With Spain," "Capture of Santa Cruz," and "Phillipine-American War," *New World Encyclopedia*, http://www.newworldencyclopedia.org/entry/Philippine-American_War; "Light on Canal Frauds," "More Rioting at Pana," and "F. H. Croker Examined," *New York Tribune*, April 11, 1899; "Investigating the New York Building Department," *Engineering News and American Railway Journal*, vol. 41 (New York: Engineering News, 1899), 285.
5. Booker T. Washington, *The Negro in Business* (Chicago: Hertel & Jenkins, 1907), 201.
6. U.S. Department of Commerce and Labor, *Twelfth Census of the United States*, 1900, *Manhattan, New York, New York*, Enumeration District 0157, p. 9, FHL microfilm 1241087.
7. *Springfield (Mass.) Republican*, October 13, 1900; "Charles E. Schuyler Real Estate," in *A History of Real Estate, Building and Architecture in New York City, During the*

2. THE PROVINCIAL IN NEW YORK CITY

Last Quarter of a Century (New York: Record and Guide, 1898/Arno Press, 1967), 212; author interview with Dr. Robert Brown, March 8, 2017.
8. Washington, *The Negro in Business*, 201.
9. U.S. Department of Commerce and Labor, *Tenth Census of the United States*, 1880, Hampden County, Westfield, Enumeration District 295, sheet 13; *Twelfth Census of the United States*, 1900, Hampden County, Westfield, Enumeration District 608, sheet 12; National Register of Historic Places Application, Westfield Center Historic District, May 10, 2013, 7.
10. U.S. Department of Commerce and Labor, *Tenth Census of the United States*, 1880, Raleigh, SW Division, County of Wake, Supervisor's District 2, Enumeration District 268, 43.
11. Roy Rosenzwig and Elizabeth Blackmar, *The Park and the People: A History of Central Park* (Ithaca, N.Y.: Cornell University Press, 1992), 379–81; Marcy Sacks, *Before Harlem: The Black Experience in New York Before World War I* (Philadelphia: University of Pennsylvania Press, 2013), 72–76.
12. Washington, *The Negro in Business*, 203.
13. Gilbert Osofsky, "Race Riot, 1900: A Study in Ethnic Violence," *Journal of Negro Education* 32, no. 1 (Winter 1963): 16–24; J. Martschukat and Silvan Niedermeier, eds., *Violence and Visibility in Modern History* (New York: Palgrave Macmillan, 2013), 73–90.
14. Amy V. Collins, "New York City Riot, 1900," in *Encyclopedia of American Race Riots*, vol. 1, ed. Walter C. Rucker and James N. Upton (Westport, Conn.: Greenwood Press, 2006), 474–76.
15. *Springfield Republican*, October 13, 1900; Census of Population, 1880, Schedule I, Springfield, Mass., Hampden County, Enumeration District 314, 26.
16. "Here and There," *Colored American Magazine* 6, no. 2 (December 1902), 126, 154.
17. Washington, *The Negro in Business*, 201–2.
18. "Questions and Answers, Brokers' Fees," *Real Estate Record and Builders Guide* (*RRBG*), March 22, 1913, 613.
19. "Questions and Answers, Brokers' Fees," 613; $\$12 \times 0.02 = \$0.24$; $\$20 \times 0.02 = \$0.40$; $\$15 \times 10 \times 12 = \$1,800 \times 0.05 = \$90$.
20. Joseph J. Korom, *The American Skyscraper, 1850–1940: A Celebration of Height* (Wellesley, Mass: Branden Books, 2008), 85.
21. "Flats and Apartments to Let," *(New York) Evening World*, May 12, 1892, June 16, 1894; "Flats and Apartments to Let," *(New York) Sun*, February 25, 1892; Sacks, *Before Harlem*, 72–73.
22. David M. Scobey, *Empire City: The Making and Meaning of the New York City Landscape* (Philadelphia: Temple University Press, 2003), 89.
23. Scobey, 89.
24. Washington, *The Negro in Business*, 204.
25. Raymond Smock, *Booker T. Washington: Black Leadership in the Age of Jim Crow* (Lanham, Md.: Ivan R. Dee, 2009), 83–97, 107–23, 153–55.
26. Robert Jefferson Norrell, *Up From History: The Life of Booker T. Washington* (Cambridge, Mass.: Harvard University Press, 2009), 221–24; Smock, *Booker T. Washington*, 146–47.
27. *Proceedings of the National Negro Business League, August 23rd and 24th, 1900* (Boston: J. R. Hamm, 1900), 7.

28. Nora N. Nercessian, *Against All Odds: The Legacy of Students of African Descent at Harvard Medical School Before Affirmative Action, 1850–1968* (Boston: Harvard Medical School, 2004), 86–87.
29. "Negroes in Business," *Colored American Magazine* 5, no. 5 (September 6, 1903).
30. Thomas V. DiBacco, "When Typhoid Was Dreaded," *Washington Post*, January 25, 1994.
31. Donald F. Joyce, "Colored Co-operative Publishing Company," in *Black Book Publishers in the United States: A Historical Dictionary of the Press, 1817–1900* (Westport, Conn.: Greenwood, 1991), 80–82.
32. James Warren Payton, "Some Experiences and Customs at Yale," *Colored American Magazine* 1, no. 2 (June 1900): 80–87.
33. "Here and There," *Colored American Magazine* 6, no. 2 (December 1902): 154.
34. New York City Register, Conveyances, sec. 6, liber 68, 181; *Deaths Registered in the Town of Westfield in the Year 1902*, 94; "Resolutions of Respect and Appreciation for the Worth of Prof. James Warren Payton," *Colored American Magazine* (March 1903): 126.
35. New York City Register, Conveyances, sec. 6, liber 80, 476–77.
36. Edith Wharton, *A Backward Glance* (Redditch, UK: Read Books, 2013), 3.
37. Floor plan for 13 West 131st Street, Robert Pugh, 1990s.
38. New York City Register, Conveyances, sec. 6, liber 74, 163.
39. Washington, *The Negro in Business*, 204.
40. Afro-American Realty Company, Partnership Papers, New York County Archives, 1903.
41. Sterling Stuckey, *Slave Culture: Nationalist Theory and the Foundations of Black America* (New York: Oxford University Press, 1987), 195–97; Stephanie E. Smallwood, *Saltwater Slavery: A Middle Passage from Africa to American Diaspora* (Cambridge, Mass.: Harvard University Press, 2009), 9–10.
42. T. Thomas Fortune, *After War-Times: An African American Childhood in Reconstruction Era Florida* (Tuscaloosa: University of Alabama Press, 2014), 66; Adam Fairclough, *Better Days Coming: Blacks and Equality, 1890–2000* (New York: Penguin, 2002), 20–21.
43. Hannah Rosen, *Terror in the Heart of Freedom: Citizenship, Sexual Violence, and the Meaning of Race in the Postemancipation South* (Chapel Hill: University of North Carolina Press, 2009), 235–41; Khalil Gibran Muhammad, *The Condemnation of Blackness: Race, Crime, and the Making of Modern Urban America* (Cambridge, Mass.: Harvard University Press, 2010), 35–87; Douglas Blackman, *Slavery by Another Name: The Re-enslavement of Black Americans from the Civil War to World War Two* (London: Icon, 2012).
44. David Levering Lewis, *W. E. B. DuBois: Biography of a Race, 1868–1919* (New York: Holt, 1994), 265–96.
45. Afro-American Realty Company, "Certificate of Partners Constituting the Afro-American Realty Company," June 22, 1903, New York County Archives; Washington, *The Negro in Business*, 104–9; "Overheard on the Avenue," *New York Age*, August 20, 1908.
46. "Certificate of Partners Constituting the Afro-American Realty Company"; "James E. Garner," *Colored American Magazine* 10, no. 3 (March 1906): 182–84; New York State Census, 1905, Twenty-third Assembly District, Borough of Manhattan,

3. ENTERING THE FIELD OF BATTLE

Fifteenth Election District, Block A, 19; U.S. Department of Commerce and Labor, *Ninth Census of the United States*, 1870, New York, New York, 13th Election District, Ward 12, p. 13; *Thirteenth Census of the United States*, 1910, New York, New York, Bronx 32nd Assembly District, Enumeration District 1484, sheet 4A.

47. Raymond Smock, ed., *Booker T. Washington in Perspective: Essays of Louis R. Harlan* (Jackson, Mississippi: University of Mississippi Press, 2006), 114; Louis R. Harlan, "The Secret Life of Booker T. Washington, *Journal of Southern History* 27, no. 3 (August 1971): 398; J. Clay Smith, Jr., *Emancipation: The Making of the Black Lawyer, 1844–1944* (Philadelphia: University of Pennsylvania Press, 1999), 346–47.
48. "National Negro Business League Opens Its Fourth Convention at the Capitol," *(Nashville) Tennesseean*, August 20, 1903.
49. "National Negro Business League Opens Its Fourth Convention."
50. Ida B. Wells, *The Red Record: Tabulated Statistics and Alleged Causes of Lynching in the United States*, 1895, Project Gutenberg e-book, https://www.gutenberg.org/files/14977/14977-h/14977-h.htm#chap4.
51. *Report of the Fourth Annual Convention of the National Negro Business League* (Wilberforce, Ohio: Charles Alexander, 1903), 53.

3. ENTERING THE FIELD OF BATTLE

1. "Noisy Greeting for New Year," *(New York) Evening World*, January 1, 1904.
2. New York City Register, Conveyances, sec. 6, liber 77, 484–88; liber 82, 223; liber 86, 382–83; "In the Real Estate Field: Church Buys on 134th Street," *New York Times*, February 2, 1904.
3. Map of New York City, sec. 6 (New York: G. W. Bromley, 1897).
4. Frederick Jackson Turner, "The Significance of the Frontier in American History, 1893," paper presented at meeting of the American Historical Association, Chicago, July 12, 1893, during the World Columbia Exposition, http://nationalhumanitiescenter.org/pds/gilded/empire/text1/turner.pdf.
5. "Real Estate Review," *Harlem Reporter and Bronx Chronicle*, April 9, 1904.
6. Jonathan Gill, *Harlem: The Four Hundred Year History from Dutch Village to Capital of Black America* (New York: Grove Press, 2011), 49, 97–99.
7. Jeffrey S. Gurock, *The Jews of Harlem: The Rise, Decline, and Revival of a Jewish Community* (New York: New York University Press, 2016), 27–74.
8. Map of New York City, sec. 6.
9. Elizabeth Blackmar, *Manhattan for Rent*, (Ithaca, N.Y.: Cornell University Press, 1991), 213–14; "Negro Families Must 'Move On,'" *New York Herald*, May 2, 1904.
10. "M. Morgenthau, 89, Realty Man, Dies," *New York Times*, December 14, 1936; Hudson Realty Company, Certificate of Incorporation, February 9, 1893; Hudson Realty Company, Annual Meeting Minutes, January 13, 1902; Alfred Theodore Andreas, *The History of Chicago: From the Fire of 1871 to 1885* (Chicago: A. T. Andreas, 1886), 719.
11. Hudson Realty Company, Certificate of Incorporation; Hudson Realty Company, Annual Meeting Minutes, January 13, 1902; New York Register, Conveyances, sec. 6, liber 85, 198; liber 84, 307.

3. ENTERING THE FIELD OF BATTLE

12. "Among the Churches: Mercy Seat Baptist Church," *New York Age*, December 17, 1908; "Accused of Clubbing the Rev. N. S. Epps," *New York Times*, September 10, 1901; "Devery Judges Policemen," *New York Times*, October 25, 1901; James Bronson Reynolds, *Civic Bibliography for Greater New York* (New York: Charities Publication Committee, 1911), 189.
13. "Harlem Negro Colony to Fight Evictions," *New York Times*, May 2, 1904.
14. New York City Register, Conveyances, sec. 6, liber 86, 346; liber 119, 414; "Real Estate Transfers: Recorded Mortgages," *New York Times*, June 16, 1903.
15. New York City Register, Conveyances, sec. 6, liber 87, 95; liber 88, 183; liber 86, 346–47; liber 84, 379–80; liber 87, 342–43; liber 90, 388–89; *Real Estate Record and Builders Guide*, May 14, 1904, 1127.
16. *Trow's General Directory of the Boroughs of Manhattan and the Bronx, City of New York*, 1907; U.S. Department of Commerce and Labor, *Thirteenth Census of the United States*, 1910, New York City, Enumeration District 536, sheet 4A; *Twelfth Census of the United States*, 1900, Schedule No. 1, Population New York City, Enumeration District 851, sheet 15; Andreas, *The History of Chicago*, 719; "A Feast of German Song," *New York Times*, April 21, 1895.
17. Unsigned letter to Philip Payton, May 3, 1904, Booker T. Washington Papers, reel 248, box 245; the letter could have been written by Washington or his assistant Emmettt J. Scott, who often wrote letters on Washington's behalf and was also a friend of Payton's.
18. AARC, Incorporation Papers, New York County Archives.
19. AARC, Incorporation Papers.
20. AARC, Prospectus, 2, 4.
21. "An Afro-American Co. with $100,000 Paid Up," *Colored American Magazine*, August 20, 1904, 6.
22. AARC, Prospectus, 4.
23. AARC, Prospectus, 6–7.
24. "An Afro-American Co. with $100,000 Paid Up," 6.
25. AARC, Incorporation Papers, 1; New York, State Census, 1905, 22nd Election District, 15th Assembly District, p. 27; U.S. Department of Commerce and Labor, *Twelfth Census of the United States*, 1900, Schedule 1, Population New York, Manhattan, Supervisor's District 1, Enumeration District 419, sheet 12; "The News of Greater New York: Brooklyn," *New York Age*, July 25, 1907; "Baptist Flock May Disband," *New York Age*, September 14, 1905.
26. Consumer Price Index Inflation Calculator, https://www.in2013dollars.com/us/inflation/1904?amount=100.
27. "To Make Color Line Costly in New York," *New York Times*, July 26, 1904; Rose Helper, *Racial Policies and Practices of Real Estate Brokers* (Minneapolis: University of Minnesota Press, 1969), 271.
28. S. Laing Williams, *Report, Fifth Annual Convention, National Negro Business League* (Pensacola, Fla.: M. M. Lewey, 1904), 56–57.
29. New York City Register, Conveyances, sec. 6, liber 96, 4–5; liber 96, 9–10.
30. "1905 Comes in With a Roar," *(New York) Sun*, January 1, 1905.
31. "Private Sales Market," *Real Estate Record and Builder's Guide*, February 18, 1905, 363; March 12, 1905, 530; March 25, 1905, 640, 650; April 22, 1905, 882; "In the Real Estate Field," *New York Times*, February 17, 1905.

32. Raymond Smock, ed., *Booker T. Washington in Perspective: Essays of Louis R. Harlan* (Oxford: University Press of Mississippi, 2006), 101; Andrew M. Kaye, "Colonel Roscoe Conkling Simmons and the Mechanics of Black Leadership," *Journal of American Studies* 37, no. 1 (April 2003): 83–87.
33. Roscoe Conkling Simmons, "The Afro-American Realty Company: Has It Justified the Support Given It?," *Colored American Magazine* (May 1905): 264–75.
34. Simmons, 268.
35. Mary White Ovington, *Half a Man: The Status of the Negro in New York* (London: Longmans, Green, 1911), 199; "Bloody Rioting in City Streets," *(Rochester, N.Y.) Democrat and Chronicle*, July 15, 1905.
36. "To Defend Civil Rights," *New York Age*, August 24, 1905.
37. "Ex-Chief Devery Speaks," *New York Age*, July 26, 1905, "Police Force of New York City," in *World Almanac and Encyclopedia* (New York: Press Publishing Company/New York World, 1905), 526.
38. "Cooney Mildly Punished," *New York Age*, November 16, 1905.
39. Ralph E. Luker, *The Social Gospel in Black and White: American Racial Reform, 1885–1912* (Chapel Hill: University of North Carolina Press, 1998), 300.
40. "A Dixon Pamphlet Stirs Negro Clergy," *New York Times*, December 18, 1905.
41. "Ask Clergymen to Condemn 'The Clansman'—Mass Meeting to Be Called," *New York Age*, December 21, 1905.
42. "Against 'The Clansman,'" *New York Age*, December 28, 1906; Jon Scott Logel, *Designing Gotham: West Point Engineers and the Rise of Modern New York, 1817–1898* (Baton Rouge: Louisiana State University Press, 2016).

4. BATTLES IN THE STREETS AND THE COURTROOM

1. "Thousands Greet New Year in Times Square," *New York Times*, January 1, 1906.
2. Clifton Hood, *722 Miles: The Building of the Subways and How They Transformed New York* (Baltimore: Johns Hopkins University Press, 2004), 103.
3. "Private Sales Market," *Real Estate Record and Builders Guide* (*RRBG*), January 27, 1906, 153; "In the Real Estate Field," *New York Times*, February 1 and 7, 1906.
4. "The Growth of the Afro-American Realty Company," *Colored American Magazine*, February 1906, 103.
5. "Growth of the Afro-American Realty Company," 104; AARC, Prospectus, 1904, 6–7.
6. "Growth of the Afro American Realty Company," 112–13.
7. "Growth of the Afro-American Realty Company," 113.
8. "Growth of the Afro-American Realty Company," 118.
9. "Growth of the Afro-American Realty Company," 118.
10. "In the Real Estate Field," *New York Times*, January 21, March 28, June 1, 1906; "Private Sales Market," *RRBG*, March 3, 1906, 374; March 24, 1906, 526, 552; March 31, 1906, 578; "Conveyances," *RRBG*, April 7, 1906, 644.
11. Khalil Gibran Muhammad, *The Condemnation of Blackness: Race, Crime and the Making of Modern Urban America* (Cambridge, Mass.: Harvard University Press, 2010), 3–12; Luigi Laurenti, *Property Values and Race: Studies in Seven Cities* (Berkeley: University of California Press, 1960), 5.

12. "Negro Invasion Averted: House Leased to Afro-American Co. Is Bought by Neighboring Owners," *New York Times*, August 8, 1906.
13. "'23' the Mystic Sign on Negro Flathouse," *New York Times*, July 22, 1906.
14. Manhattan Conveyances, sec. 7, liber 117, 484–85; Inflation Calculator, https://www.officialdata.org/1906-dollars-in-2020?amount=1000.
15. "'23' the Mystic Sign on Negro Flathouse."
16. "New York Letter," *(Pendleton) East Oregonian*, August 2, 1906.
17. "Private Sales," *RRBG*, August, September, October, November 1906; David Fort Godshalk, *Veiled Visions: The 1906 Atlanta Race Riot and the Reshaping of American Race Relations* (Chapel Hill: University of North Carolina Press, 2006), 1–8.
18. Theda Perdue, *Race and the Atlanta Cotton States Exposition of 1895* (Athens: University of Georgia Press, 2011), 8.
19. Godshalk, *Veiled Visions*, 35–56.
20. Summons, *Charles J. Crowder Against Afro American Realty Company, a Domestic Corporation, and Philip A. Payton, Jr.*," October 25, 1906, New York City Archives.
21. Summons, October 25, 1906.
22. Summons, October 25, 1906.
23. Association of the Bar of the City of New York, "Arthur Covell Bostwick," in *Yearbook* (New York, 1919), 139–40.
24. *Charles J. Crowder Against Afro-American Realty Company, a Domestic Corporation, et al. Defendant*, Supreme Court, N.Y. County, undated, New York County Archives.
25. Bret Sentf, "If You Are Thinking of Living in Tribeca, the Catalyst for Change," *New York Times*, September 26, 1993.
26. City of New York, "A Brief History of the Tweed Court House," http://www.nyc.gov/html/om/html/tweed_courthouse.html.
27. Joseph F. Mulqueen, "Hon James Fitzgerald," *Journal of the American-Irish Historical Society*, vol. 23 (New York: American-Irish Society, 1924), 251; "James Fitzgerald Buried," *New York Times*, December 21, 1922; *Charles J. Crowder, Plaintiff, Against Afro-American Realty Company and Philip A. Payton, Jr., Defendants*, Demurrer, November 13, 1906, New York Supreme Court, New York County Archives, p. 1.
28. *New York Age*, December 13, 20, 27, 1906; *Real Estate Record and Builders Guide*, January–December 1906; "In the Real Estate Field," *New York Times*, January–June 1906.
29. "Abreast of the Times," *New York Age*, January 3, 1907.
30. "Negroes Charge Payton with Realty Fraud," *New York Times*, January 30, 1907; "Mr. Payton Arrested," *New York Age*, January 31, 1907.
31. "Mr. Payton's Defence," *RRBG*, February 2, 1907, 266.
32. "The Growth of the Afro-American Realty Company," *Colored American Magazine*, February 1906, 103.
33. Conveyances, sec. 7, liber 128, 145–50; Evan McKenzie, *Privatopia: Homeowner Associations and the Rise of Residential Private Government* (New Haven, Conn.: Yale University Press, 1994), 31–36.

34. McKenzie, *Privatopia*, 31–36; Karen Brodkin, *How Jews Became White Folks and What That Says About Race in America* (New Brunswick, NJ: Rutgers University Press, 1998), 47.
35. New York City Register, Manhattan Conveyances, sec. 7, liber 108, 204–5; liber 120, 425, 427; liber 121, 473, 474; liber 128, 145–50,
36. Manhattan Conveyances, sec. 7, liber 128, 146.
37. Manhattan Conveyances, sec. 7, liber 128, 147.
38. Manhattan Conveyances, sec. 6, liber 133, 39–41; *Trow's General Directory of the Boroughs of Manhattan and the Bronx, City of New York* (New York: Trow Directory Printing and Bookbinding, 1907), 1215; *Trow's General Directory of the Boroughs of Manhattan and the Bronx, City of New York* (New York: Trow Directory Printing and Bookbinding, 1908), 1325.
39. Hampden Realty and Construction Company, Incorporation Papers, New York County Archives.
40. "Conveyances," *RRBG*, March 16, 1907, 554; April 13, 1907, 747; June 22, 1907, 1215; November 2, 1907, 734.
41. Conveyances, liber 127, sec. 7, 365–68, June 18, 1907.
42. "Afro-American Realty Company Declares Dividend," *New York Age*, June 20, 1907.
43. "Afro-American Realty Company," classified advertisement, *New York Age*, October 10, 1907.
44. "The Panic of 1907," EH.net, https://eh.net/encyclopedia/the-panic-of-1907/; "Panic of 1907: J. P. Morgan Saves the Day," U-S-History.com, http://www.u-s-history.com/pages/h952.html; Robert F. Bruner and Sean D. Carr, *The Panic of 1907: Lessons Learned from the Market's Perfect Storm* (Hoboken, N.J.: Wiley, 2009), 37–150.
45. "New Year Welcomed With Wild Acclaim," *New York Times*, January 1, 1908; "A.P. Mitchell, Loser in Stocks, a Suicide," *New York Times*, January 2, 1908; "Suit to Dissolve Harriman System," *New York Times*, January 2, 1908; "Seaboard Air Line Asks for Receivers," *New York Times*, January 2, 1908.
46. Conveyances, sec. 6, liber 145, 148–49.
47. Mary White Ovington, *Black and White Sat Down Together: Reminisences of an NAACP Founder* (New York: Feminist Press at City University of New York, 1996), 57.
48. "Death of Old Resident," *(Westfield, Mass.) Valley Echo*, October 17, 1908.
49. "Death of Old Resident."
50. *Charles J. Crowder Against Afro-American Realty Company and Philip A. Payton, Jr.*, Verdict, New York Supreme Court, February 16, 1909, 3–44.
51. *Crowder v. AARC and Payton*, Verdict, 10.
52. *Crowder v. AARC and Philip Payton*, Verdict, 10.
53. *Crowder v. AARC and Philip Payton*, New York Supreme Court, December 28, 1906, 1–40.
54. John Clay Smith, *Emancipation: The Making of a Black Lawyer, 1844–1944* (Philadelphia: University of Pennsylvania Press, 1999), 346; R. Volney Riser, *Defying Disfranchisement: Black Voting Rights Activism in the Jim Crow South, 1890–1908* (Baton Rouge: Louisiana State University Press, 2010), 180; Kerrell L. Hall, *Freedom and Equality: Discrimination and the Supreme Court* (London: Taylor & Francis, 2000), 188.
55. Emmett Scott, letter to Philip Payton, 1908.

5. TO LIBERIA AND BACK

1. "Reduced Rents to Let," *New York Age*, January 14, February 4, 1909; "Office of Philip A. Payton, Jr. Company, to Let," *New York Age,* May 13, June 24, July 1, August 12, October 7, 1909.
2. "Business to Save American Negroes," *New York Age*, June 7, 1909.
3. "Negroes Banquet Matthew Henson," *New York Age*, October 21, 1909.
4. "Afro-American Notes," *New York Age*, October 20, 1909; "Negroes Banquet Matthew Henson."
5. "A Noisy Welcome Brings in New Year," *New York Times*, January 1, 1909.
6. "Farewell Dinner to Philip A. Payton," *New York Age*, January 27, 1910.
7. Raymond Smock, *Booker T. Washington in Perspective: Essays of Louis R. Harlan* (Oxford: University Press of Mississippi, 2006), 122.
8. "Farewell Dinner to Philip A. Payton"; Gilbert Osofsky, *Harlem: The Making of a Ghetto: Negro New York, 1890–1930* (New York: Harper and Row, 1966), 94.
9. Smock, *Booker T. Washington*, 79–80.
10. Sei Rubel Gehyeka, *Inside the People's Redemption Council Government of Liberia: The Untold Story* (Bloomington, Ind.: LifeRich, 2018), 9; Smock, *Booker T. Washington*, 80.
11. James Ciment, *Another America: The Story of Liberia and the Former Slaves Who Ruled It* (New York: Hill and Wang, 2014), 99–120.
12. "Weather Summary," *New York Tribune*, January 26, 1910; "New Chelsea Piers Open Tomorrow," *New York Times*, February 20, 1910. The piers had been used for several years before the formal opening that acknowledged the completion of all buildings along the pier. See also John E. Fleming, "Alexander Walters," in *Dictionary of Negro Biography*, 630–31; "Isaiah B. Scott," Notable Kentucky African Americans Database, http://nkaa.uky.edu/nkaa/items/show/441.
13. Measuring Worth, https://www.measuringworth.com/calculators/uscompare/relativevalue.php; L. Diane Barnes, *Frederick Douglass: Reformer and Statesman* (Abingdon, UK: Routledge, 2013), 54; Glenwick-Gjonvick Archives, https://www.gjenvick.com/Brochures/1910-TravelGuide/BookingASteamshipVoyage.html.
14. Bishop Alexander B. Walters, *My Life and Work* (London: Revell, 1917), 149.
15. "Ernest Lyon," in *Herringshaw's Library of American Biography* (Chicago: American Publisher's Association, 1914), 591; Walters, *My Life and Work*, 149.
16. Walters, *My Life and Work*, 150–51.
17. "Crossings," *Liberian Register*, May 15, 1910.
18. "The News of Greater New York," *New York Age*, May 12, 1910, 7; "Real Estate News," *New York Age*, June 16, 1910.
19. Randy Roberts, *Papa Jack: Jack Johnson and the Era of White Hopes* (New York: Simon and Schuster, 1985), 85–110; "Eight Killed in Fight Riots," *New York Times*, July 5, 1910.
20. "News from the Capital City," *New York Age*, September 1, 1910. James Lawson was a physician and the son of Rosetta and Jesse Lawson, who in 1917 would found Frelinghuysen University to educate black working people in Washington, D.C. In 1930 Anna Julia Cooper would become president of Frelinghuysen. Jesse Carney Smith, ed., *Notable Black American Women*, book 2, 400; "The News of Greater New York," *New York Age*, September 8, 1910, 7.

5. TO LIBERIA AND BACK

21. Conveyances, liber 151, sec. 7, 134–46.
22. "'The 'Wizard' Welcomed Home," *National Forum*, October 22, 1910; "Friends Banquet Dr. Washington," *New York Age*, October 20, 1910.
23. Kevin McGruder, *Race and Real Estate: Conflict and Cooperation in Harlem, 1890–1920* (New York: Columbia University Press, 2015), 74.; U.S. Department of Commerce and Labor, *Twelfth Census of the United States*, 1900, Westfield, Hampden, Massachusetts, p. 12, Enumeration District 0608; *Thirteenth Census of the United States*, 1910, Manhattan Ward 12, New York, New York, p. 1B, Enumeration District 0501.
24. "William T. Francis," MNopedia, http://www.mnopedia.org/person/francis-william-t-1869-1929; "Nellie Francis," http://www.mnopedia.org/person/francis-nellie-1874-1969.
25. "McDougald's Dinner, Sure," *New York Age*, December 29, 1910; Herb Boyd, *Baldwin's Harlem: A Biography of James Baldwin's Harlem* (New York: Simon and Schuster, 2008), 13.
26. "Brilliant Social Function," *New York Age*, December 24, 1910.
27. "The Broad Ax," Library of Congress, https://chroniclingamerica.loc.gov/essays/371/.
28. "Prof. and Mrs. Washington Entertained in New York City," *Broad Ax*, December 24, 1910.
29. "Notes About Town," *New York Age*, December 29, 1910.
30. "Negroes and Negroes," *New York Age*, January 10, 1911.
31. Geneva Smitherman, *Talkin and Testifyin: The Language of Black America* (Detroit: Wayne State University Press, 1986), 39–40.
32. *New York Age*, January 26, 1911; Gail Lumet Buckley, *The Hornes: An American Family*, (Milwaukee: Hal Leonard), 63; "The Public Schools of New York," *Crisis*, vols. 14–15, 132.
33. *Thirteenth Census of the United States*, 1910, Population, Borough of Manhattan, Enumeration District 501, sheet 2B, 2A.
34. "Segregation Case Thrown Out of Court," *New York Age*, February 9, 1911; Matthew A. Crenson, *Baltimore: A Political History* (Baltimore: Johns Hopkins University Press, 2017), 340–41.
35. "The Real Estate Field," *New York Times*, February 24, 1911.
36. *New York Age*, March 31, 1911; *Brooklyn Daily Eagle*, March 31, 1911.
37. Manhattan Conveyances, sec. 7, liber 152, 297–301; liber 156, 365–72; John G. Taylor identification card, New York City Police Museum; *Twelfth Census of the United States*, Schedule No.1 Population, Enumeration District 100, sheets 1, 2.
38. *Twelfth Census of the United States*, 1900, Schedule 1, Population, Enumeration District 100, sheet 1, 2; John H. Hewitt, Jr., *Protest and Progress: New York's First Black Episcopal Church Fights Racism* (New York: Routledge, 2018), 138–43; classified advertisements, *New York Age*, February 9, 23, 1911; Shannon King, *Whose Harlem Is This, Anyway? Community Politics and Grassroots Activism During the New Negro Era* (New York: New York University Press, 2017), 21.
39. Edwin Rogers Embree, ed., *History of the Class of 1906, Yale College*, Class Secretaries Bureau (New Haven: Yale University Press, 1911) 255; *Trow's General Directory of the Boroughs of Manhattan and the Bronx* (New York: Trow Directory Printing and Bookbinding, 1911), 1206.

5. TO LIBERIA AND BACK

40. Robert E. Pinkerton, "The First Woods Cure," *The Crusader of the Wisconsin Anti-Tuberculosis Association* 1, no. 14 (May 1911): 9–10; Philip L. Gallos, *Cure Cottages of Saranac Lake: Architecture and History of a Pioneer Health Resort* (Saranac Lake, N.Y.: Historic Saranac Lake, 1985), 4; Irving Fisher, "The Modern Crusade Against Consumption," *New Outlook* 75 (1903): 691–97; Thomas Goetz, *The Remedy: Robert Koch, Arthur Conan Doyle, and the Quest to Cure Tuberculosis* (New York: Penguin, 2014); "Edward Samuel Payton Dead," *New York Age*, June 27, 1912.
41. "New York Letter," *(Pendleton) East Oregonian*, August 2, 1906; "Edward Samuel Payton," Record of Deaths, Franklin County, New York, no. 1692; "Ollie E. Moody," Obituaries, *(Saranack Lake, N.Y.) Adirondack Daily Enterprise*, August 10, 1970; "Burton F. Moody," Obituaries, *Adirondack Daily Enterprise*, January 19, 1956; Gallos, *Cure Cottages of Saranac Lake*, 20.
42. Sally E. Svenson, *Blacks in the Adirondacks: A History* (Syracuse, N.Y.: Syracuse University Press, 2017), 121–50; Gallos, *Cure Cottages of Saranac Lake*, 75; "Edward Samuel Payton," Record of Deaths; "Edward S. Payton Dead," *New York Age*, June 27, 1912.
43. "Many Attend Funeral of Mrs. M. Roberts," *New York Age*, July 18, 1912; "Historical Society Closes," *New York Age*, July 4, 1912; "News of Greater New York," *New York Age*, October 31, 1912.
44. "Whitehead Cottage, Asbury Park, N.J.," *New York Age*, August 15, 1912; 25 Atkins Ave., Asbury Park, N.J., located on Mapquest.com.
45. "Negro Co. Buys Mount Vernon Dwelling," *New York Times*, August 25, 1912; *Thirteenth Census of the United States*, 1910, Population, Westchester County.
46. Henry Mitchell MacCracken, Ernest Gottlieb Sihler, and Willis Fletcher Johnson, *New York University: Its History, Influence, Equipment and Characteristics, with Biographical Sketches and Portraits of Founders, Benefactors, Officers and Alumni*, vol. 2 (Boston: R. Herndon, 1903), 197; Supreme Court of the State of New York, County of New York, Appellate Division, *First Department Papers on Appeal*, 264, 1913.
47. Local Realty Men Doing Big Business," *New York Age*, December 5, 1912.

6. FIFTY YEARS OF FREEDOM NATIONAL

1. "Nation Celebrates 50th Anniversary of the Emancipation Proclamation," *New York Age*, January 9, 1913; Allen C. Guetzo, *Lincoln's Emancipation Proclamation* (New York: Simon and Schuster, 2004).
2. "Nation Celebrates 50th Anniversary"; Brittney C. Cooper, *Beyond Respectability: The Intellectual Thought of Race Women* (Champaign: University of Illinois Press, 2017).
3. "Nation Celebrates 50th Anniversary"; M. C. Lawton, "Uplift Work in New York," *Indianapolis Recorder*, June 15, 1912.
4. "Nation Celebrates 50th Anniversary."
5. Manhattan Conveyances, sec. 7, liber 156, 365–72.
6. "To Test Legality of the Covenant," *New York Age*, February 13, 1913.
7. Clement E. Vose, *Caucasians Only: The Supreme Court, the NAACP, and the Restrictive Covenant Cases* (Berkeley: University of California Press, 1967), 1–3.

6. FIFTY YEARS OF FREEDOM NATIONAL

8. Booker T. Washington, Geraldine E. McTigue, and Louis R. Harlan, *Booker T. Washington Papers*, vol. 10 (Champaign: University of Illinois Press, 1981), 316–17.
9. "Free Renting: Organizations Formed to Kill This Practice," *Real Estate Record and Builders' Guide*, August 25, 1900, 235.
10. "Lucy Laney Reception," *New York Age*, March 20, 1913.
11. "Status of Harlem Negroes," *New York Times*, March 28, 1913; Gilbert Osofsky, "Race Riot, 1900: A Study in Ethnic Violence," *Journal of Negro Education* 32, no. 1 (Winter 1963): 16–24; Mary White Ovington, *Half a Man: The Status of the Negro in New York* (London: Longmans, Green, 1911), 199; David Fort Godshalk, *Veiled Visions: The 1906 Atlanta Race Riot and the Reshaping of American Race Relations* (Chapel Hill: University of North Carolina Press, 2006), 1–8; Roberta Senechal de la Roche, *In Lincoln's Shadow: The 1908 Race Riot in Springfield, Illinois* (Carbondale: Southern Illinois University Press, 2008).
12. U.S. Department of Commerce and Labor, *Twelfth Census of the United States*, 1900 Enumeration District 419, sheets 3A, 2B; *Trow's General Directory of Manhattan and Bronx, City of New York, for the Year Ending August 1, 1914* (New York: Trow Directory Printing and Bookbinding, 1914), 883; "Real Estate Transfers," *New York Times*, April 30, 1902.
13. U.S. Department of Commerce and Labor, *Thirteenth Census of the United States*, 1910, New York County, Enumeration District 1726, sheets 1B, 2B.
14. "Regiment Bill Passed, Awaiting Sulzer Signature," *New York Age*, May 8, 1913; "Gov. Sulzer Signs Regiment Bill," *New York Age*, June 5, 1913; "First Company for New Regiment Formed," *New York Age*, July 3, 1913.
15. "Housing Bureau Established," *New York Age*, January 2, 1913.
16. Gunnar Myrdal, *An American Dilemma*, vol. 2 (Abingdon, UK: Transaction, 1996), 837.
17. "Realty Men Oppose Housing Bureau Idea," *New York Age*, June 26, 1913.
18. "Realty Men Oppose Housing Bureau Idea."
19. "Negroes Form a Civic League," *New York Age*, September 18, 1913; "Royall Indorsed for Alderman," *New York Age*, September 25, 1913; "Ministers Write Letter for Royall," *New York Age*, October 23, 1913; Manhattan Assembly District Map, 1905.
20. *New York Age*, January 1, 1914, 1.
21. "Race Is Dancing Itself to Death," *New York Age*, January 8, 1914.
22. U.S. Department of Commerce and Labor, *Fourteenth Census of the United States*, 1920, New York City, Manhattan, Enumeration District 978, sheet 1A; "News of Greater New York," *New York Age*, January 8, 1914, 8; author interview with Cecil Forster, Bessie's grandson, July 2014.
23. "News of Greater New York."
24. Willard B. Gatewood, *Aristocrats of Color* (Fayetteville: University of Arkansas Press, 2000), 209.
25. Hearing to Review the Smith-Lever Act, on Its 100th Anniversary, Serial No. 113-9, March 4, 2014, 113-2 Hearing (Washington, D.C.: U.S. House Agriculture Committee, 2014).
26. "Payton Protests Smith-Lever Bill," *New York Age*, February 5, 1914; O. H. Benson, "Meeting America's Peculiar Needs in Education," *Journal of Education* 90 (1919).
27. "Pastor Bolden Celebrates Birthday," *New York Age*, March 5, 1914; "Richard Manuel Boldnen," in *Who's Who of the Colored Race: A General Biographical Dictionary*

of Men and Women of African Descent, vol. 1, ed. Frank Lincoln Mather (Chicago, 1915), 29.
28. "73 Families Lose Homes in Harlem Fire," *New York Age*, March 19, 1914.
29. "Lucy Laney League Reception a Success," *New York Age*, March 19, 1914.
30. "Taylor, Advocate of Segregation, Dead," *New York Age*, February 19, 1914.
31. "Races in Harlem Will Cooperate," *New York Age*, March 19, 1914.
32. "Races in Harlem Will Cooperate."
33. "Men of the Month," *Crisis*, August 1911, 147.
34. Jeffrey B. Perry, *Hubert Harrison: The Voice of Harlem Radicalism, 1883–1918* (New York: Columbia University Press, 2008), 377.
35. Perry, 377.
36. Rose Helper, *Racial Policies and Practices of Real Estate Brokers* (Minneapolis: University of Minnesota Press, 1969), 220–22.
37. "Hon. John Lewis Morris," *New York Age*, July 2, 1914.
38. Carl Patrick Burrowes, *Power and Press in Liberia, 1830–1970: The Impact of Globalization and Civil Society on Media-Government Relations* (Trenton, N.J.: Africa World Press, 2004), 121.
39. "Heir to Austria's Throne Is Slain with His Wife by Bosnian Youth to Avenge Seizure of His Country," *New York Times*, June 29, 1914.
40. Christopher Clark, *The Sleepwalkers: How Europe Went to War in 1914* (New York: Harper Perennial, 2014), 121–241; "Fillmore Names New Board for Regiment," *New York Age*, July 2, 1914; David A. Jasen and Gene Jones, *Spreadin' Rhythm Around: Black Popular Songwriters, 1880–1930* (New York: Routledge, 2013), 127–28; John Christopher Walter, *The Harlem Fox: J. Raymond Jones and Tammany, 1920–1970* (Albany, N.Y.: SUNY Press, 1989), 51; Ralph Crowder, *John Edward Bruce: Politician, Journalist, and Self-Trained Historian of the African Diaspora* (New York: NYU Press, 2004), 215.
41. "Mandamus to Compel Adj-General to Act," *New York Age*, July 16, 1914.
42. *New York Times*, July 17, August 1, 1914; *New York Age*, August 6, 1914.
43. "Beauty Contest Awards Made," *New York Age*, October 8, 1914.
44. "Children's Neighborhood Party," *New York Age*, October 15, 1915.
45. "Study Problem of Land Restrictions," *New York Times*, November 15, 1914.
46. "Annual Meeting of Urban League," New York Urban League, December 3, 1914; Ronald Herder, *500 Best-Loved Song Lyrics* (North Chelmsford, Mass.: Courier, 2013), 176.

7. THE LAST BIG DEAL

1. "City Work Up Tired After Celebration," *New York Times*, January 2, 1915.
2. "Whitman Goes in as Bell Tolls 12," "Stubborn Battles as the Year Ends," "Kaiser Sends 1915 Greeting to America," and "Keep Literacy Test by Vote of 47 to 12," *New York Times*, January 1, 1915.
3. Classified advertisements, *New York Age*, January 7, 1915.
4. New York State Census, 1915, New York City, Block 1 Election District 15, p. 7; Block 2 Election District 19, p. 17.
5. NNBL Annual Meeting Report, 1915, 4.

6. NNBL Annual Meeting Report, 7.
7. NNBL Annual Meeting Report, 145.
8. NNBL Annual Meeting Report, 291–92.
9. "Booker T. Washington Dies Within Tuskegee's Walls." *New York Age*, November 18, 1915.
10. "Booker T. Washington Dies Within Tuskegee's Walls."
11. "The Real Estate Field," *New York Times*, December 18, 1915; Oakwood Cemetery, Montgomery, Ala., https://www.facebook.com/oakwoodcemeterymontgomeryalabama/posts/alabama-voices-cemeteries-help-keep-history-aliv; stenographer classified ad, *New York Age*, October 28, 1907.
12. "New Year Revelers Crowd the Hotels," *New York Times*, January 1, 1916.
13. "Canada Doubles Her Army Making Its Total 500,000," "British Warship Blows Up in Port, 300 May Be Lost," "King George Tells President Poincare He Is Sure of Ultimate Victory," and "Lusitania Settlement Now Likely Following Austria's Compliance with All Our Demands on Ancona," *New York Times*, January 1, 1916.
14. "Mrs. Annie M. Payton Dead," *New York Age*, January 20, 1916; "Died, Annie M. Payton," *New York Times*, January 16, 1916.
15. "Private Realty Sales," *Real Estate Record and Builders Guide (RRBG)*, February 12, 1916, 257; "Mechanic's Liens," *RRBG*, February 19, 1916, 103; "The Real Estate Field," *New York Times*, February 13, 1916.
16. "Ten Year Old Boy Helps Fund," *New York Age*, February 24, 1916; Glossary for *Annual Report of the M.C. Lawton Civic and Cultural Club*, February 10, 1918, New York State Archives, Education, http://digitalcollections.archives.nysed.gov/index.php/Detail/Occurrence/Show/occurrence_id/2142.
17. "Transactions Recorded: Uptown," *(New York) Sun*, March 15, 1916; *RRBG*, March 18, 1916.
18. "Howard Dined," *New York Age*, March 19, 1916; Howard P. Drew, https://howarddrew.com.
19. "Dr. and Mrs. McKerrow Entertained," *New York Age*, April 20, 1916; *Journal of the National Medical Association*, vols. 5–6 (New York: Appleton-Century-Crofts, 1913), 189.
20. Craig Steven Wilder, *A Covenant with Color: Race and Social Power in Brooklyn, 1636–1990* (New York: Columbia University Press, 2000), 149.
21. "Testimonial Dinner to Bert Williams," *New York Age*, May 25, 1916; Camille F. Forbes, *Introducing Bert Williams: Burnt Cork, Broadway, and the Story of America's First Black Star* (New York: Basic Books, 2008), 193–98.
22. W. E. B. Du Bois, *The Souls of Black Folk* (Chicago: A. C. McClurg, 1903), 3.
23. "Pays Tribute to Washington," *New York Age*, June 1, 1916.
24. "Pays Tribute to Washington."
25. In March 1918 Duke Hobby would board the *President Lincoln* at Hoboken, New Jersey, along with his fellow soldiers in Company B of the 312 Labor Battalion, Quartermaster Corps of the Army. See "U.S. Army Transport Services, Passenger Lists, 1910–39," sheet 7.
26. "Tender Dinner to Dr. Moton," *New York Age*, November 23, 1916.
27. "High Rentals' Meeting Warm," *New York Age*, December 28, 1916.

28. State of New York Certificate and Record of Marriage, Certificate 759, December 30, 1916, City of New York Department of Health; "Saint Mark's Episcopal Church," *Encyclopedia of the Harlem Renaissance: K–Y* (Oxford: Taylor & Francis, 2004), 1078.
29. "1917, In on Tiptoes, Keeps the Sabbath," *New York Times*, January 1, 1917.
30. State of New York Certificate and Record of Marriage, Certificate 2763, January 17, 1917, City of New York Department of Health; Census of Population, 1920, Brooklyn, Enumeration District 336, p. 7A; "Conference of Church Workers Among Colored People," *Living Church* 47 (1912): 739.
31. "Growing Interest in Race Books," *New York Age*, February 8, 1917.
32. "Trades Flat for Loft," *New York Herald*, April 18, 1917; *Real Estate Directory, 1912–13* (New York: Jay M. Jackson, 1912), 665; New York State Census 1915, Islip, Assembly District 2, Suffolk County, p. 17; "Mortgages," *RRBG*, vol. 110 (1922): 553.
33. Judith Wellman, *Brooklyn's Promised Land: The Free Black Community of Weeksville, New York* (New York: NYU Press, 2017), 167–74; Kenneth T. Jackson, Lisa Keller, and Nancy Flood, eds., "Brooklyn Howard Orphan Asylum," *Encyclopedia of New York City, Second Edition* (New Haven, Conn.: Yale University Press, 2010), 158.
34. "Women's Auxiliary Gains Members," *New York Age*, June 21, 1917.
35. "Apartment Row for Negro Homes," *Sun*, July 11, 1917.
36. "Six Negro Apartments in Deal," *RRBG*, July 14, 1917, 47.
37. Display advertisement, *New York Age*, August 16, 1917.
38. "Apartment Row for Negro Homes."
39. "Manhattan and the Bronx," *New York Age*, August 30, 1917.
40. Philip A. Payton Jr. Death Certificate, State of New Jersey, Office of Registrar of Vital Statistics, Borough of Allenhurst, August 29, 1917; Tamra Orr, *Liver Cancer: Current and Emerging Trends in Detection and Treatment* (New York: Rosen Publishing Group, 2009), 17–20; Joseph C. Bottino, Franco M. Muggia, and Richard W. Opfell, *Liver Cancer* (Berlin: Springer Science & Business Media, 2012), 100; Rosamond Rhodes, *The Trusted Doctor: Medical Ethics and Professionalism* (New York: Oxford University Press, 2020), 162–65; letter from Nathan H. (an assistant of Emmett Scott) to Susan P. Wortham, confirming the forwarding to Emmett Scott of her letter of August 17 conveying the news of Payton's illness, August 20, 1917, Emmett Scott Collection, Morgan State University; Susan P. Wortham letter to Emmett Scott, August 23, 1917, Emmett Scott Collection, Morgan State University
41. "Payton Buried at Westfield," *New York Age*, September 6, 1917; Ronald Herder, *500 Best-loved Song Lyrics* (North Chelmsford, Mass.: Courier, 1998) 238
42. Wesleyan Methodist Church, *The Methodist Sunday-School Hymn Book* (Wesleyan-Methodist Sunday-School Union, 1879), 269; "Payton Buried at Westfield"; Nellie Melba, *Melodies and Memories* (Cambridge: Cambridge University Press, 2011), frontispiece.

EPILOGUE

1. "Payton Buried at Westfield," *New York Age*, September 6, 1917.
2. "In the Matter of Proving the Last Will and Testament of Philip A. Payton," Surrogates Court, County of New York, February 6, 1918; Last Will and Testament of Philip A. Payton, Surrogates Court, County of New York, June 25, 1910.

EPILOGUE

3. Kevin McGruder, *Race and Real Estate Conflict and Cooperation in Harlem, 1890 to 1920* (New York: Columbia University Press, 2015), 187.
4. McGruder, 187.
5. McGruder, 187.
6. Payton Apartments Corporation, Incorporation Papers, New York County Archives.
7. Gargi Bhatcharyya, *Rethinking Racial Capitalism: Questions of Reproduction and Survival* (New York: Rowman and Littlefield, 2018), ix–16.
8. Afro-American Realty Company, Prospectus, 1904, 4; Brian Goldstein, *The Roots of Urban Renaissance: Gentrification and the Struggle Over Harlem* (Cambridge, Mass.: Harvard University Press, 2017), 238–77; Mamadou Chinyelu, *Harlem Ain't Nothin' But a Third World Country: The Global Economy, Empowerment Zones and the Colonial Status of Africans in America* (New York: Mustard Seed Press, 1999), 45–49; Marie Gørrild, Sharon Obialo, and Nienke Venemo, "Gentrification and Displacement in Harlem: How the Harlem Community Lost Its Voice en Route to Progress," Humanity in Action, https://www.humanityinaction.org/knowledge_detail/gentrification-and-displacement-in-harlem-how-the-harlem-community-lost-its-voice-en-route-to-progress/; Marian McPherson, "'Ri-dam-diculous': Compass Agents' Harlem Ad Prompts Blowback," September 23, 2019, Inman.com, https://www.inman.com/2019/09/23/ri-dam-diculous-compass-harlem-ad-prompts-blowback/.
9. Conveyances, New York City Register; William L. Andrews, Frances Smith Foster, and Trudier Harris, *The Oxford Companion to African American Literature* (New York: Oxford University Press, 1997), 539; "Detectives Get 4 Trunks Stolen Furs, & Dresses Arrest 2."
10. James Baldwin, *Notes of a Native Son* (Boston: Beacon Press, 1984), 85.
11. Brian D. Goldstein, *The Roots of Urban Renaissance* (Cambridge, Mass.: Harvard University Press, 2017) 153–96; 13 W. 131st Street Payton House Proposed Development Budget, January 27, 1995, author's collection; letter from Kevin McGruder, director of Real Estate Development, Abyssinian Development Corporation to Lamont Blackstone, African American Real Estate Professionals of New York, February 17, 1995; letter from Kevin McGruder to Robert Pugh, April 17, 1995, author's collection.
12. U.S. Department of Commerce and Labor, *Sixteenth Census of the United States*, 1940, Enumeration District 44-4, sheet 8A; "Mrs. B. P. Parker, Welfare Employee Succumbs at 59," *New York Amsterdam News*, July 24, 1954.
13. Thomas Yenser, ed., *Who's Who in Colored America, 1941–1944*, 6th ed. (Brooklyn, N.Y.: Thomas Yenser, 1942); U.S. Department of Commerce and Labor, *Fourteenth Census of the United States*, 1920, Manhattan, Enumeration District 1439, sheet 54B; Cheryl Greenberg, *Or Does it Explode? Black Harlem in the Great Depression* (New York: Oxford University Press, 1997), 3–4; David Dunlap, *From Abyssinian to Zion: A Guide to Manhattan's Houses of Worship* (New York: Columbia University Press, 2004), 226; "Final Respects Paid to Mrs. Wortham," *New York Amsterdam News*, January 17, 1953.
14. "William H. Wortham," *Raleigh (N.C.) News and Observer*, August 9, 1958; author's visits to Pine Hill Cemetery.
15. Paul Laurence Dunbar, "Beyond the Years," Poets.com, https://poets.org/poem/beyond-years.

CHRONOLOGY

1874	Philip A. Payton Sr. and Maggie Ryans married in Westfield, Mass.
1876	Philip A. Payton Jr. born.
1893–1894	Payton attends his junior year of high school at Livingstone College, Salisbury, N.C.
1894–1896	Payton returns to Westfield, where a football injury leads him to drop out of high school.
1899	Payton moves to New York City seeking his fortune.
1900	Payton hired as a porter in the office of Upper West side developer Charles Schuyler.
1900	Payton partners with Springfield, Mass., native Alan Brown to form Brown and Payton Real Estate.
1901	Brown leaves the firm, and Payton continues on his own.
1902	James Warren Payton dies.
1903	Payton joins with several black entrepreneurs to form the Afro-American Realty Company (AARC), a partnership.
1904	Payton announces the incorporation of the AARC.
1906	Some white Harlem residents respond to the AARC's purchase of white-occupied buildings by placing restrictive covenants in their deeds, prohibiting black ownership or residency.

1907	Disgruntled AARC shareholders sue Payton and the AARC.
1908	Philip A. Payton Sr. dies.
1909	In shareholder lawsuit, court finds Payton not guilty but fines the AARC and requires it to refund some shareholders' investments.
1909	Payton forms the Philip A. Payton Jr. Company (PAP).
1910	Payton spends several months seeking business opportunities in Liberia.
1912	Edward Payton dies.
1913	Payton and his Equity Congress colleagues raise money for legal costs to challenge restrictive covenant usage in Harlem.
1915	Philip and Maggie Payton maintain separate homes.
1916	Annie Ryans Payton dies.
1916	Susan Payton marries William H. Wortham.
1917	Bessie Hobby marries Robert Lattimore in January.
1917	Philip Payton Jr. dies at Allenhurst, N.J., in August.

BIBLIOGRAPHY

MANUSCRIPT COLLECTIONS

Payton, Philip/Afro-American Realty File. Schomburg Center for Research in Black Culture, New York City.
Payton Family Collection. Westfield Athenaeum, Westfield, Mass.
Price, J. C., Collection. Livingstone College Archives.
Scott, Emmettt J., Collection. Morgan State University.
Washington, Booker T., Papers. Library of Congress.

GOVERNMENT DOCUMENTS

Afro-American Realty Company. Certificate of Partners Constituting the Afro-American Realty Company. June 22, 1903. New York County Archives.
——. Partnership Papers. 1903. New York County Archives.
——. Prospectus. 1904. New York County Archives.
City of New York. "A Brief History of the Tweed Court House." http://www.nyc.gov/html/om/html/tweed_courthouse.html.
Deaths Registered in the Town of Westfield in the Year 1902. Westfield, Mass.
Franklin County, N.Y. Record of Deaths. 1912.
Hudson Realty Company Annual Meeting Minutes, January 13, 1902. New York County Archives.
——. Certificate of Incorporation, February 9, 1893. New York County Archives.
Map of New York City. New York: G. W. Bromley, 1897.
Marriages Registered in the Town of Westfield in the Year Eighteen Seventy-four. *Massachusetts Marriage Records, 1840–1915*.

National Archives and Records Administration (NARA). Passport Applications, 1795–1905.
New York City Department of Finance. City Register's Office, Manhattan Conveyances, Sections 6–7, 1880–1925
New York State Census. *Albany, New York; State Population Census Schedules.* 1905, 1915.
135 Broadway Holding Corporation Certificate of Incorporation. New York County Archives.
State of New Jersey, Office of Registrar of Vital Statistics. Philip A. Payton Jr. Death Certificate. Borough of Allenhurst, August 29, 1917.
Supreme Court of the State of New York, County of New York, Appellate Division. *First Department Papers on Appeal.* 1913.
Supreme Court of the State of New York, County of New York. *Charles J. Crowder Against Afro-American Realty Company.*
U.S. Bureau of Census. *A Century of Population from the First Census of Population to the Twelfth, 1790–1900.* Washington, D.C.: U.S. Department of Commerce.
U.S. Department of Commerce and Labor. *Eighth Census of the United States. Population.* Washington, D.C.: U.S. Department of Commerce and Labor, 1860.
———. *Ninth Census of the United States. Population.* 1870.
———. *Tenth Census of the United States. Population.* 1880.
———. *Eleventh Census of the United States. Population.* 1890.
———. *Twelfth Census of the United States. Population.* 1900.
———. *Thirteenth Census of the United States. Population.* 1910.
———. *Fourteenth Census of the United States. Population.* 1920.
U.S. Department of State. *Compendium of the Enumeration of Inhabitants and Statistics of the United States as Obtained at the Department of State from the Returns of the Sixth Census.* Washington, D.C.: Department of State, 1841.

BOOKS AND ARTICLES

"An Afro-American Co. with $100,000 Paid Up." *Colored American Magazine,* August 20, 1904.
Andreas, Alfred Theodore. *The History of Chicago: From the Fire of 1871 to 1885.* Chicago: A. T. Andreas, 1886.
Annual Catalogue Virginia Union University. Richmond, Va.: Clemmitt & Jones, 1922
Association of the Bar of the City of New York. *Yearbook.* New York, 1919.
"Atlanta Race Riot." *New Georgia Encyclopedia.* http://www.georgiaencyclopedia.org/articles/history-archaeology/atlanta-race-riot-1906.
Atlas of Hampden County, Massachusetts. New York: Beers, Ellis, and Soule, 1870.
Automobile Club of Rochester, N.Y. "Chief Points of Interest in Upper Manhattan." Map. 1920.
Baldwin, James. *Notes of a Native Son.* Boston: Beacon Press, 1984.
Barrett, John G. *The Civil War in North Carolina.* Chapel Hill: University of North Carolina Press, 1995.
Benson, O. H. "Meeting America's Peculiar Needs in Education." *Journal of Education* 90 (1919).

BIBLIOGRAPHY

Bhatcharyya, Gargi. *Rethinking Racial Capitalism: Questions of Reproduction and Survival.* New York: Rowman and Littlefield, 2018.

Bivins, D. Lawrence. *North Carolina: The State of Minds.* Encino, Calif.: Cherbo, 2004.

Blackman, Douglas. *Slavery by Another Name: The Re-enslavement of Black Americans from the Civil War to World War Two.* London: Icon, 2012.

Blackmar, Elizabeth. *Manhattan for Rent.* Ithaca, N.Y.: Cornell University Press, 1991.

Bottino, Joseph C., Franco M. Muggia, and Richard W. Opfell. *Liver Cancer.* Berlin: Springer Science & Business Media, 2012.

Boyd, Herb. *Baaldwin's Harlem: A Biogrpahy of James Baldwin's Harlem.* New York: Simon and Schuster, 2008.

Brodkin, Karen. *How Jews Became White Folks and What That Says About Race in America.* New Brunswick, N.J.: Rutgers University Press, 1998.

Bruner, Robert F., and Sean D. Carr. *The Panic of 1907: Lessons Learned from the Market's Perfect Storm.* Hoboken, N.J.: Wiley, 2009.

Buckley, Gail Lumet. *The Hornes: An American Family.* Milwaukee, Wis.: Hal Leonard, 2002.

Burrowes, Carl Patrick. *Power and Press in Liberia, 1830-1970: The Impact of Globalization and Civil Society on Media-Government Relations.* Trenton, N.J.: Africa World Press, 2004.

Butler, Douglas J. *North Carolina Civil War Monuments: An Illustrated History.* Jefferson, N.C.: McFarland, 2013.

Channing, Steven A. *Crisis of Fear: Secession in South Carolina.* New York: Norton, 1974.

"Charles E. Schuyler Real Estate." In *A History of Real Estate, Building and Architecture in New York City, During the Last Quarter of a Century.* New York: Record and Guide, 1898/Arno Press, 1967.

Chinyelu, Mamadou. *Harlem Ain't Nothin' but a Third World Country: The Global Economy, Empowerment Zones and the Colonial Status of Africans in America.* New York: Mustard Seed Press, 1999.

Ciment, James. *Another America: The Story of Liberia and the Former Slaves Who Ruled It.* New York: Hill and Wang, 2014.

Clark, Christopher. *The Sleepwalkers: How Europe Went to War in 1914.* New York: Harper Perennial, 2014.

Collins, Amy V. "New York City Riot, 1900." In *Encyclopedia of American Race Riots*, vol. 1, ed. Walter C. Rucker and James N. Upton. Westport, Conn.: Greenwood Press, 2006.

Cooper, Brittney C. *Beyond Respectability: The Intellectual Thought of Race Women.* Champaign: University of Illinois Press, 2017.

Crenson, Matthew A. *Baltimore: A Political History.* Baltimore: Johns Hopkins University Press, 2017.

Crowder, Ralph. *John Edward Bruce: Politician, Journalist, and Self Trained Historian of the African Diaspora.* New York: NYU Press, 2004.

Deskins, Donald Richard, Hanes Walton, and Sherman C. Puckett. *Presidential Elections, 1789-2008: County, State, and National Mapping of Election Data.* Ann Arbor: University of Michigan Press, 2010.

DiBacco, Thomas V. "When Typhoid Was Dreaded." *Washington Post*, January 25, 1994.

Du Bois, W. E. B. *Black Reconstruction in America, 1860-1880.* New York: Atheneum, 1992.

BIBLIOGRAPHY

Dunbar, Paul Laurence. *The Sport of the Gods.* New York: Dodd, Mead, 1902.
Dunlap, David. *From Abyssinian to Zion: A Guide to Manhattan's Houses of Worship.* New York: Columbia University Press, 2004.
Edmonds, Helen G. *The Negro and Fusion Politics in North Carolina.* Chapel Hill: University of North Carolina Press, 2015.
Eicher, David. *The Longest Night: A Military History of the Civil War.* New York: Simon and Schuster, 2002.
Embree, Edwin Rogers, ed. *History of the Class of 1906, Yale College.* Class Secretaries Bureau. New Haven, Conn.: Yale University Press, 1911.
Fabre, Genvifer, and Robert O'Meally, eds., *History and Memory in African American Culture.* New York: Oxford University Press, 1994.
Fairclough, Adam. *Better Days Coming: Blacks and Equality, 1890–2000.* New York: Penguin, 2002.
Fisher, Irving. "The Modern Crusade Against Consumption." *New Outlook* 75 (1903): 691–97.
Fortune, T. Thomas. *After War-Times: An African American Childhood in Reconstruction Era Florida.* Tuscaloosa: University of Alabama Press, 2014.
Franklin, John Hope. *The Free Negro in North Carolina, 1790–1860.* Chapel Hill, N.C.: University of North Carolina Press, 2000.
Freund, David. *Colored Property: State Policy and White Racial Politics in Suburban America.* Chicago: University of Chicago Press, 2007.
Gallos, Philip L. *Cure Cottages of Saranac Lake: Architecture and History of a Pioneer Health Resort.* Saranac Lake, N.Y.: Historic Saranac Lake, 1985.
Garret-Scott, Shennette. *Banking on Freedom: Black Women in U.S. Finance Before the New Deal.* New York: Columbia University Press, 2019.
Gatewood, Willard B. *Aristocrats of Color.* Fayetteville: University of Arkansas Press, 2000.
Gehyeka, Sei Rubel. *Inside the People's Redemption Council Government of Liberia: The Untold Story.* Bloomington, Indiana: LifeRich, 2018.
Gill, Jonathan. *Harlem: The Four Hundred Year History from Dutch Village to Capital of Black America.* New York: Grove Press, 2011.
Godshalk, David Fort. *Veiled Visions: The 1906 Atlanta Race Riot and the Reshaping of American Race Relations.* Chapel Hill: University of North Carolina Press, 2006.
Goetz, Thomas. *The Remedy: Robert Koch, Arthur Conan Doyle, and the Quest to Cure Tuberculosis.* New York: Penguin, 2014.
Goldstein, Brian. *The Roots of Urban Renaissance: Gentrification and the Struggle Over Harlem.* Cambridge, Mass.: Harvard University Press, 2017.
Gørrild, Marie, Sharon Obialo, and Nienke Venemo. "Gentrification and Displacement in Harlem: How the Harlem Community Lost Its Voice en Route to Progress." *Humanity in Action.* https://www.humanityinaction.org/knowledge_detail/gentrification-and-displacement-in-harlem-how-the-harlem-community-lost-its-voice-en-route-to-progress/.
Greenberg, Cheryl. *Or Does it Explode? Black Harlem in the Great Depression.* New York: Oxford University Press, 1997.
Greenwood, Janette Thomas. *First Fruits of Freedom: The Migration of Former Slaves and Their Search for Equality in Worcester, Massachusetts, 1862–1900.* Chapel Hill, N.C.: University of North Carolina Press, 2009.

BIBLIOGRAPHY

"The Growth of the Afro-American Realty Company." *Colored American Magazine* 10, no. 2 (February 1906).
Guetzo, Allen C. *Lincoln's Emancipation Proclamation.* New York: Simon and Schuster, 2004.
Gurock, Jeffrey C. *The Jews of Harlem: The Rise, Decline, and Revival of a Jewish Community.* New York: New York University Press, 2016.
Hall, Kerrell L. *Freedom and Equality: Discrimination and the Supreme Court.* London: Taylor & Francis, 2000.
Harlan, Louis R. "The Secret Life of Booker T. Washington." *Journal of Southern History* 27, no. 3 (August 1971): 393–416.
Harter, Jim. *World Railroads of the Nineteenth Century: A Pictorial History in Victorian Engravings.* Baltimore: Johns Hopkins University Press, 2005.
Helper, Rose. *Racial Policies and Practices of Real Estate Brokers.* Minneapolis: University of Minnesota Press, 1969.
Herder, Ronald. *500 Best-loved Song Lyrics.* North Chelmsford, Mass: Courier, 1998.
"Here and There." *Colored American Magazine* 6, no. 2 (December 1902).
Hewitt, John H., Jr. *Protest and Progress: New York's First Black Episcopal Church Fights Racism.* 2000. New York: Routledge, 2018.
Hilton, Raymond Pierre. *Virginia Union University.* Mt. Pleasant, S.C.: Arcadia Press, 2014.
History of the Connecticut Valley in Massachusetts. 2 vols. Philadelphia: Louis H. Everts, 1879.
Hood, Clifton. *722 Miles: The Building of the Subways and How They Transformed New York.* Baltimore: Johns Hopkins University Press, 2004.
"Investigating the New York Building Department." *Engineering News and American Railway Journal,* vol. 41. New York: Engineering News, 1899.
Jackson, Kenneth T., Lisa Keller, and Nancy Flood, eds. "The Brooklyn Howard Orphan Asylum." *Encyclopedia of New York City.* 2nd ed. New Haven, Conn.: Yale University Press, 2010.
"James E. Garner." *Colored American Magazine* 10, no. 3 (March 1906).
Johnson, James Weldon. *Black Manhattan.* 1930. Cambridge, Mass.: DeCapo Press, 1991.
Joyce, Donald F. "Colored Co-operative Publishing Company." *Black Book Publishers in the United States: A Historical Dictionary of the Press, 1817–1900.* Westport, Conn.: Greenwood, 1991.
Kaye, Andrew M. "Colonel Roscoe Conkling Simmons and the Mechanics of Black Leadership." *Journal of American Studies* 37, no. 1 (April 2003): 79–98.
Kerr, Audrey Elisa. *The Paper Bag Principle: Class, Colorism, and Rumor and the Case of Black Washington,* part 3. Knoxville: University of Tennessee Press, 2006.
King, Shannon. *Whose Harlem Is This, Anyway? Community Politics and Grassroots Activism During the New Negro Era.* New York: New York University Press, 2015.
Knight, Edgar Wallace. *Public School Education in North Carolina.* New York: Houghton Mifflin, 1916.
Korom, Joseph J. *The American Skyscraper, 1850–1940: A Celebration of Height.* Wellesley, Mass: Branden Books, 2008.
Laurenti, Luigi. *Property Values and Race: Studies in Seven Cities.* Berkeley: University of California Press, 1960.

BIBLIOGRAPHY

Lewis, David Levering. *W. E. B. DuBois: Biography of a Race, 1868–1919*. New York: Holt, 1994.
———. *When Harlem Was in Vogue*. New York: Penguin, 1997.
Logel, John Scott. *Designing Gotham: West Point Engineers and the Rise of Modern New York, 1817–1898*. Baton Rouge: Louisiana State University Press, 2016.
Luker, Ralph E. *The Social Gospel in Black and White: American Racial Reform, 1885–1912*. Chapel Hill: University of North Carolina Press, 1998.
MacCracken, Henry Mitchell, Ernest Gottlieb Sihler, and Willis Fletcher Johnson. *New York University: Its History, Influence, Equipment and Characteristics, with Biographical Sketches and Portraits of Founders, Benefactors, Officers and Alumni*. Vol. 2. Boston: R. Herndon, 1903.
Martschukat, J., and Silvan Niedermeier, eds. *Violence and Visibility in Modern History*. New York: Palgrave Macmillan, 2013.
McClurken, Jeffrey W. *Take Care of the Living: Reconstructing Confederate Veteran Families in Virginia*. Charlottesville: University of Virginia Press, 2009.
McGruder, Kevin. *Race and Real Estate: Conflict and Cooperation in Harlem, 1890–1920*. New York: Columbia University Press, 2015.
McKenzie, Evan. *Privatopia: Homeowner Associations and the Rise of Residential Private Government*. New Haven, Conn.: Yale University Press, 1994.
McPherson, Marian. "'Ri-dam-diculous': Compass Agents' Harlem Ad Prompts Blowback." Inman.com, September 23, 2019. https://www.inman.com/2019/09/23/ri-dam-diculous-compass-harlem-ad-prompts-blowback/.
Melba, Nellie. *Melodies and Memories*. Cambridge, UK: Cambridge University Press, 2011.
Miller, Tom. "The Lost Church of the Messiah—Park Avenue and 34th Street." *Daytonian in Manhattan* (blog), October 4, 2015. http://daytoninmanhattan.blogspot.com/2015/10/the-lost-church-of-messiah-park-avenue.html.
Moller, Joanne E. "1876: Local Observance of the Centennial." *Historical Journal of Western Massachusetts* 5, no. 1 (Spring 1976).
Muhammad, Khalil Gibran. *The Condemnation of Blackness: Race, Crime, and the Making of Modern Urban America*. Cambridge, Mass.: Harvard University Press, 2010.
Mulqueen, Joseph F. "Hon. James Fitzgerald." *Journal of the American-Irish Historical Society*. Vol. 23. New York: American-Irish Society, 1924.
Myrdal, Gunnar. *An American Dilemma*. Vol. 2. Abingdon, UK: Transaction, 1996.
National Center for Education Statistics. *120 Years of American Education: A Statistical Portrait*. Darby, Pa.: Diane, 1993.
National Register of Historic Places Application. Westfield Center Historic District, May 10, 2013.
"Negroes in Business." *Colored American Magazine* 5, no. 5 (September 6, 1903).
Nercessian, Nora N. *Against All Odds: The Legacy of Students of African Descent at Harvard Medical School Before Affirmative Action, 1850–1968*. Boston: Harvard Medical School, 2004.
Norrell, Robert Jefferson. *Up From History: The Life of Booker T. Washington*. Cambridge, Mass.: Harvard University Press, 2009.
North Carolina History Project. "Rowan County." *Encyclopedia of the Old North State*. http://northcarolinahistory.org/encyclopedia/rowan-county-1753/.

BIBLIOGRAPHY

Orr, Tamra. *Liver Cancer: Current and Emerging Trends in Detection and Treatment.* New York: Rosen Publishing Group, 2009.

Osofsky, Gilbert. *Harlem, the Making of a Ghetto: Negro New York, 1890–1930.* Chicago: Ivan R. Dee, 1996.

——. "Race Riot, 1900: A Study in Ethnic Violence." *Journal of Negro Education* 32, no. 1 (Winter 1963): 16–24.

Our Story, Westfield State University. Vol. 4. Westfield, Mass: Westfield State University, 2010.

Outland, Robert B., III, *Tapping the Pines: The Naval Stores Industry in the American South.* Baton Rouge: Lousiana State University Press, 2004.

Ovington, Mary White. *Black and White Sat Down Together: Reminisences of an NAACP Founder.* New York: Feminist Press at City University of New York, 1996.

——. *Half a Man: The Status of the Negro in New York.* London: Longmans, Green, 1911.

Payton, James Warren. "Some Experiences and Customs at Yale." *Colored American Magazine* 1, no. 2 (June 1900): 80–87.

Perry, Jeffrey B. *Hubert Harrison: The Voice of Harlem Radicalism, 1883–1918.* New York: Columbia University Press, 2008.

Pierson, Sharon Gayle. *Laboratory of Learning: HBCU Laboratory Schools and Alabama State College Lab High in the Era of Jim Crow.* Bern, Switz.: Peter Lang, 2015.

Pinkerton, Robert E. "The First Woods Cure." *Crusader of the Wisconsin Anti-Tuberculosis Association* 1, no. 14 (May 1911).

Proceedings of the National Negro Business League, August 23rd and 24th, 1900. Boston: J. R. Hamm, 1900.

Pugh, Robert. Floor Plan for 13 West 131st Street, 199?. Author's collection.

"Questions and Answers, Brokers' Fees." *Real Estate Record and Builders Guide*, March 22, 1913.

Real Estate Record and Builders Guide. 1900–1917.

Record and Guide. *A History of Real Estate, Building and Architecture in New York City, During the Last Quarter of a Century.* New York: Record and Guide, 1898/Arno Press, 1967.

Report of the Fourth Annual Convention of the National Negro Business League. Wilberforce, Ohio: Charles Alexander, 1903.

Reynolds, James Bronson. *Civic Bibliography for Greater New York.* New York: Charities Publication Committee, 1911.

Riser, R. Volney. *Defying Disfranchisement: Black Voting Rights Activism in the Jim Crow South, 1890–1908.* Baton Rouge: Louisiana State University Press, 2010.

Roberts, Randy. *Papa Jack: Jack Johnson and the Rea of White Hopes.* New York: Simon and Schuster, 1985.

Rosamond Rhodes. *The Trusted Doctor: Medical Ethics and Professionalism.* New York: Oxford University Press, 2020.

Rosen, Hannah. *Terror in the Heart of Freedom: Citizenship, Sexual Violence, and the Meaning of Race in the Postemancipation South.* Chapel Hill: University of North Carolina Press, 2009.

Rosenzwig, Roy, and Elizabeth Blackmar. *The Park and the People: A History of Central Park.* Ithaca, N.Y.: Cornell University Press, 1992.

Rountree, Louise M. *Blue Bear Trax: Highlights of the Livingstone College Blue Bear Football Record and Gridiron Greats, and a Documented Scoreboard 1892–1966*. Salisbury, N.C.: Livingstone College, 1967.

Rucker, Walter C., and James N. Upton, *Encyclopedia of American Race Riots*. Greenwood Publishing Group, 2007.

Sacks, Marcy. *Before Harlem: The Black Experience in New York Before World War I*. Philadelphia: University of Pennsylvania Press, 2013.

Scobey, David M. *Empire City: The Making and Meaning of the New York City Landscape*. Philadelphia: Temple University Press, 2003.

Senechal de la Roche, Roberta. *In Lincoln's Shadow: The 1908 Race Riot in Springfield, Illinois*. Carbondale: Southern Illinois University Press, 2008.

Sentf, Bret. "If You Are Thinking of Living in Tribeca, the Catalyst for Change." *New York Times*, September 26, 1993.

Simmons, Roscoe Conkling. "The Afro-American Realty Company: Has It Justified the Support Given It?" *Colored American Magazine* (May 1905).

Simmons, William J., and Henry McNeal Turner. *Men of Mark: Eminent, Progressive, and Rising*. Cleveland: George M. Rewell, 1887.

Sketch Book of Livingstone College and East Tennessee Industrial School. Salisbury, N.C., 1903.

Smallwood, Stephanie E. *Saltwater Slavery: A Middle Passage from Africa to American Diaspora*. Cambridge, Mass.: Harvard University Press, 2009.

Smith, J. Clay, Jr. *Emancipation: The Making of the Black Lawyer, 1844–1944*. Philadelphia: University of Pennsylvania Press, 1999.

Smitherman, Geneva. *Talkin and Testifyin: The Language of Black America*. Detroit: Wayne State University Press, 1986.

Smock, Raymond. *Booker T. Washington: Black Leadership in the Age of Jim Crow*. Lanham, Md.: Ivan R. Dee, 2009.

———, ed. *Booker T. Washington in Perspective: Essays of Louis R. Harlan*. Jackson: University of Mississippi Press, 2006.

Stuckey, Sterling. *Slave Culture: Nationalist Theory and the Foundations of Black America*. New York: Oxford University Press, 1987.

Svenson, Salley E. *Blacks in the Adirondacks: A History*. Syracuse, N.Y.: Syracuse University Press, 2017.

Talbot, Edith Armstrong. *Samuel Chapman Armstrong: A Biographical Sketch*. New York: Doubleday, Page, 1904.

Taylor, Keeanga-Yamahtta. *Race for Profit: How Banks and the Real Estate Industry Undermined Black Homeownership*. Chapel Hill, N.C.: University of North Carolina Press, 2019.

Thompson, Charles Manfred. *History of the United States: Political, Industrial, Social*. Boston: Sanborn, 1917.

Trow's General Directory of the Boroughs of Manhattan and the Bronx, City of New York. New York: Trow Directory Printing and Bookbinding, 1907, 1908.

Turner, Frederick Jackson. "The Significance of the Frontier in American History, 1893." Paper presented to meeting of the American Historical Association, Chicago, July 12, 1893. http://nationalhumanitiescenter.org/pds/gilded/empire/text1/turner.pdf.

Van Camp, Louis. *Washington, North Carolina*. Mt. Pleasant, S.C.: Arcadia, 2000.

BIBLIOGRAPHY

Vose, Clement E. *Caucasians Only: The Supreme Court, the NAACP, and the Restrictive Covenant Cases.* Berkeley: University of California Press, 1967.
Walter, John Christopher. *The Harlem Fox: J. Raymond Jones and Tammany, 1920–1970.* Albany, N.Y.: SUNY Press, 1989.
Walters, Bishop Alexander B. *My Life and Work.* London: Revell, 1917.
Washington, Booker T. *The Negro in Business.* Chicago: Hertel & Jenkins, 1907.
Washington, Booker T., Geraldine E. McTigue, and Louis R. Harlan. *Booker T. Washington Papers.* Vol. 10. Champaign: University of Illinois Press, 1981.
Wellman, Judith. *Brooklyn's Promised Land: The Free Black Community of Weeksville, New York.* New York: NYU Press, 2017.
Wells, Ida B. *The Red Record: Tabulated Statistics and Alleged Causes of Lynching in the United States,* 1895. Project Gutenberg e-book. https://www.gutenberg.org/files/14977/14977-h/14977-h.htm#chap4.
Westfield Athenaeum, *Westfield: Images of America.* Charleston, S.C.: Arcadia, 1996.
Westfield Directory. Westfield, Mass.: Ridley's, 1874.
Westfield Directory. Albany, N.Y.: R. S. Dillon, 1881, 1885.
Westfield, Hampden County, 1870, Massachusetts. New York: Frederick W. Beers, 1870.
"Westfield, Massachusetts." *Lost New England.* http://lostnewengland.com/category/massachusetts/westfield-massachusetts/.
Wharton, Edith. *A Backward Glance.* Redditch, UK: Read Books, 2013.
Williams, S. Laing. *Report, Fifth Annual Convention, National Negro Business League.* Pensacola, Fla.: M. M. Lewey, 1904.
Winford, Brandon K. *John Hervey Wheeler, Black Banking, and the Economic Struggle for Civil Rights.* Lexington: University Press of Kentucky, 2020.
World Almanac and Encyclopedia. New York: Press Publishing Company/New York World, 1905.
Writer's Program. *The State Teacher's College at Westfield.* Westfield, Mass.: Jerome Press, 1941.
Yenser, Thomas, Ed. *Who's Who in Colored America, 1941–1944.* 6th ed. Brooklyn, N.Y.: Thomas Yenser, 1942.
Zatarga, Michael P. *The Battle of Roanoke Island: Burnside and the Fight for North Carolina.* Mt. Pleasant, S.C.: History Press, 2015.

INDEX

Page numbers in italics signify graphics.

Aaron, Louis, 36
Abyssinian Baptist Church, 60, 135, 174
Abyssinian Development Corporation, 174
Adler, Felix, 143
Advisory Council of Real Estate Interests, 143
African Americans: beliefs in inferiority of, 15, 140; Jim Crow laws against, 21–22, 23, 100, 135; lynchings of, 48, 52, 96, 135, 148; and post–Civil War period, 17–18, 21, 23, 48, 49–50, 70, 126; terms used for, 47–48, 114–15; in Westfield, MA, 18, 19–20; white backlash against, 3, 126, 128–29, 131–32, 138–40. *See also* black communities; black tenants; race riots
African Methodist Episcopal Zion Church, 22, 107
African Society of Redemption, 117
Afro-American League, 22, 48, 107
Afro-American Realty Company (AARC): closing of, 101; *Colored American Magazine* on, 67–68, 75–76; dividends issued by, 94; eviction of white tenants by, 71–72, 78–79, 80, 83, 171; financing terms of, 65; formation of, 1–2, 11, 47, 49; and Hampden Realty, 93–94; incorporation of, 61–62, 66; national ambitions of, 77; net earnings of, 75, 90; *New York Times* attacks on, 65–66, 78–79; office of, 86; and Panic of 1907, 95; partners in, 49–51, 64–65, 86; Payton's relationship to, 84, 87–88; prospectus of, 62, 63, 64, 123, 171; as race enterprise, 4, 64, 76–77, 171, 172; real estate deals of, 60, 67, 79–80, 81, 86, 87–88; and rent increases, 76, 80; vision and goals of, 1–2, 62, 64, 74, 171. *See also Crowder v. Afro-American Reality Corporation*
Agard, D. P., 139
Aked, Charles F., 135
Amend, Edward B., 88
American Colonization Society (ACS), 106
Anderson, Charles W., 104, 111–12, 113, 154, 155
Anti-Saloon League, 158
Armstrong, Samuel Chapman, 27, 28
"Atlanta Compromise" (Washington), 28, 40, 81–82

INDEX

Atlanta race riot, 81–82
Attucks, Crispus, 161–62
Autumn Exposition and Amusement Festival, 142

Bailey, S., 139
Baldwin, James, 173
Baltimore, MD, 116
Banking on Freedom (Garret-Scott), 6–7
Barnes, J. S., 16
Battle, Samuel, 155
Beckett, George E., 148
Bell, John, 12
Bennet, Stephen A., 86
Bhatcharyya, Gargi, 4, 170
Bishop, Hutchens C., 120, 137, 139
black business history, 6–7
Black Codes, 48
black communities: history of in New York City, 1, 9, 34–35, 56; portrayed as vectors of crime and disease, 3–4, 59, 140, 170–71; restrictive covenants to prevent, 90–92, 94, 111, 112, 116, 117, 127; San Juan Hill, 4, 9, 35, 68–69, 82, 130; Tenderloin, 4, 9, 34–36, 37, 74, 146. *See also* Harlem; residential segregation
Black Manhattan (Johnson), 5–6
black tenants: evictions of, 57–61; higher rents charged to, 3, 38, 76, 123, 140, 156–57; organizing efforts of, 123, 132–34, 156–57; restrictive covenants against, 90–92, 94, 111, 112, 116, 117, 127
Blauner, Jacob, 91–92
blockbusting, 80
Bloomingdale, Joseph, 58, 60–61
Bolden, Richard Manuel, 137, 156
Bomzon, Wolf, 91
Booker T. Washington Memorial Fund, 153–55
Bostwick, Arthur C., 85, 86, 88, 93, 94
Bowen, Richard, 16
Breckenridge, John, 12
Briggs, Cyril, 138
Brooks, William H., 120, 158–59, 166–67
Brown, Albert N., 36, 37
Brown, E. C., 149, 169

Brown, Joseph, 99–100
Brown and Payton firm, 36–37
Bruce, Joseph H., 50
Bryan, William Jennings, 42
Bulkley, W. L., 156
Burdett, Cyril H., 168
Burnside, Ambrose, 14
Butler, C. Leroy, 70

Caffey, Dickie F., 153
Caffey, Frank, 151–52
Carnegie, Andrew, 150
Chinese immigrants, 19
Citizens Club, 154
Civic League, 133–34
Civil War, 13–15
Clansman, The (Dixon), 70–71
Clark, John T., 132
Clark, Melissa, 173
Clark, T. J., 139
Clinton, Arthur W., 99–100
Cohn, Wolf, 153
Colored American Magazine, 42–43, 62, 64, 67–68, 75–77
Colored Citizens' Protective League, 69, 70, 71
Colored Property (Freund), 7
Committee for Improving the Industrial Conditions Among Negroes, 132
Committee on Urban Conditions Among Negroes, 132
Conference of Workers Among Girls, 126
Congamond Holding Company, 175
convict lease system, 48–49
Cooke, Frank L., 168
Cooney, John, 69–70
Cooper, Anna Julia, 111
Courtney, Cornelia, 27
Courtney, Samuel, 27, 28, 41, 51, 112, 151
Crowder, Charles J., 83, 84, 92–93, 100
Crowder v. Afro-American Realty Company: civil trial in, 85–86; filing of, 83–85; judgment in, 98–100; motivation for, 100–101; Payton arrest in, 88–89; Payton's reputation damaged by, 101, 105

INDEX

Cunard, Samuel, 108
Curtis, James L., 126

Dabney, Winston, 64
Dade, Miss E., 23
DaSilva, Mrs. C., 156
Davis, Floyd W., 168
Dawley, William, 93
Declaration of Independence, 17–18
Devery, William S., 59
Dixon, Thomas, 70–71
double-consciousness, 155
Douglas, Stephen, 12
Douglass, Frederick, 40–41, 108, 162
Dowling, Justice, 99
Drew, Howard, 154
Du Bois, W. E. B., 10, 23, 36, 97, 155; and Niagara Movement, 107–8, 115; *The Souls of Black Folk*, 49
Dunbar, Paul Laurence, 118, 161–62; "Beyond the Years," 176, 177; *The Sport of the Gods*, 30, 31
Duncan, Samuel A., 141

Earle, John, 166
Eicher, David, 14
Elkay, Lewis, 19
Ellis, John, 13
Emancipation Proclamation, 124–25
Empire City (Scoby), 38–39
Enoch, May, 35
Epps, Norman, 59–60
Equity Congress, 126–27, 130, 131, 155
Europe, James Reese, 155, 156
evictions: of black tenants, 57–61; of white tenants, 71–72, 78–79, 80, 83, 171

Falkner, Roland P., 106
Fauset, Jessie, 10
Fitzgerald, James, 85–86
Folsom, C. M., 146
football, 25, 26
Fork, William H., Josephine, and Grace, 19
Forster, Cecil and Sandra, 175
Forster, Evelyn, 175
Fortune, T. Thomas, 22, 48, 107

Francis, Nellie Griswold, 113
Franz Ferdinand, Archduke, 141
Freund, David, 7
Fugitive Slave Law, 12

Garner, James E., 50, 68, 139
Garnet, Henry Highland, 168
Garret-Scott, Shenette, 6–7
Georgia State College for Negroes, 136
Gibson, Peter B., 42
Gilbert, M. W., 70
Goldstein, Brian, 6
Green, J. M., 157
Greenwich Village, 34, 117

Hamilton, Miss D., 23
Hampden Realty and Construction Company, 92–94, 96
Hampton Institute, 143
Handy, Walter E., 50
Harlem: black population in, 112; brownstones in, 56–57; contemporary real estate development in, 172, 173–74; development boom in, 1, 55; eviction of black tenants in, 57–61; history of African American presence in, 1, 9, 56, 82–83; housing shortage in, 161–62; Payton move to, 38; racial animosity toward blacks in, 38, 126, 128–29, 131–32, 138–40; real estate deals in, 36–37, 40, 54, 67, 75, 77, 79–80, 81, 86, 87–88, 116–17, 121–22, 129–30, 151–52, 154, 155; restrictive covenants in, 90–92, 94, 111, 112, 116, 117, 127; scholarship on, 5–6; walk-up apartment buildings in, 56
Harlem, the Making of a Ghetto (Osofsky), 6
Harlem Board of Commerce, 128–29
Harlem Home Protective Association, 126–27, 128
Harlem Renaissance, 10, 173
Harlem Reporter and Bronx Chronicle, 55
Harris, Arthur, 35
Harris, George W., 139
Harris, Lewis, 93

INDEX

Haynes, George E., 166
Hayward, William, 156
Heinze, Auguste, 95
Henderson, W. L., 23
Henson, Matthew, 103–4
Herbert, Rufus, 139
Herman Raabe's Sons, 78
Herndon, Alonzo, 151
Hill, Richard, 51–52
Hobby, Duke, 116, 136, 146, 155, 160; after Payton death, 174; in Payton will, 168
Hobby (Lattimore), Mary Elizabeth (Bessie), 116, 146, 160; debutante party for, 135–36; later life of, 175; marriage of, 158–59; in Payton will, 168
Horne, Edwin F. and Edna Scottron, 115–16
Horton, Loton, 79, 80
Housing Bureau (Urban League), 131–32, 133, 157
Howard, C. D., 23
Howard, Frank, 148
Howard, Oliver, 159
Howard Orphanage, 159–60
Howell, Clark, 82
Hudson Realty Company, 58, 65, 66, 117, 170
Hughes, Langston, 173
Hunter, M. L., 113
Hurston, Zora Neale, 173
Hutchinson, Charles, 118
Hutchinson, Clarence, 122, 146
Hyder, Frank, 157

immigration restrictions, 145–46
Independent, 97
Infants of the Spring (Thurman), 173

Jarmulowsky, Meyer, 138, 139
Jim Crow, 100, 135; in North Carolina, 21–22, 23
John Hervey Wheeler (Winford), 7
John Royall Real Estate, 118
Johnson, Charles S., 10
Johnson, E. A., 166
Johnson, Jack, 36, 110–11, 151
Johnson, James Weldon, 5–6, 154

Johnson, J. Rosamond, 156
Johnson, Mrs. E. A., 117
Jones, Eugene Kinckle, 143, 154
Jones, P. E., 103

Karney, Henry, 147
Kenney, John, 150
King, Shannon, 6
Kingsland, James L., 174–75
Klein, David, 46
Koch, Erduin von der Horst, 128, 129
Koch, Robert, 119
Kroehle, Charles, 60, 61
Kuehne, Gerhard, 168
Ku Klux Klan, 70

Ladson, Robert, 146
Lane, Frank T., 59
Langston, Ralph, 146
Lattimore, George, 136
Lattimore, Robert Pinkerton, 158–59
Lawson, James F., 111, 190n20
Lawson, Josephine F., 111
Lawton, Marie C., 126, 154–55
Lawton, W. R., 120
League for Protection of Colored Women, 132
League of Urban Conditions Among Negroes, 131–32, 133
Leavelle, Louis, 166
Leonard, Mrs. C. R., 156
Lever, Asbury, 136
Levy, Morris, 94
Liberia, 140–41; and African Americans, 105, 106; Payton trip to, 107–10; U.S. official delegation to, 106–7
Liggan, Julia, 60, 118
Lincoln, Abraham, 12, 124
"Little Africa" (Harlem), 1, 9, 112
"Little Africa" (Lower Manhattan), 34
Livingstone College, 21, 22, 23–25
Lucy Laney League, 128, 137–38
Luker, Ralph, 70
lynchings, 48, 52, 96, 135, 148
Lyon, Ernest, 108–9, 140
Lyon, Maude, 140

INDEX

Manhattan: blacks in, 34–35, 56, 112; real estate market in, 38–39, 55. *See also* Harlem; San Juan Hill neighborhood; Tenderloin neighborhood
Mann, Horace, 26
Martin, David, 113
Martin, Eugene, 113
McAdoo, Maybelle, 118
McAdoo, William, 69–70
McArthur, Allis, 19
McClellan, George B., Jr., 71, 73
McClendon, Rose, 154–55
McDougald, Cornelius, 113
McElligent, William, 19
McKerrow, H. G. and Eva, 154
McKinley Realty and Construction Company, 74
McLaughlin, William, 69–70
McNeill, F., 23
McPherson, Richard C., 141
Mercy Seat Baptist Church, 54, 59–60
Meyer, Louis, 78, 79–80
Miller, George F., 159
Miller, Horace G., 120
Minck, Matilda, 129–30, 153
Mitchell, Archibald P., 96
Moody, Burton and Ollie, 119
Moore, Charles H., 148
Moore, Fred R., 126, 139, 156, 160; and B. T. Washington, 104, 111–12; as *Colored American Magazine* publisher, 67, 76, 98; on lynchings, 148; on "new Negro," 41–42; as Payton friend and business partner, 3, 67, 76–77, 98
Morganthau, Maximilian, Jr., 121–22
Morgenthau, Maximilian, Sr., 58, 60–61
Morris, Charles Satchell, 60, 70
Morris, John Lewis, 140
mortgage financing, 52–53
Moton, Robert Russa, 143, 156–57
Mount Vernon, NY, 121–22

Nail, John B., 160
Nail, John E., 6, 127, 133, 137, 146, 154, 156, 159; *New York Times* on, 128–29; as partner in AARC, 86; and racial tensions, 138, 139; partnership with Parker formed by, 117–18, 122
Nail and Parker Real Estate, 117–18, 122, 146
National Association for the Advancement of Colored People (NAACP), 97, 115
National Association of Real Estate Boards (NAREB), 140
National Guard regiment, 130–31, 141, 155; Women's Auxiliary of, 160
National League for Urban Conditions Among Negroes, 143
National Medical Association, 154
National Negro Business League (NNBL), 40, 41–42, 51–52, 66, 107, 147–49; and Payton, 47, 52, 53, 103
"Negro" term, 114–15
Nelson, Mrs. Cole K., 115
New Bern, NC, 14–15
Newman, Rosa, 92
New Year's Eve celebrations, 54, 66–67, 86–87, 102, 104, 158; *New York Times* on, 73–74, 95–96, 104, 114, 145, 152
New York Age, 86–87, 104, 106, 113, 132–33; articles on Payton in, 88–89, 98–99, 110, 114–15, 122–23, 167; on black protests, 134–35, 156; and B. T. Washington, 82, 150; Payton advertisements in, 74, 86, 146, *147*; on Payton death and funeral, 164, 166; Payton letter in, 136–37; Payton's ties to, 114, 128
New York City: anti-black hostility in, 77–78; Draft Riots in, 97, 159; growth of African American population in, 55, 56; history of black communities in, 1, 9, 34–35, 56; Payton move to, 29, 31–33; residential segregation in, 34, 38, 56, 64, 77–78, 118; subway line in, 55, 57; Tammany Hall in, 85; traveling to, 30–31. *See also* Harlem; Manhattan
New York Times, 44, 115, 128; on New Year's Eve celebrations, 73–74, 95–96, 104, 114, 145, 152; on Payton and AARC, 36, 65–66, 71–72, 78–79, 80

New York Tribune, 32, 102, 104
Niagara Movement, 108, 115
Norman, Conrad, 141
North Carolina, 12-13, 21-22, 23
Notes of a Native Son (Baldwin), 173
Nugent, Richard Bruce, 173

Ochs, Adolph S., 73
Oppenheim, Alfred and Benjamin, 116
Osofsky, Gilbert, 6
Ovington, Mary White, 68, 97

Panic of 1907, 95
Parker, Henry, 86, 122-23, 127, 138, 146, 156
Partzchefeld, Louis, 60, 61
Patterson, Louis, 174
Payne, Charles H., 166
Payton, Annie M. Ryans (mother), 19, 120, 147; death of, 152-54; marriage of, 16
Payton, Edward (brother), 104-5, 176; birth of, 19; illness and death of, 118-20; as real estate partner, 86, 118, 168
Payton, James (brother), 26, 39, *44*, 176; birth of, 18; death of, 42-43; at Yale, 28, 33, 42
Payton, Maggie Lee (wife), *46*, 96, 121, 136, 151; dinner parties of, 3, 104-5, 112-13, 115-16; later life of, 174-75; marriage to Philip, 33-34; in Philip's will, 167-68; in real estate business, 43, 44; separation from Philip, 146-47, 159, 164
Payton, Philip, Jr.: AARC formed and closed by, 1-2, 11, 47, 49, 101; AARC's relationship to, 84, 87-88; advertisements by, 44, *45*, 74, 86, *89*, 146, *147*; black tenants of, 3, 76, 80, 123, 133, 134, 140, 156-57; and B. T. Washington, 2-3, 5, 61, 104, 107, 111, 115, 137, 150-51, 171; death of, 163-65; education of, 1, 4-5, 21, 23-26; eviction of white tenants by, 71-72, 78-79, 80, 83, 171; as football player, 25, 26; funeral of, 166-67; homes of, 35, 38, 39, 45-46, *46*, 92-93, *147*; housing vision of, 1-2, 62, 64, 74, 129, 163, 171; jobs worked by, 1, 28-29, 33; lawsuit against, 83-86, 88-89, 98-101; as leader of Harlem organizations, 69, 70, 131, 141, 142; legacy of, 4, 10, 120, 166-67, 175; and Liberia, 104-10, 140-41; at Livingstone College, 21, 23-25; marriage of, 33-34; media skills of, 71, 114, 171-72; move to New York by, 29, 31-33; and National Negro Business League, 47, 52, 53, 103; *New York Times* on, 36, 65-66, 71-72, 78-79, 80; and Payton Apartments, 162-63; personality of, 24, 29; philanthropic activities of, 142-43, 152, 154-55, 156, 160-61; photos, 26, *27*, *46*, *68*, *89*, *147*; "Possibilities for the Negro in the Real Estate Field" speech, 52, 53; public profile of, 11, 77, 81, 125, 136; real estate business entered by, 36; real estate deals of, 36-37, 40, 43, 44, 54, 67, 75, 77, 79-80, 81, 86, 87-88, 116-17, 121-22, 129-30, 151-52, 154; relationship network of, 2-3, 11, 33, 111--13, 115-16, 154-55; social activities of, 120, 128, 135-36, 137-38, 140-41, 151, 154-57; will of, 167-68. *See also* Afro-American Realty Company; Philip A. Payton Jr. Company
Payton, Philip Anthony, Sr. (father), 15-16, 19, 20-21, *98*; barbershop of, 18, 19; birth and childhood of, 12; death of, 97-98; at Wayland Seminary, 16, 24, 27
Payton (Wortham), Susan Ann Wesley (sister), 104-5, 120, 141, 157, 176; birth of, 18; later life of, 175; marriage of, 157-58; and Philip death, 164-65; in Philip's will, 167, 168; in school, 20, 26-27
Payton Apartments, 162-63, 169
Payton Apartments Corporation, 169
Peace, Harold, 174
Peary, Robert, 103-4
Pell, Margaret, 19

INDEX

Pendleton, Anna, 173
Philip A. Payton Jr. Company, 102–3, 117, 121, 133, 146, *147*; after Payton's death, 167–68, 169, 175; founding of, 101
Philippine War, 32
Philton Realty Company, 161
Pinchback, P. B. S., 151
Pine Hill Cemetery, 98, 163, 167, 175–76, *176*
Poincare, Raymond, 152
police, 4, 34–36, 59, 68, 69–70
Powell, Adam Clayton, Sr., 132, 135, 137, 142, 154
Prayer, Paul G., 139
Price, Joseph C., 22, 23, 24, 48
Progressive Party, 134
Property Owner's Improvement Corporation, 138–40
Property Owners Protective Association, 128, 129
Pugh, Robert, 174

Race and Real Estate (McGruder), 6, 168
Race for Profit (Taylor), 7
race riots: in Atlanta, 81–82; New York Draft Riots, 97, 159; in San Juan Hill, 68–69, 82; in Springfield, Il, 96–97; in Tenderloin, 35–36
racial capitalism, 4, 5, 10, 169–71, 170
real estate practices: evictions of black tenants, 57–61; evictions of white tenants, 71–72, 78–79, 80, 83, 171; mortgage financing, 52–53; and rents, 3, 38, 76, 80, 123, 140, 156–57; restrictive covenants, 90–92, 94, 111, 112, 116, 117, 127, 143. *See also* residential segregation
Real Estate Record and Builders' Guide, 93, 153, 161; article about Payton in, 44–45; establishment of, 39; Payton advertisements in, *45*, 89; Payton letter to, 89–90
Reconstruction, 17–18, 21, 23, 70
Red Record, The (Wells), 52
residential segregation: in Baltimore, 116; in New York City, 34, 38, 56, 64,
77–78, 118; and Payton business model, 2, 3, 10, 123; scholarship on, 7
restrictive covenants: advisory committee to investigate, 143; in Harlem, 90–92, 94, 111, 112, 116, 117, 127
Rethinking Racial Capitalism (Bhatcharyya), 170
Revenue Realty Company, 121
Reynolds, David I., 168
Rice, Mrs. Daniel J., 156
Riddick, Bettie E., 23
Roanoke Island campaign (Civil War), 14
Roanoke Times, 114–15
Roberts, Mollie, 120
Robinson, A.M., 157
Roosevelt, Theodore, 32, 106
Root, Elihu, 136, 137
Roots of Urban Renaissance, The (Goldstein), 6
Rosenberg, Millie, 159
Rosenberg, Montgomery, 91
Roth, P.M., 78
Royall, John, 127, 134, 137, 154–55; advertisements for, 118, 169; and Housing Bureau, 132–33; and tenants' campaign, 157
Ruff, August, 54, 61
Ruff, Mena, 60, 61

Sale, George, 106
Salisbury, NC, 21–22
San Juan Hill neighborhood, 4, 9, 35, 130; race riot in, 68–69, 82
Scarborough, W. S., 156
Schloss, Leo, 168
Schuyler, Charles E., 33
Scoby, David, 38–39
Scott, Emmett, 101, 104, 151, 156, 164, 166; and National Negro Business League, 148–49; and Payton's Liberia trip, 106, 107
Scott, Isaiah B., 107–8, 110
Sears, Ellen B. and Horace, 27
segregation. *See* Jim Crow; residential segregation

Simmons, Roscoe Conklin, 67–68
slavery, 12–13, 51–52
Smith, Hoke, 82, 136
Smith, Wilford H., 68, 69, 156; biographical information, 51, 100; and suit against Payton, 83, 84, 88–90, 100
Smith-Lever Act, 136–37
Souls of Black Folk, The (Du Bois), 49
Spanish American War, 32
Sport of the Gods, The (Dunbar), 30, 31
Springfield, IL, 96–97
Stanley, Edward, 15
Steuart, Frank A., 64–65
Stevens, Andrew F., 169
Stevenson, John, 50
Stewart, Gilchrist, 69, 139, 155
St. Mark's Methodist Episcopal Church, 120, 153, 154, 158, 166–67, 175
Strong, Abiah Root, 34, 112
subway, 55, 57
Sulzer, William, 131
Sun (New York), 104, 161–63
Supreme Liberty Life Insurance Company of Chicago, 175

Taft, William H., 106
Tammany Hall, 85
Tandy, Vertner, 113, 136
Taylor, John G., 117, 129, 138
Taylor, Julius F., 113
Taylor, Keeanga-Yamahtta, 7
Tenderloin neighborhood, 4, 9, 37, 74, 146; about, 34–35; race rioting in, 35–36
Ten Eyck, William, 33, 50
Terrell, Robert H., 42, 112
Terry, Watt, 149, 166, 168
Theobold, Hanna, 91
13 West 131st Street townhouse, 46, 146; after Payton's death, 172–73, 174; Payton's purchase of, 45; transfer of ownership of, 92–93
Thomas, James C., 68, 104, 127, 133–34; as Payton business partner, 50, 60
Thompson, George R., 36
Thorpe, Robert J., 35

Thurman, Wallace, 173
Tillman, Sarah A., 159
Times Square, 104, 114, 145, 152, 158; development of, 73–74
Toney, Charles, 141
Toots, Charles, 99–100
Toussaint L'Ouverture, 161
Trudeau, Paul, 119
Turner, Richard F., 99–100
Tuskegee Institute, 28, 40, 136, 137, 153–54, 156
Tweed, William "Boss," 85
Twichell, David C., 119

Up from Slavery (Douglass), 40–41
Urban League. *See* Committee on Urban Conditions Among Negroes; League of Urban Conditions Among Negroes; National League for Urban Conditions Among Negroes

van Vechten, Carl, 10
Vollhart, Rosina, 129

Walker, Ada Overton, 138
Walker, George, 155
Walker, Maggie Lena, 6–7
Wallace, Walter, 42
Walling, William English, 97
Walters, Alexander, 107–8, 109, 110, 117, 154
Warren, Edward A., 139
Washington, Booker T., 24, 87, 103, 106, 162; "Atlanta Compromise" speech of, 28, 40, 81–82; on Atlanta race riot, 82; black activists' challenge to, 97, 107–8, 113; on black economic progress, 126; death of, 150–51; and National Negro Business League, 40, 41, 52, 148; and Payton, 2–3, 5, 61, 104, 107, 111, 115, 137, 150–51, 171; Smith as attorney for, 51, 100; and Westfield school, 27, 28; whites' criticisms of, 70–71, 114–15
Washington, Margaret Murray, 113, 150
Washington, NC, 11–12
Watkins, Jessie, 42
Wayland Seminary, 16, 24, 27, 181n13

Wells, Ida B., 52, 97
West, Samuel, 116
Westfield, MA, 11, 25–26; black population of, 18, 19–20; history of, 16–17; Pine Hill cemetery in, 98, 163, 167, 175–76, *176*
Westfield Academy, 20
Westfield State Normal School, 27, 28
Wharton, Edith, 45
Wheatley, Phillis, 161
Wheaton, J. Frank, 138
White, Joseph, 19
white backlash, 3, 126, 128–29, 131–32, 138–40
Whitehead, Mrs. L. B., 120–21
Whitehouse, Joseph A., 93
Whitfield, L. C., 123
Whitman, Charles S., 145, 155
Whose Harlem Is This, Anyway? (King), 6
Wilcox, William G., 151

Williams, Bert, 127–28, 154–56
Williams, Fannie Barrier, 42
Williams, Harry, 113
Williams, J. S., 139
Willis, William H., 166
Wilson, Estelle, 151, 153
Wilson, Mrs. R. P., 115
Wilson, Richard R., 64–65
Wilson, Woodrow, 145
Winford, Brandon K., 7
Wood, J. B., 126–27, 139
Woodson, Marion, 147
World War I, 141, 145, 152, 161
Wortham, Sadie, 175–76
Wortham, William Hilmon, 157–58, 169, 175
Wright, Clara, 112, 116
Wright, Lizzie W., 154
Wright, Mrs. A. K., 153

Young, George, 159

GPSR Authorized Representative: Easy Access System Europe, Mustamäe tee
50, 10621 Tallinn, Estonia, gpsr.requests@easproject.com

www.ingramcontent.com/pod-product-compliance
Lightning Source LLC
Chambersburg PA
CBHW021944290426
44108CB00012B/960